Cross-Cultural Readings of Chineseness

CHINA RESEARCH MONOGRAPH 51

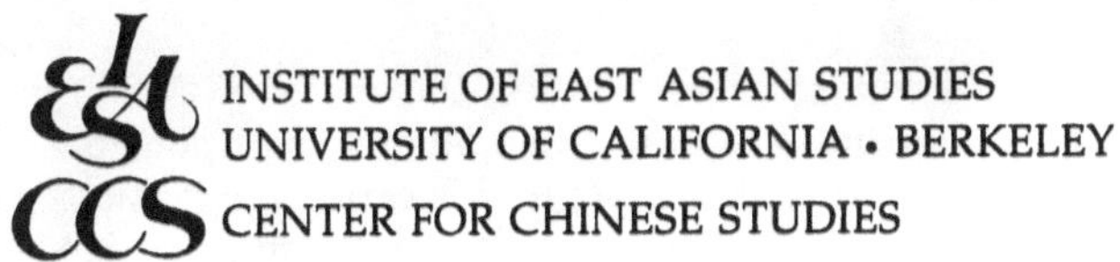
INSTITUTE OF EAST ASIAN STUDIES
UNIVERSITY OF CALIFORNIA • BERKELEY
CENTER FOR CHINESE STUDIES

Cross-Cultural Readings of Chineseness

Narratives, Images, and Interpretations of the 1990s

EDITED BY
Wen-hsin Yeh

A publication of the Institute of East Asian Studies, University of California, Berkeley. Although the Institute of East Asian Studies is responsible for the selection and acceptance of manuscripts in this series, responsibility for the opinions expressed and for the accuracy of statements rests with their authors.

Correspondence and manuscripts may be sent to:
Ms. Joanne Sandstrom, Managing Editor
Institute of East Asian Studies
University of California
Berkeley, California 94720-2318
E-mail: easia@uclink.berkeley.edu

The China Research Monograph series is one of several publications series sponsored by the Institute of East Asian Studies in conjunction with its constituent units. The others include the Japan Research Monograph series, the Korea Research Monograph series, and the Research Papers and Policy Studies series. A list of recent publications appears at the back of the book.

Library of Congress Cataloging-in-Publication Data

Cross-cultural readings of Chineseness : narratives, images, and interpretations of the 1990s / edited by Wen-hsin Yeh.
p. cm. — (China research monograph ; 51)
Collection of papers presented at the conference "Theoretical Issues in Modern Chinese Literary and Cultural Studies".
Includes bibliographical references
ISBN 1-55729-064-4
1. Chinese literature—20th century—History and criticism Congresses. 2. Arts, Chinese—20th century Congresses. 3. Motion picture—History and criticism Congresses. 4. Postmodernism—China Congresses. I. Yeh, Wen-hsin. II. Theoretical Issues in Modern Chinese Literary and Cultural Studies (1998 : Berkeley, Calif.) III. Series: China research monographs ; no. 51.
PL2303.M625 1999
700'.951'0904—dc21 99-24300

Contents

Acknowledgments

The chapters collected here were first presented at a workshop held at the Center for Chinese Studies, University of California, Berkeley, in January 1998. On that occasion Rey Chow, Stan Abe, and Michelle Yeh each gave a paper, with Wendy Larson, Patricia Berger, and Haun Saussy serving as discussants respectively. By the invitation of the editor, the commentators later developed their remarks into essays, while the presenters further revised their papers.

The contributors would like to thank all who participated at the Center for Chinese Studies workshop on that occasion. It was the questions and comments from the audience that inspired the production of this volume.

Introduction

The six essays in this volume offer interpretive readings of a film, a work of plastic art, and an essay, all products of contemporary China. The film examined here is Chen Kaige's *Temptress Moon*, the art *A Book from the Sky* by Xu Bing, and the essay Zheng Min's "Retrospect at the End of the Century: Chinese Language Reform and Modern Chinese Poetry." Chen has been a notable figure in the limelight of international film circles for more than a decade. Xu's accomplishment received recognition, most recently, in the form of a MacArthur "genius award." Zheng Min's essay did not appear in journals such as the *New York Review of Books*, but it is larded with quotations from Lacan and Derrida. These works are thus "Chinese" not just because they are by Chinese artists and writers and "from China" but because they also bear witness to cultural and intellectual imaginations both by the Chinese themselves and about China in an era of border-crossing. They constitute, in that sense, part and parcel of an interactive reconstruction of the meaning of "Chineseness" in our time.

The locus of this volume is thus not somewhere "inside China" in its territorially bounded convention, but a Chinese world that is being refashioned by its global reach. The interpretive readings are not directed at objects "out there"—museum pieces and cultural relics of discrete and delimited significance. They are examples, instead, of the possibilities of textual meanings produced through divergent practices of reading. The three sets of essays in this volume combine to show how a text can be made to yield opposing dimensions with the choice of particular strategies of reading.

What, for instance, does a Western audience see in a Chinese film or piece of art when the viewing takes place in the West? If—as is often the case—the "Chineseness" of the work inevitably surfaces as a predominant question, does this not demand of the work a certain ethnic attribute that reconstitutes its nature? What, similarly, does a Chinese audience see when the viewing takes place in China? Given the Chinese preoccupation with China's place in the world, in what way do questions of identity surface in Chinese viewing, reconstituting a piece of work that is known to have been well received as authentically "Chinese" in the West?

Rey Chow's essay, "The Seductions of Homecoming: Place, Authenticity, and Chen Kaige's *Temptress Moon*," sets the tone of this volume by posing as a problem the quest for authenticity in the search for "Chineseness" in a transnational setting. The essay offers a reading of the film that is focused on Zhongliang, an orphaned boy who becomes almost a son to Dada, the leader of a Shanghai gang. Zhongliang's story is that of a runaway from a stultifying hierarchical order, who finds his niche in Dada's underground family as the prized seducer of married women. Zhongliang's initiation to desire, to be sure, precedes Shanghai and takes place in the presence of his sister for the perverted pleasure of his brother-in-law. The urban sojourning is instrumental to his transformation from a vulnerable victim to a skilled gigolo. Rey Chow's interpretive reading moves to a new plane when the accomplished seducer heads home on the assignment of Dada to prey upon Ruyi, the virgin sister of Zhongliang's brother-in-law and the new head of the Pang clan.

By focusing on Zhongliang, Rey Chow both draws attention to the gendered dynamics between males on the run and females who are place-bound and offers a reading of *Temptress Moon* as a psychodrama of encounters between men and women. In Chow's reading, the multiple acts of entries and departures in the film mark critical transitions in a narrative about human desire rather than Chinese identity. This tale of desire, to be sure, involves subjects and objects mutually positioned in a patriarchal framework. The power relationships within this framework are radically transformed by the spatial displacement engendered by the lead characters' lateral movements between the Pang ancestral estate and Dada's Shanghai gangland. Zhongliang's journey alters his standing vis-à-vis Ruyi and enhances his ability to seduce upon homecoming. Rey Chow's interpretive reading thus foregrounds the spatial and the universal over the historical and the particular and offers a reading that is about placement and seduction instead of place and identity.

Wendy Larson's essay, written in response to Rey Chow's piece, offers an alternative reading that presents *Temptress Moon* as a tale of power. Larson follows the progression of Duanwu instead of Zhongliang and foregrounds the ascendancy of a secondary male in the patriarchal hierarchy. The act of homecoming, Larson reminds us, is a central narrative theme in modern Chinese literature that traces its origin to seminal works such as Lu Xun's short story "Guxiang" (My old home). The homecomings of Duanwu and Zhongliang are no mere recurrent motions taking place across empty space, but purposeful acts in a terrain charged with historical significance. Thanks to the "scripting," so to speak, by that history, the dissonance produced by the sojourning goes beyond mere spatial displacement; it becomes imperative that there be an iconoclastic critique of the injustices of the patriarchal order. Whereas Zhongliang's story may be a tale of desire, Duanwu's story is one of power. Zhongliang's story reaches an end when he dies an inevitable death following the logic of instrumentalized love. Duanwu's seizure of power in the final moments of the film, argues Larson, can be seen as almost a metaphorical reference to the rise of the downtrodden in China's modern revolutionary history.

Both essays pay attention to the visual history and symbolic repertoire that inform the viewing and producing of a film such as *Temptress Moon*. While Rey Chow, by referring to films made in Hong Kong, draws attention to earlier visual moments of flights and homecomings in modern Chinese cinematic production, Wendy Larson reminds us of the standard tropes and canonical texts inscribed in socialist China's literary curriculum. The choices of reading strategies by Chow and Larson may be different. But the attempt in each case is to get behind what meets the eye in the film narrative and to get into the mind's eye of the producers and consumers of these images.

No less than new-generation films, art works from China travel into non-Chinese parts of the world. The viewing of such work takes place over time and across national borders. Interpretive readings of traveling art, as Abe's and Berger's essays show, thus must engage conditions of the art's origination as well as its eventual consumption.

Xu's work, by general recognition, involves an intriguing manipulation of large numbers of Chinese characters that resist a literate reading. The work confounds conventional divisions between words and pictures, art and craft, handmade work and mechanical reproduction, high literacy and total illiteracy. It elicits a multiplicity of readings while making itself receptive to diverse inscriptions by a variety of viewers.

Abe's essay delineates a whole spectrum of interpretive positions that can plausibly be occupied by viewers in China as well as in the West. When Xu's work first went on display in Beijing in October 1988, it perplexed Chinese critics, who debated whether the work was a critique or an instantiation of Chinese culture or both. As the work seemingly poses no questions nor offers any answers, it also lends itself to a romantic celebration of the freedom in the space between the neither/nor.

When the work went on exhibition in the United States in 1991, the unstable meaning of Xu's work posed extra challenge for the attempt to find an "exact" English rendering of its title, which had gone, to be sure, through several rounds of revisions in its Chinese original. Abe argues that in the charged atmosphere after June 4, 1989, liberal ideology and cultural Orientalism converged to produce, in the pages of mainstream American media, a politicized reading of antigovernment and anti-Communist defiance. The sinological profession, armed with Chinese dictionaries, took part in the act by authenticating the Chineseness of Xu's work. Finally, as the events of June 4 recede into the background against a new tide of globalization and commercialism, Xu finds his work commodified into yet another embodiment of Chinese authenticity—this time not as a political statement in the media but as objects for commercial transaction and private ownership in the marketplace.

Abe underscores how Western readings of Xu's work can be derivative of or overly determined by an American self-positioning vis-à-vis China. The essay captures the reproduction of meaning of a finished piece of art in time and space that is considerably removed from the work's moment of origin. Patricia Berger, writing in response to Abe's reading, probes instead the artist's early life and places the making of *Tian shu* within the cultural trends in China.

Berger situates the conception of *Tian shu* in the overheated cultural atmosphere of Beijing in the late 1980s. She uses the artist's own words to draw attention to his deliberate withdrawal from an overindulgence in the modernist, postmodern, and pseudo-modern discourse in fashionable Chinese intellectual circles of the time. Xu's privileged and educated background, meanwhile, assured his membership in the establishment. The wall-like displays of unbound pages of *Tian shu*, Berger reminds us, were curiously reminiscent of the wall posters of the Democracy Wall of 1978—subversive, to be sure, yet firmly within the tradition of a socialist history of revolution. To view these productions, one stands in front of the massive walls and searches for the readable. Berger argues that Chinese viewers are just as likely as their Western counterparts to aestheticize decontextualized bits of their material past or disembedded fragments of old symbolic systems. This aestheticization is no less a misunderstanding than is an Orientalist mystification of cultural relics of the East. Xu Bing's work, in Berger's representation, grows out of a tradition in which the exoticization of the self and the audience is not unknown. The conventions of this tradition thus complicate the nature of Xu's participation in the American art scene and raise questions about whether he is more interestingly seen as a victim of Orientalist critics or a skilled participant.

Abe has suggested, in short, that there are linkages between an Orientalist characterization of Chinese culture and a Western reading of Xu's work as quintessentially Chinese. Berger strongly suggests, in contrast, that the Chineseness of Xu's work is no Orientalist imagination but well grounded in a history of Chinese painting. She points to symmetries between Xu's earlier work and Buddhist paintings of Song to support her suggestion, thereby inviting further contextualization of Xu's work in that tradition.

Is the modern West, indeed, the only possible vantage position to view China from the outside? Are there historical moments in which the Chinese find their literacy subverted as a result of their illiteracy of a fully developed writing system—a system that contains seemingly recognizable components of written Chinese yet whose meaning eludes their grasp?

Berger draws attention to the written scripts of the Khitan and the Tangut—non-Han people of different linguistic families who had developed their own writing systems. Despite the borrowing from written Han Chinese, these languages, like Xu's script, were familiar yet unreadable. Although they subverted the conventional Chinese sense of literacy, they did not corrupt the possibility of meaning. Berger suggests, therefore, that given time, even Xu Bing's ostensibly senseless scripts may accrue meaning.

What, then, are the politics and possibilities of a cross-cultural humanistic understanding? When art is viewed and thought of in contexts detached from its inception, what are the possibilities for the work to take on new contextual meaning? Are the results of such reproduction of meaning necessarily signs of categorical misunderstanding? Finally, when ideas travel across national borders and when Western trends reach China, how do they insert themselves in cultural warfare away from home?

Michelle Yeh's essay, which takes up some of these issues, is a focused critique of Zheng Min, who had published several articles in the early and mid-1990s that outlined a reassessment of the New Literature of the May Fourth period. Zheng Min deplores the iconoclasm of the vernacular movement of the 1920s that had been trumpeted, in official Party history, as the dawn of a Chinese enlightenment. Citing Lacan, Derrida, and a whole host of others as her new source of authority, Zheng laments the earlier generation's rejection of the classical tradition and argues that linguistic and literary practices were not matters of anyone's arbitrary choice. She criticizes the *forced* borrowing of vocabulary, syntax, and grammar from Western languages and regards these interrelated factors as responsible for the loss of a literary "Chineseness." Great Chinese literature of global notability, in short, must necessarily come out of China's tradition. The New Literature of the May Fourth era, by orienting itself to Western models, had compromised its authenticity.

In her reading of Zheng Min's piece, Michelle Yeh forcefully questions why issues of cultural identity should dominate readings of modern Chinese poetry. Why does the Chineseness of a piece of work matter more than any other aspects of its literary attributes? Why should it seem an inevitable compromise of a poet's Chineseness when he or she borrows from the West? A reading that privileges Chineseness, Yeh points out, assumes a reified dichotomy between "China" and the "West," "tradition" and "modernity." Those who think this way have not fully grasped the subtle and complex linkages between the past and the present. Those who insist upon a "Chineseness" that is self-contained and insulated from the West are often guilty of an essentialized conception of cultural practices that are better seen as fluid and dynamic. By Yeh's analysis, Zheng Min appears to have taken up, quite inadvertently, a position that is in full accord with that of Western sinologists who are professionally committed to the reification of China as an object of study. Despite the national audience and the "Chineseness" of Zheng's intent, in other words, the literary critic has lent her essays to a reinforcement of Western Orientalist positions when these essays are read from across the Pacific.

Haun Saussy, in his response to Michelle Yeh's reading, agrees with Yeh that Zheng may not have mastered the subject of

Western linguistic theories. He argues, however, that the misreading is just as significant, for it points to logical imperatives inherent in an environment in which postmodernism and postcolonialism flourished in China in the 1990s. Zheng's essay is an attempt, in Saussy's reading, to search for an alternative strategy in the reading of modern Chinese literary history. What she offers represents an alternative legitimization device for the writing of a new kind of literary history. To the extent that the latter focuses attention on language and literature, it is also an attempt to be apolitical, thus a departure from the age-old close connections formed between literary politics and socialist revolution.

Postcolonial and postmodern critique in China nonetheless carries the aura of an official ideology in waiting. Saussy juxtaposes his reading of Zheng Min with theoretical pieces in *Zhanlue yu guanli,* a state-sponsored journal of national visibility. Chinese "post-isms," Saussy observes, are anti-Western and inherently nationalistic, riding as they do on a repudiation of modernity and the European Enlightenment. Zheng Min's piece, critical as it may seem of the established official position of an earlier time, shares with that earlier position a refusal to allow a multiplicity of legitimization devices. In contrast to Michele Yeh's reading of their surface resemblance to a Western "Orientalist" position, Saussy argues that Chinese post-isms, Zheng Min's essay included, are in fact exercises in Chinese nationalism when placed in their transnational context.

The essays in this volume hardly exhaust the possibilities either in the choice of reading strategies or in the production of textual meaning. Each is an eloquent demonstration of how the production of specific meaning is closely connected to the choice of reading strategy. The essays underscore the instability of meaning as they highlight the dialectical interaction between the national and the transnational, the universal and the particular in everyday practices of reading.

The contribution of this volume, then, is not about definitive interpretations of any particular text, but about a heightened self-awareness when engaged in the practice of reading and viewing. Old-style objectification of China as an immobile empire has certainly endured the test of time and may very well carry on. What this volume seeks is not the rejection of that view, but a reflexive understanding of our participation in the production of "Chineseness" in a new trans-cultural context.

ONE

The Seductions of Homecoming: Place, Authenticity, and Chen Kaige's *Temptress Moon*

REY CHOW

> That sentiment accompanying the absence of home—homesickness—can cut two ways: it can be a yearning for the authentic home (situated in the past or in the future) or it can be the recognition of the inauthenticity of all homes.
>
> — Rosemary Marangoly George (75)

Even though it has been an overwhelmingly successful phenomenon worldwide, contemporary Chinese cinema is often greeted by Chinese-speaking audiences with hostility. It is as if the accomplishments of this cinema have an impossible task in returning home. The simple fact that it has traveled abroad and been gazed at with interest by "foreigners" is apparently enough to cause it to lose trustworthiness as wholly and genuinely Chinese. The films of the two most well-known directors, Chen Kaige and Zhang Yimou, for instance, have continued to be attacked for their tendencies to pander to the tastes of Western audiences eager for the orientalized, exotic images of a China

Note: This essay, which first appeared in *Narrative* 6.1 (January 1998): 1–17, is based on the version of the film *Temptress Moon* I saw in Hong Kong in the summer of 1996. Unfortunately, some of the scenes have been edited and cut from the North American version. (Places that contain discrepancies between the Asian and North American versions are marked by asterisks.) The essay was first presented as a plenary speech at the annual conference of the journal *Narrative*, at the University of Florida, Gainesville, April 1997. My sincere thanks to Elizabeth Langland not only for inviting me to speak but also for negotiating with Miramax for a showing of *Temptress Moon* at the conference, which thus became the U.S. premiere of the film. (It was released to the general public a couple of months later.) I am also grateful to Lee Edelman, my discussant, for his profoundly responsive comments, and to the audience at Gainesville for their enthusiasm. Used by permission.

whose history they ignore or falsify. This problematic, which is the problematic of authenticity, is familiar to all those engaged in cross-cultural studies.[1] In the late 1990s, when filmmaking and film watching are obviously global events involving ineluctable interaction with the "foreign," how might a film intervene in the tenacious and persistent demands for authenticity? I believe that Chen's 1996 film *Fengyue* (*Temptress Moon*) can in many ways be seen as such an intervention,[2] the director's own cultural complexes notwithstanding. A discussion of this may begin with the significance of place in the film narrative. Place, as we shall see, is not only the setting that shapes characters in action; it is also the locus of specifically filmic significations of "home" and authenticity.

The Flight from Home

Topographically, *Temptress Moon* shifts back and forth between the countryside of Jiangnan (the location of the wealthy Pang clan) and the metropolis of Shanghai, which was among the earliest Chinese cities to be opened to foreign trade in the mid-nineteenth century (as a result of the Opium War of 1839–42). In the film, visual and architectural details combine to convey the sharp differences between the two locations as "tradition" and "modernity" respectively. The Pang family house, situated by a river, is a well-endowed ancient estate with its air of unbreakable heritage and kinship order; the solemnity and reticence typical of tribal bondage find their expression in darkish interiors with their austere, muted décor. Shanghai, by contrast, is a world of bright and gaudy colors, loud and vibrant foreign dance-hall music, fast-moving vehicles, and ruthless, mercenary human relations. Contrary to the mood of languid eternality that shrouds the old books, arcane utensils, and antique furnishings in the Pang household, Shanghai's Westernized domestic spaces are characterized by a much less permanent, because much newer, sense of time. In an apartment rented for the purpose of an illicit relationship, for instance, a vase of roses, a rocking chair, a window pane, a closet

[1] This is a problematic the politics of which I have considered in detail in Chow (1995); see in particular pt. 2, chap. 4.

[2] Story by Chen and Wang Anyi; film script by Shu Qi. Please bear in mind that in the Chinese language, *fengyue* (literally "wind, moon") is a euphemism for eroticism or matters of sex.

mirror, and the occasional music of a piano from afar all suggest the aura of a larger culture in the process of change. For those living in the countryside, meanwhile, everything from the city, including clothes, shoes, and hairstyles, and personal possessions such as pocket watches, slippers, razors, soaps, hats, and photographs alike take on the historic fascination of "modernity," the legend, the sign that separates Shanghai from the rest of China's hinterland.

It is in Shanghai that we meet the adult figure of the leading male character, Yu Zhongliang. Zhongliang is by profession a special kind of gigolo. A key member of a Shanghai mafia in the 1910s, Zhongliang works at seducing and blackmailing rich married women who fall for him. Using the pseudonym "Xiao Xie,"* Zhongliang would entice a woman into a secret affair; after the affair had gone on for a while, the mafia would stage a typical scene: while Zhongliang was making love with the woman during one of their trysts, gangsters of the mafia would burst in on the scene, blindfold the woman, and threaten to report the affair to her husband unless the woman agreed to pay them a large sum of money. In the process, the woman would be told that her lover "Xiao Xie" was dead. After she was thus psychologically destroyed, Zhongliang would leave quietly with his cohorts and move on to the next target.

Zhongliang's professional success is the result of his familiarity with topography of another kind—a particular strategic spot on a woman's body. Typically, as he gains intimacy with a woman, he kisses her on one ear, nibbling at her ear until the earring comes off. The earring, like Diderot's *bijoux indiscrets,* is therefore the site of a female sexual confession.[3] For the mafia, this "memento" of a single earring exists as a repeated symbol of Zhongliang's invincibility. Although every case of extortion is carried out with the announcement that "Xiao Xie" is dead, in the next shot Zhongliang is usually alive and well, speedily departing from the scene of destruction for the next scene of conquest. Zhongliang's ease at the two subplaces that govern his life in Shanghai, married women's earlobes and the boudoirs of clandestine affairs, makes him indispensable to the mafia. Dada (or Boss), the head of the mafia, openly speaks of Zhongliang as someone he cannot do without.

---

[3] This reference to Diderot has, of course, been made famous by Foucault (77–80).

To the audience, however, the smoothness with which Zhongliang moves about in Shanghai carries a different set of connotations. When the film begins, years prior to his Shanghai career, Zhongliang has just arrived at the residence of the Pangs in the countryside of Jiangnan after the death of his parents. His only relative is his sister, Xiuyi, who is married to the young master Pang. Despite being officially the brother-in-law of the young master, Zhongliang is in effect treated as a servant. Between the lowly task of serving opium to his decrepit and perverse brother-in-law and the intimate, incestuous affection of his sister, the young boy is plunged into a confusing encounter with the adult world. The twin experiences of a cruel adult male and a desirous adult female culminate in a scene in which Zhongliang's brother-in-law orders him to kiss his sister, who, sitting alongside the bed, acquiesces smilingly by opening her arms toward the boy. Fearful and reluctant, Zhongliang approaches the older woman while holding the opium-serving tray, his hands shaking violently. Amid the unforgettable noise of the opium utensils tossing against one another, his gaze is arrested by one of Xiuyi's earrings.

The place that is supposed to be a home for the displaced orphan child thus serves, in terms of narrative structure, as the unbearable site of infantile seduction (in the etymological sense of the word *infant* as *in-fans,* the state of speechlessness).[4] Like many first encounters with sexuality, the meaning of his experience with the sadomasochistic relationship of the two adults eludes Zhongliang and leaves him speechless. Architecturally, the traumatic nature of this seduction is mirrored by the circular, labyrinthine structure of the Pang estate, where a seemingly infinite series of doors and chambers, each connected with yet indistinguishable from the others, precludes any clear notion of entry or exit. Unable to comprehend (that is, to fully enter or fully leave behind) this primary encounter with sexuality, Zhongliang retains it through a certain repeated pattern of behavior. Having illicit relationships with married women that begin with the stealing of a single earring becomes his symptom and trademark, which turns a painful remembrance virtually into an industry. Although Zhongliang is a successful seducer, therefore, his success is presented from the beginning as a façade—a cover-up and a displacement of the trauma of his own seduction.

---

[4] For an authoritative discussion of the problematic of seduction in psychoanalysis, see Laplanche, chap. 3.

Meanwhile, another incident makes it impossible for him to remain with the Pang family. Acting from resentment, he uses his opportunity of serving opium to poison his brother-in-law with a dose of arsenic, thereby causing the man to become brain-dead. Fearing that his murderous act will be discovered, Zhongliang escapes. This escape clarifies the teleological tendency of the narrative of *Temptress Moon.* As an adopted home for Zhongliang, the backward, decadent countryside of the Pangs is significant as the site of a sexual primal scene that has shaped his character negatively. To be, Zhongliang must leave. His existential autonomy, in other words, will have to be established as a flight from the shock that is supposedly "home." But where will he flee from there?

Zhongliang intends to head for Beijing, the site of the historic, student-led May Fourth Movement of 1919, which sought, among other things, to revolutionize and modernize the Chinese written language and culture. To make sure that the audience understands this point, Chen Kaige inserts a scene in which Zhongliang, like other passengers, is hurrying along the railway, shouting, "Is this the train to Beijing?" Crucially, however, this intention is frustrated when Zhongliang, robbed of all his luggage before boarding the train, is picked up by Dada's gangsters and transported to Shanghai instead. Rather than Beijing, the enlightened capital city of modern China, in which he might have been able to receive a proper education, Zhongliang is literally abducted into a new home, the depraved underground world of Shanghai, where he soon emerges as the favorite son. He is so at home in this Westernized, commercial city that Dada, who may be regarded as Zhongliang's adopted father, says to him, "You belong to Shanghai; Shanghai cannot do without you."[5]

The escape from "home" leads not to liberation and enlightenment but rather to another type of entrapment. In the decadence of Shanghai, Zhongliang remains enslaved to an autocratic,

[5] Lee Edelman commented thoughtfully that Zhongliang cannot reach Beijing because he has, literally from the outset, been "shanghaied." Hence, for Zhongliang, Beijing remains nothing more than a fantasy. This is evident in a revealing scene in which he interrogates Ruyi about her ignorance of the outside world. In his pretentious attempt to educate her, he describes Beijing in lyrical, revolutionary, but entirely bookish terms—as a place where the sky is blue, the walls are high, the girl students all have short hair and wear long black skirts, and so forth. While he has thus succeeded in seducing Ruyi with his professed enlightenment, he is painfully aware that he is, in effect, performing his own lack.

violent, and immoral patriarchal community. His two masters, the poisonous Pangs in the countryside and the poisonous gangsters in the metropolis, echo each other in the control they exert over him, and his life in Shanghai, despite its glamor and success, becomes a symmetrical double to his life in Jiangnan. We may even go so far as to say that in fact, it is precisely as he becomes existentially autonomous and seemingly acquires agency as an adult human being that the shadow of the past begins to loom the darkest. He may have physically left "home," but psychically "home" has never left him.

This unfinished relationship with home is evident, for instance, in Zhongliang's affair with a nameless woman. In one scene, in which he is waiting for her in her apartment at Tianxiangli (Heavenly Lane) in Shanghai, we as well as he are transported by hallucinatory images from his current surroundings back to his former home: first, the woman's picture, which bears a striking resemblance to Xiuyi; then, a flashback to the scene of Zhongliang's childhood seduction; finally, the woman herself appearing, putting her hands over Zhongliang's eyes from behind—a gesture that once again reminds us of the games Xiuyi used to play with her younger brother. This attachment to a figure who visually conjures the past constitutes an obstacle in Zhongliang's job: despite Dada's urging, Zhongliang is unable to bring himself to destroy this woman. He tries to delay her destruction by prolonging their relationship. In this postponement, this reluctance to execute, we recognize the prelude to his ultimate return home.

The Homecoming... As You Wish

Dada's new target is Pang Ruyi, Xiuyi's sister-in-law, whom he wants Zhongliang to seduce. After Xiuyi's husband becomes brain-dead and leaves the clan without a male to succeed the old master, the Pang elders decide to appoint Ruyi as the head of the clan. Since Ruyi is female, they also appoint Duanwu, Ruyi's younger cousin from a poor, distant branch of the family, as her male companion.

Upon receiving instructions for his new task, Zhongliang's first reaction is a firm refusal: "As you know," he says to Dada, "I will never go to the town of the Pangs." The next thing we know, he is there against his conscious will.

Strictly speaking, Ruyi is merely the latest in Zhongliang's series of targets, but what distinguishes her from the other women is precisely her topographical location. That this wealthy and powerful woman lives in his former home means that his seduction of her is inevitably commingled with a fateful revisit to the scene of his own seduction. In the course of the film we are made to understand that Ruyi is topographically distinctive in another sense. Unlike the women in Shanghai, Ruyi is a virgin, a "place" yet untouched by the rest of the world because, having been raised in an opium-filled house, she remains unwanted by most families looking for a prospective daughter-in-law. Despite her "poisonous" history, moreover, Ruyi comes across as a beautiful person with a refreshing, untainted sense of personal integrity.

Like her name, which means "as you wish" in Chinese, Ruyi likes to act according to her own wishes, which are, contrary to her conservative upbringing, entirely independent and liberatory. After becoming the head of the clan, for instance, she orders the retirement of her father's concubines, much to the anger of the clan elders. Then, after meeting Zhongliang, she is direct in her expression of interest in him: one day, she even asks him to teach her how to ride a bicycle. This occasion gives Zhongliang the opportunity to become intimate with her, but when he kisses her on the ear and comes away as usual with one of the earrings, Ruyi reacts by taking off the other earring and offering it to him as well. This unusual event, which epitomizes Ruyi's difference from all the other women Zhongliang has conquered, does not escape the notice of his cohort, who asks, "How come there are two earrings this time?"

If the possession of the single earring is Zhongliang's means of surviving the trauma of an illicit sexual experience, which he must nonetheless keep repeating—through the screening work of fetishization and continual repression—in order to attain a false sense of equilibrium, this equilibrium is now disturbed by the voluntary gift of the other earring by an unsuspecting Ruyi. By giving him the other earring, Ruyi offers Zhongliang something he had never found at home—a love that does not carry with it the connotations of enslavement, illicitness, and humiliation. As such, Ruyi's boldness and spontaneity stand as a force with the potential of pulling Zhongliang out of the stupor that is his entire existence so far. Through this "virgin territory" that is the independent-minded woman at home, Zhongliang could have found redemption. Yet in spite of this, he remains unmoved. In a scene following the offer of the second earring, we find him displaying disgust at Ruyi, who, being in love, has secretly gone into his room to look at his belongings. Instead of reciprocating her attention, Zhongliang merely feels resentful and loses his temper. Accusing her of a lack of respect for his privacy, he reminds her bitterly of the class hierarchy that used to separate them—that he was, at one time, a servant at her house.

The Seduction of the Seduced

The strong, innocent woman who offers him true love thus remains, topographically, a goal that Zhongliang has the potential of reaching but somehow misses. Instead, he continues to aim consciously at the Ruyi that is his professional target—the rich woman to be cheated, blackmailed, and then abandoned. As in the case of his journey toward Beijing, however, Zhongliang's conscious move toward Ruyi is diverted en route, bringing about an unexpected turn in his plan. This turn occurs when Ruyi asks Zhongliang to meet her in the family boathouse by the riverside one evening. For her, it is a rendezvous with a newfound love; for him, it is an opportunity to carry out his duty and finally have sex with her. As they begin to make love, Zhongliang, confident that Ruyi is inexperienced and that he should take control, suddenly hears her confess: to please him (who she believes likes women more than girls because of the picture of the nameless woman she has seen in his belongings), she says, she has already had sex with Duanwu. She has deliberately gotten rid of her virginity so that he would love her.

Zhongliang's face at this point has nothing of the look of someone who is happy at discovering that he is being loved. Instead, it is contorted with anguish. Since the film narrative does not offer any explanation, we must use the clues we have to speculate. Ruyi's independent behavior overwhelms Zhongliang, we might say, not because she has casually given her virginity to someone whom she does not really love or even because she has performed a selfless deed for his sake. Rather, it overwhelms him because she has unwittingly plunged him into the abyss of his own past. In sacrificing her virginity, her *integrity*, for him, is Ruyi not exactly like the other women, and ultimately like Xiuyi? And is Ruyi's incestuous relationship with Duanwu not a frightful mirror image of Xiuyi's incestuous relationship with Zhongliang years ago? With the blinding intensity of the unanticipated déjà vu, Ruyi's confession strikes Zhongliang as if it were his own flashback, his own involuntary memory: though (and perhaps precisely as) a picture performed by others, it forces him to recognize himself. Like the character Cheng Dieyi in Chen's *Farewell My Concubine,* who is finally tamed by the sight of a performance of the story he has been resisting, Zhongliang is finally tamed and, instead of seducing others, becomes seduced once again into playing the role that is his fate.[6]

If this chance (re)seduction of Zhongliang, which constitutes the major narrative turning point, can be described as the ultimate meaning of his homecoming, what is the relationship between seduction and home? Etymologically, "seduction" refers to a leading astray, the opposite of going home. As the paradigm of Odysseus demonstrates, a man who wishes to return home must be determined to stave off seduction—to refuse to succumb to the sirens. In *Temptress Moon* this classic opposition between home and seduction has broken down. Consciously, indeed, Zhongliang resists and rejects home, and yet in his negative, flighty mode as a professional seducer, he seems nonetheless to keep turning back, to keep clinging to something he does not fully comprehend. And, as he tries to ignore his own feelings about "home" and ventures forth with the task of seduction in cold-blooded indifference toward everyone at home, including the innocent woman who loves him, what he stumbles upon is none other than the "homely" (intimate), yet also seduced (gone-astray), part of himself.

Seductions of the former home involve the memory of and attachment to the entire scenario of Zhongliang's early encounter, a scenario composed by particular configurations of relationships in their enigmatic violence and intensity. Such violence and intensity have remained unrecognized, we may say, until Zhongliang sees it in the form of an other, an image presented by another person. If this imaging of how "others do it" may be described as a visual guide to home, then homecoming itself is, strictly speaking,

[6] In *Farewell My Concubine,* Chen takes pains to show the process in which Cheng Dieyi "becomes" the character of the concubine in the opera of the same title. While a boy-apprentice in the Beijing opera troupe with which his mother left him, Dieyi is for a long time unable to accept his role as a woman and unable to speak his lines correctly. Because of this failure, he is severely punished, and he tries to run away. He would have successfully escaped, but on his way he unexpectedly comes across a street performance of none other than the opera *Farewell My Concubine.* Completely absorbed and moved, he changes his mind and returns to the troupe. From then on, he accepts, performs, and identifies with his assigned role—and fate—of "concubine" to the end.

a seduction of the already seduced. Working by the force of memory, which erupts at the sight/site of that which has already been experienced once before, this homecoming can be extraordinarily powerful. In fact, it is lethal.

What is most interesting about this double seduction—this state of being seduced encountering itself at the sight/site of an other—is that it no longer revolves around one particular character. At the point of Zhongliang's discovery of Ruyi's relationship with Duanwu, the story line of *Temptress Moon* is no longer narratologically reducible to the relationship between the "leading" characters, Zhongliang and Ruyi, but must instead be understood as a series of compound relationships involving differentiations on multiple planes and scales, including the sexual, familial, class, rural, metropolitan, modern, and feudalist. Such differentiations, moreover, exceed any restrictive hierarchical arrangement. The following diagram helps clarify their superimposed nature.

Zhongliang and Xiuyi	: Duanwu and Ruyi	: Zhongliang and Ruyi
Zhongliang and Xiuyi	: Zhongliang and women in Shanghai	: Zhongliang and woman at Tianxiangli
Zhongliang and the Pangs	: Zhongliang and the Shanghai mafia	
Zhongliang and the Shanghai mafia	: Duanwu and the Pangs	

In these relationship-series, every character becomes the narrative hinge for the emergence and development of another character, and every relationship becomes the double of another relationship. The subjectivity of a character is, hence, no longer a matter of the character's inner world but is the result of his or her interactions with others. Accordingly, the significance of each character no longer has an independent value but can only be established through his or her entanglement with other characters. While this may be obvious, it is also worth emphasizing in consideration of our persistently essentialist ways of thinking about characterization (as if the characters were real people). In *Temptress Moon,* since "meaning" cannot stabilize upon such multilayered relationships, characterization takes on a topographical or even archaeological significance: characters themselves become intersecting places or crossroads, digs or ruins, all with multifaceted messages. In the case of Zhongliang, for instance, "character" is the meeting of a "prehistory," in which lie the remnants of a traumatic experience, which he does not understand and cannot express, and a "posthistory," which is a belated, deferred re-imaging, in the form of an other (scene), of that prehistory. If the ineluctability of this meeting is an ineluctable return home, then homecoming itself is always (the repetition of) a going-astray, a departure that has already taken place.

The Man in Flight, the Women Bound, and the Country-Bumpkin-Turned-Nouveau-Riche

As the film approaches its end, Zhongliang is unsettled by his own feelings for Ruyi but must still fulfill his duty to Dada. Dada has meanwhile sensed that Zhongliang has changed. To prevent further harm, he decides to stage a scene in which Ruyi will discover for herself Zhongliang's identity as a gigolo. Dada is convinced that, once Ruyi sees this, she will no longer love Zhongliang, and Zhongliang will have to become once again his professionally cool and efficient self. This exposure of Zhongliang happens in Shanghai. By intricate arrangements, Ruyi is indeed forced to witness Zhongliang's act from the window of an apartment opposite his in Shanghai: he is making love to the woman at Tianxiangli for the last time, with the gangsters breaking in in their usual fashion, with threats for the woman, and so forth. Only this time, the woman, who refuses to be blindfolded and insists on confronting Zhongliang, commits suicide upon learning the truth.

Contrary to Dada's expectations, Ruyi remains determined in her love for Zhongliang. Even so, she is unable to hear from Zhongliang what she wants the most—the verbal affirmation that he, too, loves her. Heartbroken, Ruyi returns to the countryside and prepares to marry another man. Upon learning that Ruyi is to get married, Zhongliang hurries back to his former home once more and confesses that he does, in fact, love her. He even proposes that the two of them elope to Beijing "for real this time." Ruyi refuses to change her mind. In despair, Zhongliang replicates the other episode that resides in the "primal scene": just as he used arsenic to poison his brother-in-law, so he now prepares a dose of opium mixed with arsenic for Ruyi, who consumes it unaware and becomes brain-dead as well. This act of poisoning completes the saga of Zhongliang's homecoming. As he tries to escape again from the countryside, he is gunned down by Dada's gangsters. If his initial arrival at the Pangs' family residence—by boat at night, through water—is a kind of birth, then the countryside now serves also as his tomb.

Throughout the film, Zhongliang's character is portrayed with a compelling depth, which is the result, ironically, of his need from the very first to escape. Like many writers of the May Fourth period (the landmark period in which Chinese literature became "modern"), Chen relies for the construction of male subjectivity on what may be called the paradigm of fright-and-flight.[7] Hence, just as in the preceding *Farewell My Concubine*, *Temptress Moon* is full of instances of exaggerated music and sound, body movements, close-ups, and dialogues, which together with the cinematography (by Christopher Doyle) of fast-moving shots and changes of shots amplify the effects of a psychologically persecuted male character who seems always on the run.[8] In narratological terms, Zhongliang is hence constituted—visually and aurally as well as through the plot—by patterns of departure that help convey the questions of his identity: "What is Zhongliang running from?" "Where is he going?" "Whom will he meet on the way?" This negative pose of a male character on the run is a kind of "resistance" that, ultimately, delivers him home against his

---

[7] For instance, the typical scenario in some of Lu Xun's short stories is that of a male narrator emotionally shocked by a spectacle of social injustice, regarding which he feels impotent; in spite of his sympathies for the victim(s), such a narrator usually takes flight in one form or another. Likewise, in Ba Jin's *Jia* (*The Family*), the predominant narrative action is placed in the characters who, feeling indignant at the corrupt nature of the feudalist patriarchal family system, attempt to rebel and take leave. Readers acquainted with modern Chinese literature are asked to see a more detailed discussion of this connection with May Fourth writings in Chow (1997), also on *Temptress Moon*, which complements the present discussion. Insofar as Chan associates home and countryside with backwardness, he is modernist in his authorial perspective, a perspective that is different from the sentimental idealization or romanticization of the countryside as the place of simple and eternal truths that also runs throughout modern and contemporary Chinese literary culture. A recent example of this latter tendency is found in Zhang Yimou's 1995 film *Shanghai Triad*, in which the point-of-view character, a child, fascinated by Shanghai, nonetheless sees truth at the end through his experience in the countryside.

[8] This can perhaps be described by way of the phrase "motion and emotion" (first used by Wim Wenders); see Tony Rayns's brief discussion, which is based on some of the rushes rather than on the finished film. The North American version of the film, because it has been heavily edited with many abrupt shifts of scenes, comes across as even more discontinuous and discomforting than the version shown in Hong Kong and Taiwan. In "Bulunbulei de youhuo," I offer a related discussion of the effects generated by Chen's use of motion in terms of melodrama.

will. At the same time, if such a male "psyche" is the legacy of a mainstream modernism that defines itself in opposition to the *socius*, then what is revealed in the seductions of Zhongliang's homecoming is perhaps the unviability of this dissident masculinity as inscribed in the paradigm of fright-and-flight, a paradigm that is being subverted by the network of characters and relationships that sprawl around Zhongliang like a labyrinth. In the light of this unwilling captivity—and demise—of the Man in Flight, the women characters become very interesting.

Unlike Zhongliang, the women characters are all place-bound, in terms of both their physical and their mental locations: Xiuyi is stuck in the countryside and in her bond to a brain-dead husband; the women of the metropolis are trapped by the Shanghai way of life and by their own illicit sexual desires; even Ruyi, who is the most independent of all, remains a prisoner of her home and her heart. (Even though she is about to get married at the end, she consumes opium one more time simply because it has been prepared by Zhongliang, the man she once loved.) However, if these women are ultimately victimized in various ways by their topographical and bodily confinement (a loveless marriage, psychological destruction, suicide, and brain damage), the bold defiance of patriarchal culture expressed by each of them nevertheless signifies a different concept of flight and departure that may, in due course, not have to lead back to the "home" that is the original place of captivity. As I have commented elsewhere, Chen is typically ambiguous and ambivalent in the way in which he handles questions regarding women. Here, as always, he has left the implications of the women characters' fates in the form only of a suggestion, a possibility in all its open-endedness.[9]

Indirectly, Zhongliang's homecoming causes the power of the Pang clan to pass to Ruyi's servant-companion Duanwu. Like Zhongliang, Duanwu has been exploited by an older female for sexual purposes, but unlike Zhongliang, he seems to be unperturbed by this "initiation." He remains loyal to Ruyi until they reach Shanghai, where he discovers, he says, the war between the sexes. After Ruyi fails to confirm that Zhongliang loves her, Duanwu rapes her. Later, as they arrive home, he even exposes her relationships with both him and Zhongliang to the man she is about to marry. At the end, as Ruyi becomes permanently brain-

[9] For more elaborate discussions of the status of women in Chen's other films, see the relevant sections in Chow (1995).

damaged by arsenic, Duanwu logically succeeds her as the head of the clan. Like most characters in the film, that of Duanwu is far from being well-developed (his transformation in Shanghai, for instance, lacks persuasiveness), but he is thought-provoking as a type. What Duanwu stands for, in contrast to Zhongliang, is a new type of man—a new class perhaps—who has been abused but who somehow manages not to have repressed and internalized such abuse; instead, when the right moment occurs, this type of man turns the violence he has experienced to his own advantage by directing it at fresh victims. Lacking the sensitivity and self-doubt, and hence vulnerability, of Zhongliang, Duanwu makes it to the top through petty cunning, hypocrisy, and opportunism. His success is, Chen's film seems to say, the vulgar success of the country-bumpkin-turned-nouveau riche.

Filmmaking as Homecoming

For a filmmaker, the paths of seduction lie not only in narrativization or characterization but also in film language itself. Is the movie screen not the ultimate place of an irresistible allure? If China and Chinese history are the home to which Chen attempts to return, what might be said about this particular homecoming that is filmmaking?

The story of *Temptress Moon* takes place at a crucial moment in the historical meeting between East and West—the 1911 Revolution, after which China shifted from the imperial to the republican era. Having been documented, described, debated, narrativized, and fantasized countless times, this moment can indeed be rewritten—schematically, of course—as a certain "primal scene" in which violence and progress converge, and in which the traditional, imperial patriarchal society gives way, albeit sluggishly, to a Westernized, feminized, and modernized state, henceforth to be ruled by the will of "the people." A contemporary Chinese director's revisit of this, modern China's critical historical moment, much like Zhongliang's revisit of his former home at the Pangs, cannot be naive or simplistically nativist. This is probably why, besides the convoluted narrative and the superimposed effects of characterization, Chen's film is also remarkably reminiscent of other films about modern China. To that extent, *Temptress Moon* stands as an assemblage of allusions, often calling to mind previous films that one has seen.

To cite a striking example of pure screen resemblance: in the scene in which Duanwu is to receive the honor of being appointed as the companion to Ruyi, who has just been made the head of the clan, the young boy is shown to be running into the ancestral parlor while the entire clan stands in observation of the ceremony. In a great hurry, Duanwu throws his proper clothes on while running. In the context of the story of *Temptress Moon,* this demonstration of haste is illogical—there is no reason why Duanwu should need to be rushed in the manner he is—until we realize that the scene is probably an allusion to a scene in the older Chinese director Li Hanxiang's *Huoshao yuanming yuan.*[10] In Li's film, which is set during the reign of the late Qing emperor Xian Feng, there is a scene featuring Prince Kung, one of the emperor's brothers, who has to rush from Beijing to attend Xian Feng's funeral in Jehol (in 1861). Since, by historical account, clothing for different imperial occasions was greatly ritualized, and since the prince was coming from Beijing, the character in Li's film is shown to be throwing on the proper funereal garb befitting the brother of the emperor as he dashes into the funeral parlor. Chen probably so liked the compelling ambience of that scene that he had to recreate it in his own work, even when it is not contextually necessary.

But the film that has left its marks most vividly on Chen's is, interestingly, not one made by a Chinese director—Bernardo Bertolucci's *The Last Emperor* (a film in which Chen was an extra, playing one of the anonymous guards standing at the entrance to the palace). It is from this film that Chen has made copious imaginative borrowings, from the construction of characters and narrative episodes to the use of architecture, interior décor, lighting,

[10] This is one of a series of films made by Li on the late Qing during the 1970s and 1980s. Others include *Chuilian tingzheng, Xi tai hou, Qing guo qing cheng, Ying tai xi xue,* and *Huo long.* Li, a director who left mainland China in the 1950s, worked in both Taiwan and Hong Kong. He died in 1996 in the midst of making a film in Beijing. Li first became well known in the 1960s with films he made for Shaw Brothers Ltd. (in Hong Kong) and for his own company Guo Lian (in Taiwan). When box office trends no longer favored the styles of his early works, he made a series of pornographic films to stay in the business; because of the success of these pornographic films, he received funding for his major historical films featuring the late Qing. One of his pornographic films was titled *Fengyue bao jian* [Precious lessons in matters of sex], which plays on the Chinese term *fengyue,* which, as I pointed out, is a euphemism for "matters of sex." Since Li's film, I believe, pornographic films have often been referred to as "Fengyue pian" in Chinese. Is it a coincidence that Chen adopted *Fengyue* as the title of his film?

and individual screen images. For instance, just as the bulk of the story of *The Last Emperor* is historically situated in the transition period between the Qing dynasty and the Republic of China, so the story of *Temptress Moon* begins with the 1911 Revolution, when the Qing dynasty officially ended, and lasts until about 1920.[11] The poignancy of this epochal moment is in both cases portrayed through the life of a child—Pu Yi, the boy emperor, in one case, and Ruyi, the future successor to the "throne" of the Pang clan, in the other. Both children are held captive in a privileged environment that is represented, with fascination, as out of sync with modern times. Like the little Pu Yi, Ruyi is full of mischief. In an early scene, she has to be chased out of the ancestral parlor where girls are not allowed; the doors the elders close to shut her inside her quarters are, in terms of cinematographic angles, a clear imitation of the high imperial gates that shut Pu Yi in the Forbidden City.*

Like Pu Yi also, Ruyi ascends to power by accident, when a proper male heir has failed to appear at the necessary moment. When she becomes the head of the Pang clan, Ruyi, once again reminding us of Pu Yi, introduces unprecedented policies that cause great consternation. Her order to retire her father's concubines, an act that is reminiscent of Pu Yi's historic retiring of the eunuchs of the palace, is shown to be a futile attempt at household reform. (The scene in which the concubines leave the family estate is visually reminiscent of the one in Bertolucci's film in which the royal family, led by the grown emperor, is forced to leave the forbidden city.) Above all, being cloistered in the prison-like world of her family town, Ruyi is ignorant of and longing for the new, modernized world outside. The arrival of Zhongliang from Shanghai, then, is not unlike the arrival of Reginald Johnston, Pu Yi's Scottish tutor, who brings Western education to the young emperor, including the fashionable item of a bicycle—an important detail that Chen does not neglect to include in his story.

The point of mentioning some of the borrowings Chen has obviously made from other films is not to accuse him of lack of

---

[11] Rayns offers the following account: "In Beijing in 1993, while he was still searching for a scriptwriter for *Temptress Moon* and trying to deal with the Film Bureau's demands for cuts in *Farewell My Concubine*, Chen joked to me that he would definitely set his next film in 1920—a year before the Chinese Communist Party held its first (underground) congress in Shanghai. That way, he implied, his scenario couldn't possibly be accused of misrepresenting the Party's role. So much for jokes in present-day China: the film is indeed set in 1920" (13).

originality. Rather, it is to emphasize that filmmaking, like writing, is conditioned by the utterances of others, the references others have made in and of the past. In the case of film, of course, the more accurate word to use is "gazes," and what I mentioned as "allusions" a moment ago should be understood not simply as contents of the story but also as ways of gazing that have been inscribed in previous films. For a contemporary Chinese director making a film about modern China, the questions are especially complex: if making a film about one's own culture is a certain kind of homecoming, how does one go about mediating between the desire for portraying that "home" exactly as one thinks one knows it and the allure of multiple images that have already been made of it by others and seen by millions more? In the light of the thematics of place, then, the older films of Li, Bertolucci, and others must be regarded as so many versions of a topos in its dual resonance as geography and as knowledge. Capturing the physical place, modern China, on film, these directors' works have also become sites of learning—visual archives on which directors such as Chen draw for their own work of imaging China. As these others' gazes beckon in their orientalist, exoticizing, or meticulously historical modes, the homecoming that is filmmaking inevitably becomes a process of citation and review, and—even as one produces a new collage of perspectives—of being (re)seduced with the sights/sites of others.

To return to the question of "authenticity" that I raised at the beginning, it is virtually impossible for a director such as Chen to be "authentic"—if by "authenticity" we mean the quality of being bona fide to the point of containing no impurities, no traces of others. Once this is understood, we will see that, paradoxically, the impossibility of being authentic is exactly the reason Chen's work can be so provocative. Not-being-authentic here translates into a remarkable filmic self-consciousness, reflecting and refracting the ways modern China has been looked at by others, Chinese and non-Chinese, in the past century and a half.

The Final Image of Homesickness

And yet, despite offering a self-conscious statement of what filmmaking amounts to in the postcolonial age by incorporating into his own film others' gazes and perspectives, Chen seems unable to overcome a familiar kind of emotion in relation to home—nostalgia. He expresses this emotion as he has often done in his previous works, through children. For his concluding image, Chen inserts an early scene from the childhood years of Ruyi, Duanwu, and Zhongliang: Ruyi and Duanwu are playing and running with their backs to the audience; Zhongliang, slightly older, is coming from the opposite direction facing us. As Ruyi and Duanwu turn their heads, the three children are looking at us at the same time. This moment is frozen as the final still. The gazes of the three children are a reminder of an exclamation made earlier by Zhongliang: "How nice it would be," he says, "if only we didn't have to grow up!" In terms of theorizations of the gaze, this visual conclusion confirms the ontological-representational relation that can, according to Slavoj Žižek, be asserted between nostalgia and children. Žižek argues that in the nostalgic mode, what is fascinating is not so much the displayed scene as "a certain gaze, the gaze of the 'other,' of the hypothetical, mythic spectator" who was still able to "take it seriously." "The innocent, naïve gaze of the other that fascinates us in nostalgia," he writes, "is in the last resort always the gaze of the child" (Žižek 112, 114).

In terms of place, meanwhile, what the gaze of the child (as explained by Žižek) signifies is the longing for a utopia, a non-place, a place that does not exist. In the context of *Temptress Moon,* this is borne out by the fact that the three children were, even as children, never allowed to be innocent, naive, or happy; childhood for them was not idyllic but filled with abuse and loneliness. In spite of the knowledge that his film has presented, however, the ending Chen supplies can be read only as a deliberate erasure of such knowledge. By invoking (and fetishizing) the gaze of the child, Chen forces certain narrative elements that have hitherto run quietly parallel to one another to crystallize and converge. The final image makes it possible to articulate these elements for the first time as tendencies of idealization that are present throughout the story from the beginning. And what is being idealized, whether by way of plot, characterization, or final screen image, is the nonexistent. Like Zhongliang's journey toward Beijing, and like his designs on Ruyi, the invocation of childhood is a maneuver that is doomed to fail. The enlightened, revolutionary capital city of modern China, the pure virgin woman in the countryside, and the still, innocent gazes of children all turn out to be unreachable places. Yet precisely because they are unreachable, they seem all the more "authentic," all the more to be longed for. We thus have the vicious circle of a cultural complex in which idealism leads, as it always does, to homesickness, and vice versa.

Ironically, the implications of Chen's concluding image bring him much closer to the critics who accuse him of forsaking the "authentic" China. In their reluctance to give up what is irretrievably lost, be it a hypothetical childhood or a mythical Chineseness, the director and his critics are finally united as perpetrators of the seductions of a certain kind of homecoming, a well-trodden path familiar to all. As they probably know only too well, such paths lead nowhere. But that, it should be added, is also probably why their homesickness persists.

Works Cited

Ba Jin. 1931. *Jia.* Hong Kong: Tiandi tushu, 1985.

Chow, Rey. 1995. *Primitive Passions: Visuality, Sexuality, Ethnicity, and Contemporary Chinese Cinema.* New York: Columbia University Press.

______. 1997. "Bulunbulei de youhuo—mantan Chen Kaige dianying Fengyue zhong de aimeixing." In *Dangdai wenhua lunshu: rentong, chayi, zhutixing—cong nuxing zhuyi dao houzhimin wenhua xiangxiang* [Contemporary cultural discourse: Identity, difference, and subjectivity—from feminism to postcolonial cultural imagination], 217–36. Taipei: Fujen University.

Edelman, Lee. 1997. Comment (on Rey Chow's paper), delivered at the Annual Conference of Narrative. University of Florida. April.

Foucault, Michel. 1980. *The History of Sexuality.* Vol. 1 (1976). Trans. Robert Hurley. New York: Vintage.

George, Rosemary Marangoly. 1992. "Traveling Light: Of Immigration, Invisible Suitcases, and Gunny Sacks." *Differences: A Journal of Feminist Cultural Studies* 4.2 (Summer): 72–99.

Laplanche, Jean. 1989. *New Foundations for Psychoanalysis* (1987). Trans. David Macey. Cambridge, Mass.: Basil Blackwell.

Rayns, Tony. 1996. "Motion and Emotion." *Sight and Sound* (March): 11–13.

Žižek, Slavoj. 1991. *Looking Awry: An Introduction to Jacques Lacan through Popular Culture.* Cambridge: MIT Press.

TWO

Duanwu Goes Home: Chen Kaige's *Temptress Moon* and the Politics of Homecoming

WENDY LARSON

The act of returning home is a central narrative theme in modern Chinese literature. In story after story of the May Fourth period, authors represent homecoming in different ways, but they always situate it as a contradictory and unsettling event in the establishment and construction of Chinese modernity. To return home means negotiation with the Chinese past, both that still existing within the present and that within the narrator's oft idealized memory. In this internalized past, the narrator experiences homecoming as a psychological crisis. In this essay I interpret the meaning of homecoming in Chen Kaige's 1997 film *Fengyue* (Temptress moon) and use the film to look back at homecoming within May Fourth enlightenment thought as it is expressed in Lu Xun's seminal stories "Guxiang" (My old home) and "Zhufu" (New year's sacrifice). I argue that in *Temptress Moon,* Chen continues a long discourse on homecoming and through the character of Duanwu, takes on, responds to, and deconstructs the May Fourth enlightenment narrative.[1] Duanwu provides a new

[1] This paper originated as a commentary on Rey Chow's article "The Seductions of Homecoming: Place, Authenticity, and Chen Kaige's *Temptress Moon,*" which is included in this volume. My debt to her argument, which shows how the theme of coming home again, presented vividly in the return of the character Zhongliang to the Pang residence in the countryside, is parallel to a structure implicit in the act of filmmaking, should be obvious. As part of my original comments, I used other publications by Rey for comparison and contrast. I have maintained those sections in this paper when they shed light on the character of Duanwu. I thank Rey for her work and for encouraging me to write a paper focusing on Duanwu's role in the film.

interpretation of homecoming and its relationship to the past by insisting on experiencing the past as history rather than as psychological trauma. In particular, Duanwu rejects the embodiment of the past as the trauma of loving and being loved, watching and being watching, desiring and being desired. What for others within the film is the trauma of psychological angst, becomes for Duanwu an opportunity to reject being "set up" by the enlightenment narrative and to substitute in its place a gendered politics of power. Although we see little of Duanwu's future, I try to investigate what a gendered politics of power means in terms of his actions and to interpret Chen Kaige's "trauma versus history" structure within that context. Here, I argue that the Duanwu character establishes homecoming, or the creation of a Chinese modernity, as an issue of male power, something hinted at throughout Lu Xun's stories but basically undeveloped. In this kind of homecoming discourse, negotiation with the past and the stance that must be taken for a future to emerge is constructed as an act of male will and a reorganizing of gender relations that works against the modern liberatory ideas of women's emancipation and equality between the sexes. By refusing the idea and practice of gender equality or more specifically by accepting gender inequality as the basis through which to act, Duanwu can say no to the crisis and its ensuing angst. Even more important, he displaces a problematic feminine seizure of power as something temporary and moves China toward a more unproblematic future. Gender difference becomes the basis for power difference and replaces the old-fashioned family structure that pushed Ruyi into power in the first place.

Lu Xun and the Experience of Homecoming

Homecoming is the quintessential act of meeting the past, which is the past within the present as it exists in the people, buildings, processes, language, and objects of the home village and in the narrator's mind and memory as it is triggered through his encounters with the people and places of his childhood. Lu Xun's male intellectual characters frequently experience a jarring dislocation when they go home, a dislocation that gives rise to their stark realization not only that they are seemingly contaminated by the past, but also that the mind-set born of this past blocks their ability to put change into effect. To use the common leftist interpretation directed at May Fourth liberalism, these intellectual vanguards of the revolution—the future—can only partially revolt; they lack the sensibilities and skills that could take them past a block of passivity and numbness. They cannot adequately grasp or in any way express the ideals of liberty, equality, science, and democracy, let alone put them into practice.

The protagonists of "Guxiang" and "Zhufu" (New year's sacrifice)[2] are hesitant narrators riddled with complex, contradictory distress because they cannot figure out how to respond to or even interpret the now distant yet intimately internalized feelings of their childhood. Ultimately they displace their discomfort with utopian rationalizations or through brief participation in rituals of

---

[2] Another homecoming work is "Kuangren riji" (Diary of a madman), where a man who has come home to discover that his brother has gone mad begins the tale in a brief paragraph written in classical Chinese, only to disappear completely into the madman's vernacular subjectivity. If we consider these stories chronologically ("Madman" was published in 1918, "Old Home" in 1921, and "Sacrifice" in 1924), we see a shift of emphasis into the uneasy mind of the narrator. Theodore Huters notes that this direction is above all a "focus on the question of self-knowledge" and locates seven stories in which Lu Xun emphasizes the "compromised narrator" (65, 72). See "Blossoms in the Snow: Lu Xun and the Dilemma of Modern Chinese Literature," *Modern China* 10, 1 (January 1984): 9–77. In showing the increasing "focus" on self-knowledge, Huters shows a path to the more extreme psychologization of characters that we find in the early Ding Ling and in Yu Dafu and also to the materialist critique of modernism that has lasted throughout the century.

Critiques of Lu Xun ran throughout the 1920s and have continued throughout the contemporary era. Lu Xun's work also has been an early object of study for Western scholars, and critics have found material for interpretations that enriches contemporary theoretical studies based on new understandings in feminist theory, postcolonial studies, and the like. In the 1920s, objections to Lu Xun's writing include criticism of his lack of a sense of national character (*guomin xing*), the vagueness of urban characters in his work, his emphasis on typical characters at the expense of finely and individually detailed representations, his excessive humanism, and his emphasis on the minds of intellectuals. In the late 1920s debate on revolutionary literature, Feng Xuefeng criticized Lu Xun for refusing to link the national character shown in "A Q zhengzhuan" (The true story of A Q) and other fictional works to China's economic system under the assaults of capitalism. Feng also faulted Lu Xun for his inability to get into the minds of the proletariat. Feng's conclusion, that Lu Xun is a thinker, not a revolutionary, was overturned by Mao Zedong in 1937 when he characterized Lu Xun as a writer, thinker, and revolutionary who refused to adopt the fawning stance desired by colonial powers. For a detailed study of these critics and much more, see the series of articles by Wang Furen that begins with "Zhongguo Lu Xun yanjiu de lishi yu xianzhuang" (The history and circumstances of Lu Xun research in China) in *Zhongguo xiandai wenxue* (Chinese modern literature), 8 (August 1993): 1–16, and continues in *Lu Xun yanjiu yuekan* (Lu Xun research monthly) in 1994, beginning with vol. 2 (February): 33–43; 3 (March): 29–40; 4 (April): 29–38; 5 (May): 7–53; 6 (June): 43–52; 7 (July): 49–57; 8 (August): 47–54; 9 (September): 46–52; 10 (October): 39–49; 11 (November): 42–54.

celebration. The narrators' vanguard position—the future-looking direction they occupy by virtue of their education and work "outside" their homes and the prestige it brings them—is actualized and experienced only as psychological trauma, not as a tool through which they can solidify their power within the local political or cultural structure or as a mechanism to push that culture "forward" toward acceptance of modern ideas and establishment of modern institutions and practices.

"My Old Home" is one of the purest homecoming stories in all of Lu Xun's work.[3] The nameless protagonist returns to the actual site where he grew up, exactly the same house and courtyard where his mother still lives, if not for long. The village is basically as it once was, and the local populace also is the same.

A great deal has been written about this story. Studies delve into and analyze the story's approach to some general issues that run throughout May Fourth literature: the crisis of representation, general questions directed at realism and its utopian tendencies or inappropriateness to the Chinese situation, the relationship between intellectuals and the masses, the nostalgia that infuses the May Fourth intellectual, and so on. By the late 1920s, a common leftist interpretation, directed by some critics toward Lu Xun and other writers, criticized the bourgeois inward turn that characterizes nineteenth-century European fiction and appeared in China in the 1920s.[4] This psychologizing in turn facilitates the narrator's—or more generally speaking the intellectual's—flight from recognition of poverty caused by unequal power relations. Using such a framework to evaluate Lu Xun's fiction results in some insights.

Characters such as the local woman once known as a beauty but now changed through age and poverty into a petty and irritating thief echo the story's central encounter, that of the narrator with his old childhood friend Runtu, the son of the narrator's

[3] Because the story is based on a real event in Lu Xun's life, some do not feel it belongs in a collection of short stories. Others, however, find it the most successful of all of Lu Xun's stories in overall conception and artistic achievement. See William Schultz, "Lu Hsun: The Creative Years" (Ph.D. diss., UCLA, 1955), 230.

[4] See Wang Furen, *Lu Xun yanjiu yuekan*, especially his essay in vol. 2 in which he describes intellectuals' critiques of Lu Xun in 1926–27. In the context of my essay here, it also is interesting to note that one Lu Xun critic, Li Changzhi, pointed out that the characteristics of Lu Xun's writing that are most admired are its sense of loneliness, its intellectuality, and its sadness, and that through these qualities it projects a feminine flavor. Ibid., 3:33. Another word frequently encountered in criticism from the 1920s and later is "pessimism," which is interpreted by leftist critics as an inward direction or a psychologizing of experience. Ibid., 4:32–34.

parents' former household servant. Even more than the former beauty, Runtu has been altered through aging, through the raising of six children, and through the poverty that allows him to eke out nothing more than a life of continual hardship. Runtu is more important to the narrator than the woman is because (as the story's "I" tells us directly) the narrator paid little attention to this famous beauty when he was small, but his entire mental landscape was changed by his fleeting relationship with the child Runtu. It is this narrowing of the village scene to Runtu and the expansion of Runtu into the narrator's entire experience of coming home that produce the lopsided emphasis on psychological trauma that we find in this story. At the same time, what Lu Xun foregrounds about Runtu, when the focus is on him rather than on the narrator, is his extreme poverty.

Centering psychological angst as a crucial modern experience for elites has a solid literary following in the 1920s. Ding Ling's character Sophia in "Shafei nüshi de riji" (Sophia's diary) and Yu Dafu's protagonist in "Chenlun" (Sinking) go further than Lu Xun's narrators in projecting inconsolable melancholy and depression as essential characteristics of their identity.[5] They also include and develop heightened sexual awareness and frustration as one aspect of the modern character, showing how sexuality, with its befuddling constructions of desiring and being desired, emerges as a key element in the modern person—an approach readily taken up in *Temptress Moon,* where much of the action revolves around the significance of sexual relationships. As if anticipating the later leftist critiques of such psychological trauma as bourgeois, foreign-originated, and individualistic, Lu Xun situates his story, if not his main character, somewhere in between those defined by a total plunge into subjective emotions and those that focus on the way in which relations formed through material production construct experience.[6] Thus the protagonist in "My Old Home" is trapped by nostalgia and an inability to act, yet at the same time he lays out for the reader to see the conditions of poverty, making

---

[5] The ideological meaning of Chinese writers' creation of characters with well-developed psychologies is taken up by Tani E. Barlow and Rey Chow in their interpretations of Ding Ling's Sophia. I have discussed this debate in my *Women and Writing in Modern China* (Stanford, Calif.: Stanford University Press, 1998), 138–40. See also my discussion of the problem as it has been treated by others immediately following, 140–44.

[6] For examples of such critiques leveled at women writers, see ibid., 177–94.

it clear to us that Runtu's problems are almost entirely economic in origin.[7]

Because I am reading back from my interpretation of *Temptress Moon,* what I want to emphasize here is this one particular aspect of the narrator's difficulty, his experience of homecoming as a psychological trauma. This is the crisis that the act of coming home engenders. The narrator's learning (which we must infer from his class and the fact that he has been away), itself the result of May Fourth enlightenment thought and its focus on education as a basis of change, is ineffective in relieving the poverty of Runtu or even giving the narrator a means of approaching or understanding it. Slowly the reader sees that the narrator's youthful experience, as well as the child's viewpoint, has caused the narrator to subtly idealize Runtu's life. As soon as his mother mentions Runtu, the narrator visualizes a stunning image of the seashore, shells, watermelon fields, and the chase for the fruit-stealing *zha.* He recalls ingenious traps set in the snow to catch birds. The materiality of life in all of its glory, denied to the bookish child who is kept within courtyard walls, unfolds before him. Yet we discover that the narrator fondly remembers something he has never seen: the vista that comes to represent Runtu's free and exciting life was merely described to him by the child Runtu. Although Runtu invited him to visit, the narrator never actually did, and in fact even the child Runtu visited the narrator only once, during the symbolically significant ancestor sacrifice time.

The authenticity of the vision comes under question, as does the narrator's memory of home. Home itself turns into a swirling mass of deceptive recollections, which one by one are dismantled by what the narrator sees as a returned adult. The magic of a material life has been overtaken by the innate resistance of matter, the transformation of which becomes a heartbreaking obstacle as Runtu tries to maintain or increase agricultural production in the

---

[7] Lin Zhihao, a contemporary critic of Lu Xun, underlines this point, showing how Lu Xun brings out the economic basis behind Runtu's appearance as a boy, when his father was able to buy a nice felt hat and a protective silver necklace for him. Lin writes, "Economics is the foundation; the change in Runtu's image cannot be separated from this foundation.... The change in Runtu's image is basically a reflection of the change in economic conditions. To deny this is to deny materialism. Naturally, change in appearance is the expression of change in spirit, and even more profound and tragic is the change in spirit; he has become a complete idiot, slow and mute." See *Lu Xun yanjiu (xia)* (Lu Xun research, vol. 2) (Beijing: Zhongguo renmin daxue chubanshe, 1986), 2:167.

face of natural calamities, tax collectors, and sundry money-grubbers. The woman who formerly attracted customers to her bean-curd shop with her beauty now slips in and steals from the narrator's house; she is not atypical, however, but merely representative of the other villagers, all of whom try to run off with things.

The impoverished reality of village life may not have been so extreme for the child Runtu's family, but surely it existed in more general terms when the narrator was a child—he met Runtu because Runtu's father brought him in to guard sacrificial vessels during ancestor sacrifice, hinting clearly that they could easily be stolen—but was invisible.[8] As a child and not responsible for taking care of basic necessities such as food and shelter, the narrator translated Runtu's life into a magical realm. As an adult, the narrator sees that Runtu has grown into a man much like his father, with creased face, calloused hands, and an air of exhaustion. Thus Lu Xun shows us that the hardship of peasant life is nothing new and in fact is a repeating reality, but one that the narrator simply could not see when he was young.

It is typical of Lu Xun's fiction to show but a glimmer of any positive future. Weighing in heavily on the side of darkness and despair, Lu Xun sometimes adds some symbolic hope—the crow flying off in "Yao" (Medicine), the nonappearing but challenging girl students in "Feizao" (Soap), the cry of "Save the children!" in "Kuangren riji" (Diary of a madman)—which he called his concession to the young. In "My Old Home," the narrator makes his now famous reference to hope as a road walked by many but as yet available only to children. Children, of course, can live within fantasy worlds because, lacking responsibility for their physical needs, they can transform the physical world into their own play realms.

But Lu Xun's reference is a form of deceiving the reader and perhaps also himself, since the reader knows that children will grow up and be educated, like the narrator, or succumb to the struggle for survival that constrains Runtu. Despite their education, their rejection of the past, and their allegiance to the idea of

---

8 In a recent reading of "My Old Home," Tang Xiaobing perceptively points to the fact that the mere idea of "old home" is an adult concept that children do not need, an idea produced by adults after they have become alienated (205–6). See "Xiandai jingyan yu neizai de jiayuan—du Lu Xun de 'Guxiang'" (Modern experience and the internal home: A reading of Lu Xun's "My Old Home"), *Jintian* 2 (1997): 204–20.

progress, Lu Xun's intellectual characters have no way to influence material life; other than "writing," an activity to which Juansheng in "Shangshi" (Regret for the past) is devoted and that more or less engages the others, the characters do not engage in other visible forms of work. Writing in the worst cases turns out to be hypocritical indulgence, simply ineffectual in the best. The crisis of homecoming, therefore, is not only the disappearance or destruction of an imagined past but also the striking lack of an imagined future.

The various terms that scholars have concocted to describe the moment of hope that springs in the mind of the narrator—the "lyrical epiphany," "ironic epiphany," "lyrical mediation," or "imaginary nostalgia"—best illustrate the fantastical and seductive sense that the narrators grasp: despite all evidence to the contrary, maybe things at least have a chance of being all right in the future. From my point of view, what is important is that this moment, short as it is and yet occupying the crucial position at the story's end from which all can be summed up, comes from an absolute refusal to recognize the reality of material life laid out before us in the story.[9] The moment of hope is, in other words, a psychological pacifier that displaces the poverty of Runtu and allows the narrator to go about his business. In the character A Q of "The True Story of A Q" and in his ability to reconstruct frequent beatings from other villagers as signs of his own success, Lu Xun created a sharp critique of mind over matter; furthermore, because we have the bulk of his other stories laid out before us and can clearly see the self-deceit his narrators must produce to push themselves forward, and because he is known for his pessimism, lack of hope, and darkness, we can hardly accuse Lu Xun of promoting this psychological trick. Yet he presents for us the mechanism, and in many of his stories the epiphany's position allows an ambivalence not evident in "The True Story of A Q." Interpreted ideologically, "My Old Home" presents two choices of modernity: a hard recognition of and commitment to changing the material conditions (poverty) that determine the lives of most rural people, or a flight to the city and the displacement of this reality through a psychologically produced euphoria.

---

[9] As Huters aptly puts it, "In each case, the access of lyricism at the conclusion is markedly at odds with what is represented in the story" ("Blossoms in the Snow," 71).

"New Year's Sacrifice" presents the same basic structure, baring for the reader the way in which those with cultural and economic capital sacrifice those without, thus perpetuating a system that will always bar resources to some to make them available to others. Xianglin Sao, herself the sacrifice, becomes the narrative nucleus with which others interact and gain currency. Stigmatized as dirty, she can be sacrificed to honor those who are clean; her oft repeated and finally ridiculed story of her son's being eaten by a wolf shows the absurd voice of the poor and ill-trained, who cannot effectively construct a narrative to tell their story and thus, through their lack, open a space for other stories including "New Year's Sacrifice." The sale of Xianglin Sao as wife to a second husband provides funds for her in-laws so they can purchase a wife for another son, and her failure to kill herself when she dashes her head against a table gives rise to the moral sensibilities of the village women, who blame her for living on to marry again.

The "I" of "New Year's Sacrifice" falls into even worse psychological angst than does the narrator of "My Old Home." Fretting endlessly about his answer "I'm not sure," which he gives Xianglin Sao when she asks about the existence of hell, the narrator cannot find even a moment of peace, as does the narrator in "My Old Home," by creating an image from a fantasized past.

When Xianglin Sao is prohibited from handling sacrificial vessels, Lu Xun again sets up for us the process of richer people using the poor during the family's organized rituals of sacrifice—hereby refusing Xianglin Sao's help and thus branding her as unclean in contrast to the family's cleanliness—effectively grinding their poverty into symbolic meaning for the wealthy. It is this elite processing of material impoverishment into symbolic ritual that is, for the narrator, the structure into which he should insert a challenge that calls for change. But he cannot. Instead, the narrator's education allows him to partially comprehend and despise his own role in this process and yet does not provide a way out.

Much more than "My Old Home," "New Year's Sacrifice" highlights the disproportionately large burden of shouldering elite cultural production that is borne by poor women. We never see Runtu's wife, presumably home and working. From a narrative point of view, Runtu shoulders the difficult act of representation and becomes its inarticulate spokesman. In "New Year's Sacrifice," on the other hand, Xianglin Sao emerges as a character because her husband dies; she is forced to become a servant when she is widowed and her son dies. With her irritating repetition of the story of her son's being eaten by a wolf, Xianglin Sao's narrative answers the question, What would Runtu say if he could talk? Without access to culture-producing symbolic logic, the impoverished can tell no stories, can only make repetitive noises.

It is significant, however, that Lu Xun locates this story-creating impulse in a female character. Is Lu Xun projecting a common view of women that finds in them a tendency toward useless talk and an inability to construct abstract arguments?[10] Or does Xianglin Sao provide us with a tiny step beyond what Runtu can do because as a woman, she has liberties that Runtu does not? In her reading of Lu Xun's story "Feizao" (Soap), Carolyn Brown claims that the story revolves around Lu Xun's critique of the far-ranging influence of the *caizi jiaren* (scholar and beauty) trope that runs through classical literature.[11] Within the story, Mrs. Siming has the ability to "reread the male text" and is thus empowered to understand China's future in ways in which Siming, befuddled by romantic ideals from the literature of the past, is not. Brown calls this the wisdom of those at the bottom and yet insists that Mrs. Siming's power, limited as it is, does not emerge from or embody an ideological position: she just wants Siming to direct his attention toward her. Mrs. Siming, in other words, is far from a revolutionary herself; she just wants to claim a beneficial position within the gender hierarchy.

Brown analyzes the scene of the Siming family at the table, where Siming, with irritation, watches his son snatch up a tantalizing morsel of food that he desired. This scene, Brown writes, subtly illustrates the repression of desire hidden in the theory and practice of filial piety that orders Siming's entire worldview. Significantly, Brown begins her essay with a reference to Lu Xun's own article on what happens to Ibsen's Nora after she leaves home. The options open to women of the times, Lu Xun cautions, are prostitution or simply giving up and returning home. Women's homecoming discourse, in other words, differs from men's. Whereas men must confront and interact with the past in the present, women are engulfed by past definitions of the female role or, if they choose to stay away, encompassed within sexual

---

10 See my discussion of May Fourth debates on the innate natures of men and women in *Women and Writing in Modern China*, 63–68.

11 See "Woman as Trope: Gender and Power in Lu Xun's 'Soap,'" *Modern Chinese Literature* 1 and 2 (Spring and Fall 1988): 55–70.

servitude as organized by men, who profit from it. Such an early-twentieth-century gendered distinction in the meaning of home-coming sheds light on Duanwu's behavior when we arrive at his transformation from loyal servant to his "sister" at home to violent rapist in Shanghai. In the film and in Lu Xun's stories, sexual relationships and behavior insert women into meanings (wife/whore) so overladen with significance that they are unable to escape. Women seem to possess the symbolic meaning of future possibilities, or the spark of progress, but they lack the forward momentum to actualize it.

If Mrs. Siming has insight that her husband lacks, it is only because she cannot read and become overly contaminated by the sentimental world of "scholars and beauties," but can only talk. She can see through the lustful hypocrisy of Siming and his Confucian friends as they obsess about the beggar girl, thus partially voicing a critique of Confucian patriarchy that would beome common in the discourse of May Fourth intellectuals.

I believe we see several strands of May Fourth thought in Lu Xun's subtle privileging of women's ability to see through things, or to voice even ineffectual or countereffectual tales, like that of Xianglin Sao. Brown has shown how "Soap" gives Mrs. Siming revelatory powers within the narrative because she is at the bottom of the social hierarchy, and to a great extent that position is a function of being female. Xianglin Sao possesses the same quality of being a female at the bottom, but lacking a husband or a son to anchor her relational position, she is in even worse shape than Mrs. Siming or the nonexistent Mrs. Runtu. One of Xianglin Sao's biggest problems is that without a male connection through which she can voice her discontent, she has to speak out in the more public arena, thus making herself the laughingstock of the village by her unsophisticated, repetitive rant. Of course, the structure behind Xianglin Sao's oppression is invisible to her; she can hardly speak about misogyny and female roles, poverty and the elite, and the literary and textual web that supports those who kidnap and sell her. Her myopic focus is solely on her own misfortune in losing her son to a wolf.

Because she does not have a male to represent her or mediate between her and others, Xianglin Sao latches onto the educated male intellectual, and it is through this link that we have access to the story. If we translate Xianglin Sao's question "Is there a hell?" into "Will I suffer forever?" and then take her character as representative of the lowest rung on the social scale, we can see why the narrator could not answer. More than any other woman in Lu Xun's stories (with the possible exception of Zijun in "Regret for the Past"), Xianglin Sao is presented to us an an enabler, a pivot who allows other narratives to develop both abstractly and in material life. Xianglin Sao's question to the narrator also produces his traumatized state of mind, which overwhelms any story that she herself can tell or even represent.

As I compare this story to Chen Kaige's *Temptress Moon,* I see a similar position occupied by Ruyi. In *Temptress Moon,* however, the narrator's position translates into two positions and is occupied by the characters Zhongliang and Duanwu. Zhongliang sinks into mental collapse, and Duanwu spins off his relationship with Ruyi to assume a position of power. If we regard Zhongliang as one possible way of being modern and Ruyi as a second (or perhaps, because of limitations associated with being female, a modernizing impulse), we can see that Duanwu, through his switch from menial servant to master, represents a third option.

Home As You Wish It

The overarching context of *Temptress Moon* is clear in the opening narrative, which tells of the British attack on China, the Opium Wars, the importation of opium into China, and addiction to opium as part of the social crisis of the late-Qing dynasty. The beginning year, 1911, when Zhongliang is orphaned and goes to live with his sister, is the end of the Qing dynasty and the beginning of the Republic. The background of Western imperialism and colonialist intentions in China, which with the abdication of the emperor along with the Western presence now has an uncertain future, comes to the audience through a closer view at the Pang family rural estate in the Jiangnan area not far from Shanghai.

Even before this, the Pang daughter Ruyi ("as you wish it") as a child stands listening to a lecture from her father, who tells her about the joys of opium smoking. As we see a cloud of smoke envelop her, she smiles enigmatically. Later we discover that Ruyi and her older brother, the sole heirs to the Pang fortune, both smoke opium.

The next scene shows a row of older men standing, and then Zhongliang moving on a boat through lily pads to arrive at the Pang estate. The scene switches, and Ruyi is sneaking beneath tables in a large room where women are playing Mah-Jongg. The camera focuses on their long fingernails and jewels, and we hear talk of large amounts of money, giving the picture of excessive indulgence and decadence. Ruyi runs through the room, pulling tablecloths off and bringing Mah-Jongg tiles and dishes crashing to the ground. She emerges from under a table and looks directly at the viewer, as do the three main characters now and then throughout the film. As she takes off with an older man in pursuit, she runs into the ancestral hall where, we immediately hear, girls are forbidden. The scene then turns to several men who have just heard that the emperor has abdicated and are lamenting. This is the first time Duanwu appears, watching around the corner. We hear a voice telling him to catch Ruyi, because even if the emperor has abdicated, it is still unthinkable to have a girl in the ancestral hall. At this point Zhongliang joins Ruyi and Duanwu, and the three look winsomely at the camera.

These scenes establish many meaningful issues, and we understand through their direct looks that the three children are speaking to us. Ruyi's flaunting of both the decadence of traditional elite culture and the strictures against female presence in places of authority is a precursor not only to her future behavior, but also to general thematic elements in the film, especially to its continual questioning of what it means to be a man or a woman. The national and cultural power invested in the empire and overturned when the emperor abdicates are part of the general crisis—economic, military, and social—that allows a powerful underworld to develop. The enigmatic smile we see on Ruyi's face after she listens to her father call opium his inspiration and as she disappears in the hazy cloud of smoke foreshadows an important focus on human pleasure and desire that structures the film. And Duanwu's role in catching and constraining Ruyi proves prophetic as he eventually takes over her role as head of household.

As Ruyi's cousin and playmate, Duanwu has no rights to the family fortune. He is brought in when Ruyi's older brother Zhengda, who is married to Zhongliang's sister, becomes incapacitated. Actually Zhengda has been poisoned by Zhongliang. The young Zhongliang is disgusted and angered because his route to study—the carrot his sister dangled before him when she brought him into the household—has been cut off by his demanding, opium-addicted brother-in-law, who not only forces him to prepare opium for him constantly but also coerces him into sexual games with his sister under the mark of "teaching him to be a man." Zhongliang adds arsenic to the opium and destroys his brother-in-law's mental capabilities, then has to flee. Thus Duanwu is brought in by other male relatives to help the "weak" female heir; Duanwu, in other words, is supposed to be a conduit through which the men in the family can control and manipulate Ruyi into saying what they want her to say and acting as they want her to act while he himself has no opinions or power.

The ploy fails immediately when Ruyi, fully conscious of the anger her decision will inspire in family members, tells Elder Qi to send away the concubines who belonged to her father and brother. Not only does she send them away, but she chides and taunts her male relatives by telling them that she is doing the women a favor, since women don't belong in the ancestral hall anyway. Clearly Ruyi has been festering under her femaleness and the restrictions it has imposed on her since she was a child. But where did Ruyi, whose formal education undoubtedly has been traditional and, given the fierce gender concepts of the Pang family, quite possibly very limited, and who shows no understanding of modern gender roles or feminist protest, get this idea?[12] The film gives us no clue, leaving us to understand that she is by nature a rebellious and even revolutionary person with a strong concept of self-value. As a child, she already dared to upset the Mah-Jongg tables, and as an adult, she dares to upset the entire family's traditional gender relationships. Here we see a possible link to the earlier depiction of women in Lu Xun's stories. Although none of the women are as bold as is Ruyi, their lowly social position gives them knowledge unavailable to the men, knowledge that is based on a life experience against which they "naturally" struggle. Ruyi's position partially corresponds to that of Ibsen's Nora, who became a symbol for reformist intellectuals on the left such as Lu Xun; Nora fails because she has nowhere to go but to prostitution or home, and thus she can forcefully represent the constrictions placed on women by traditional social practice and the difficulties of revolutionary actions. The feminine seizure of power that underlies the actions of Ruyi, along with that of other female characters in May Fourth literature, has some connection with a more utopian future and provides us with a direction toward change.

[12] Although in a large wealthy family such as the Pang family a daughter most likely would have been educated at home, when Ruyi and Duanwu arrive in Shanghai they cannot figure out where they are, despite a large sign with the characters "Shanghai" written on it before them. Duanwu takes off and returns in a few minutes to tell Ruyi excitedly that this is Shanghai. We do not find out how he discovers this information.

And rather than go out to change society, Ruyi is changing her home.

Meanwhile, Duanwu has refused to overturn Ruyi's decision and is mocked and beaten by the men in the household, who berate him for not being a real man and mourn the loss of real men in the Pang family. Duanwu's loyalty to Ruyi appears absolute; he claims he wants not a penny, but only to serve her the rest of his life.

Viewers see the concurrent development of the three main characters as the film switches between the Pang estate and Shanghai, where Zhongliang has ended up. After he leaves the Pangs, Zhongliang tries to go to Beijing but is tricked or lured into going to Shanghai by mafia men after his suitcases are stolen—and because the men appear to help Zhongliang immediately after two boys run off with the suitcases, the whole thing appears to be a setup. Zhongliang is trying to make his way to the good and the true side of modern life that the nonappearing Beijing, with its possibilities of gaining modern knowledge through study, represents throughout the film. But he ends up in the deceitful arena where romantic love is nothing but a commodified trick and the bonds of kinship are expressed in the father-son link between Dada, the underworld boss, and Zhongliang. This scene, however, is as mystifying as Ruyi's seemingly feminist actions. Why was Zhongliang so easily deceived? On the train platform, as he is rushing about screaming "Which train goes to Beijing?" and trying to make his escape, he can't figure out which train to get on. Why doesn't he calmly ask some of the many people around him which train is correct? All we can see is that he is too anxious and confused to act intelligently. We must conclude that his terror and overwhelming desire to escape cloud his perceptions and cause him to lose his bags and his way, in the process making him an apt target for Dada's men. Although Zhongliang was victimized and traumatized by his brother-in-law and by a sister who refused to demand better treatment on his behalf but did not refuse to participate in her husband's sex games, this is the first scene where we see psychological trauma taking over on its own and ordering his actions without any apparent cause. His psychological distress has caused him to literally lose his way.

By the time we catch up with Zhongliang, it is the 1920s, the heady days of revolutionary thought in all spheres. Questions of what it means to be modern and how China can be modern and still stay Chinese surround the May 4, 1919, student revolt against foreign control of Chinese territory, and the ensuing social, political, and economic changes turn out to be immense. Zhongliang has in many ways become a modern person: he has traded his long gowns for the most contemporary Western suits, smokes cigarettes, not opium, and is a constant fixture at the bars and dance halls that bring in new-style Chinese and foreigners alike. Having been absorbed into a large underground family run by Dada, Zhongliang is to seduce women and get them into compromising situations so they can be blackmailed by Dada's men.[13] Except for one relationship he has developed with a woman who looks suspiciously like his sister, he carries out his work admirably. Dada warns him, "I fear that dreams multiply when the night is long," and indeed, Zhongliang has become emotionally attached to this woman.

When Dada orders him back to the Pang family to work his seduction on Ruyi, Zhongliang finds himself in a terrible homecoming dilemma. Here Rey Chow's interpretation of the film as using a psychological model is compelling. Chow shows us how Chen Kaige sets up the Pang household as a site of infantile seduction for Zhongliang, who throughout his life is influenced by and repeats this "primary encounter with sexuality." Through this sexual model we can see that Zhongliang's success in being modern is not authentic or creative, nor does it possess the reality that those values imply; it is simply the enactment, over and over, of this sexual trauma, a pattern that displaces the first event at least until he ends up "home" again.[14]

[13] Because Rey Chow's essay in this volume focuses on Zhongliang, I will mention only as much as necessary about his character to show how his way of being modern contrasts with that of Duanwu. See her essay for a discussion of the parallel nature of the relationship between Duanwu and Ruyi and between Zhongliang and his sister. Although Duanwu and Ruyi are not biological siblings, the male family members instruct him to call her *jiejie* (elder sister), thus setting up a symbolic sibling relationship. Significantly, Zhongliang's biological sister is impressed with Duanwu's loyalty to Ruyi, commenting enviously that rarely does one see such loyalty to a sister.

[14] Although both Chow and I focus on psychological trauma, it is for different reasons and with different interpretations. Because I believe the director has foregrounded psychological trauma as a theme with cultural specificity and national implications, I emphasize the contrast between the two stories—that of Zhongliang and that of Duanwu. I agree with Chow's analysis of Zhongliang's sexual trauma as his original crisis that is then repeated throughout his life, but my emphasis lies on the way in which that kind of existence is challenged through the character of Duanwu.

When Zhongliang finally does accept Dada's assignment and return to the Pang estate, the servants praise him, noting how study in Beijing has made him into a gentleman. The Beijing-Shanghai contrast emerges forcefully here, with Beijing standing as the true modernity based on knowledge and Shanghai as the illicit copy based on surface alone.[15] The May Fourth principles of enlightenment around which Lu Xun circles and which hypocritically serve Zhongliang's seduction of Ruyi, who is beguiled by images of liberated Beijing female students that Zhongliang poetically evokes for her despite that fact that he has never been to Beijing, materialize only as lyrical moments or hypothesized roads in Lu Xun's work.

Ruyi is "grounded" in a way that Zhongliang and Duanwu are not. After sending away the concubines, Ruyi has a moment of regret for the enjoyable times that have been lost. Her sympathy quickly switches to herself, however; with tears in her eyes she comments to Duanwu that although the others have left, she was born here and here she must die. This gendered groundedness, or the association of women with the home, extends even more fully to Zhongliang's sister, who cries over and over about the life she has led for the last ten years locked up in the Pang family estate and tries pathetically to get Zhongliang to take her to Beijing.

A comparison of Ruyi's situation with that of Duanwu leads to some interesting conclusions. As long as he binds himself loyally to Ruyi, Duanwu is as grounded as she is. Only when he breaks the tie of love that he develops with Ruyi can he be on his own, and paradoxically gain power and freedom even though he returns home again.

Zhongliang's job when he returns home is the same as before: he is to seduce Ruyi and get her to go with him to Shanghai so Dada can use her absence to blackmail or threaten the Pang family for money. This setup differs from Zhongliang's previous job in that because Ruyi is unmarried, the threat of blackmail would not seem to be so serious, but the exact plan is not divulged to us. Perhaps Ruyi's pleasure trip will be presented as a kidnaping and her family will have to pay ransom, or Dada will threaten the family with public divulging of Ruyi's moral transgressions, or the act

15 For an elaboration of the Beijing-Shanghai contrast throughout modern literature and film, see Yingjin Zhang, *The City in Modern Chinese Literature and Film: Configurations of Space, Time, and Gender* (Stanford, Calif.: Stanford University Press, 1996).

will be a simple robbery while Ruyi is away. Somehow, in some unexplained way, the goal of getting to the Pang money will be reached. Zhongliang's plan runs into problems first because he becomes attracted to Ruyi and second because although she, like all the other women, is more than happy to become involved with Zhongliang, she is different from them.

She takes it upon herself, in what to Zhongliang is a shocking reversal of his normal seduction sequence, to offer him the second earring to match the one he has stolen to show to Dada as a token of his success. Even more amazing is her decision to change herself from a girl into an attractive woman by having sex with Duanwu in anticipation of her meeting with Zhongliang. Ruyi's "let me play too" attitude, her childlike innocence in the game of love, and her uncanny agency in proffering the second earring—possibly the same quality that allowed her to turn over the Mah-Jongg tables and send away the concubines—sets her off from all the other women Zhongliang seduces. In the first part of his seduction, Zhongliang has to use the old narrative that beguiled him—study in Beijing—to lay out for Ruyi the modern changes that now characterize the urban world. Beijing and its students, especially female students, come to represent revolution, sexual equality, and the passion of youth for a political cause. Zhongliang's own seduction and betrayal show clearly on his face as he falls into reverie at his melodramatic description of the modern wonders of Beijing.

As all of this goes on, Duanwu, frustrated with Ruyi's infatuation with Zhongliang, shows a hint of change in his placid and obedient nature. When he accompanies Ruyi to what is supposed to be Beijing, Duanwu ventures off on his own the minute he arrives, returning quickly to tell Ruyi that this is Shanghai. As Ruyi is set up by Dada's men to watch Zhongliang betray his girlfriend in Heavenly Lane, Duanwu leaves and wanders around Shanghai. Although we see nothing but his first steps and his apprehension and wonder at the labyrinth of buildings and alleys, this experience is crucial for him, for he comes back totally changed. He now has synthesized what he has seen and come to the conclusion that "men and women are at war—one wins, the other loses." He also takes a powerful personal stance: "I don't want to lose." Ruyi's detached comment is, "Tonight I go to see Zhongliang," showing her failure to acknowledge Duanwu's desire for her.

Within a short time, Duanwu undergoes a complete transformation from country boy to confident master of a large and profitable estate. How does this alteration occur, and what reasons does the film provide for Duanwu's change? Like several other insufficiently explained changes or events in the film, Duanwu's revelation remains basically unexplained.[16]

What is Duanwu rejecting, what is he moving toward, what is his strategy to get there, and finally, what are the larger meanings associated with this character's actions? The short answers are that Duanwu is rejecting love and what it represents, he is moving toward a powerful future, and his strategy to get there involves grabbing power through gender hierarchy. The larger meanings are the rejection of a Western psychologized view of the world and a recognition that power determines who wins. The gendered structure of power in the film becomes a metaphor for power in the world, as well as functioning as a localized means for power to develop.

Duanwu's enlightenment, or his ability to break free of the ties that kill Zhongliang and incapacitate Ruyi, appears to come from nothing more than his wandering about Shanghai, being propositioned by prostitutes, finding his way among the alleys and gates, and finally, witnessing the suicide of Zhongliang's lover in Heavenly Lane. That these events could cause such a radical change is unbelievable in the context of the film, but this fact can lead us to a very simple interpretation: Duanwu's first encounter with the kind of modernity that is available in Shanghai staggers and permanently alters him. Of course, Duanwu has been primed for change by the same force we see envelop Zhongliang—the love he is developing for Ruyi.

Over the course of his service to Ruyi, Duanwu becomes more and more enamored of her, and after Zhongliang arrives, he shows his distress at Ruyi's oblivious disregard of his affection. But rather than be encompassed by a love story and its loyalty, passion, betrayal, jealousy, and so on, Duanwu rejects the story and gains power.

---

[16] Duanwu's name probably refers to the festival that occurs on May 5, a coincidence that could be meaningful in that Duanwu represents the position that it is power, not knowledge, that allows one to succeed. Thus his name indicates that which comes directly after May Fourth. My thanks to Samuel Cheung for pointing this out to me.

Temptress Moon reminds me of a pattern familiar to us through some of Zhang Yimou's films. Here a strong woman, always played by Gong Li as in *Temptress Moon,* is the conduit through which a man progresses toward a powerfully expressed future. Invariably another older, weaker, and more conservative man stands in the way, and the power relationships of this triangle define the success or failure of the younger man's quest. Furthermore, it is through a sexual relationship with the woman that the younger man is able to become reinvigorated and oriented toward progress.[17]

In this film, Duanwu is the younger man, and Zhongliang stands in his way. First by declaring loyalty to his "elder sister" and then by having sex with her at her request, raping her, and announcing their relationship to her fiancé, he gains both power and screen time. As is typically the case with Zhang Yimou's films, here the woman loses her mental capacity; in other films she dies or goes insane. Only in *Red Sorghum* does the victorious younger man end up in a position anywhere nearly as positive as that of Duanwu at the end of *Temptress Moon.*

The relationship between gender and the past or the modern is complicated in the film.

Beijing, the utopian, fantasized modern, is represented by female students, much as it is in Lu Xun's story "Soap," where we hear of short-haired female students but as in this film, never actually encounter them. Shanghai is where the modern goes bad, but it also is the only modern that exists; we can only infer that in the scheme of relationships within the film, Shanghai is the true or actualized modern while Beijing is imagined. The Pang estate is the Chinese past, or home. In *Temptress Moon,* the Pang household elders bemoan the loss of "true men" when Duanwu allows Ruyi to send away the concubines, implying that although once the Chinese past was the locale of power as expressed through male strength, it has become feminized and lost its power.[18] When Zhongliang arrived at the Pang family estate, it already had succumbed to symbolic Western takeover through the addiction of its heirs to opium; as we can see in the character Zhengda, this addiction effectively feminized the site, corrupting and ruining its

---

[17] See my article "Zhang Yimou: Inter/National Aesthetics and Erotics," in *Cultural Encounters: China, Japan, and the West,* ed. Søren Clausen, Roy Starrs, and Anne Wedell-Wedellsborg (Aarhus: Aarhus University Press, 1995), 192–214.

[18] The "elders" to which I refer probably are distant relatives brought in as servants, but they function as guardians of authority and tradition within the family.

ability to produce the future. Zhongliang claims that modernized Shanghai is the "place for men," a place where men do as they wish with women.[19] It is only when Duanwu discovers the war between the sexes in Shanghai and beholds a woman kill herself for love of a man that he loses his loyalty to Ruyi, eventually raping and betraying her. Patriarchal culture once had no choice but to empower Ruyi, but Shanghai allows Duanwu to capture this power from her.

In her essay, Rey Chow indicates that Duanwu represents a new type of man, someone abused by the past but who does not internalize his wounds. She calls him "unperturbed." Indeed, the post-epiphany Duanwu lacks the sensitivity and doubt of the old Zhongliang-type of character. If Duanwu represents the new China, he certainly is not feminized; rather, he has successfully used Ruyi's power and strength to set up his own regime. In that she can be used by both men for their own aims, Ruyi stands as a disposable pivot between the old and the new. The two male characters also present us with an ironic reversal: it is Zhongliang, with his constant burden of the past—yet his modern clothes and lifestyle—who destroys Ruyi, and her demise creates room for Duanwu—who wears robes and lives the most traditional lifestyle—to flourish and move toward a powerful future.

Duanwu first accepts and then makes his way out of a subservient role and into an authoritative position. Although he starts out as nothing but the country cousin, ironically it is not Duanwu, but Ruyi and Zhongliang who are crudely bewitched by material things, Zhongliang by his own beautiful appearance as well as by the brocades, embroidery, and silks of the past that he fingers as he arrives home again, Ruyi by the apparatus of modernity—razors, bicycles, and so on. These are "wannabe" intellectuals, entranced with the possibility of new knowledge yet unable to make it to Beijing. Duanwu doesn't have the same problem. Rather, the war between the sexes provides him with his own moment of enlightenment, clearly shown on his shocked face as he looks directly at the audience, and the ability to devise a warpath that leads toward social power. He's going home, not to Beijing.

Duanwu, unlike Ruyi and Zhongliang, knows nothing of the promise of new knowledge. He has no Beijing out of which to

---

19 Despite their differences, Zhengda, Zhongliang, and Duanwu all produce their power, or the "real man," through sex, centering sexual behavior as central to human identity.

construct an illusive modernity. Duanwu's only modern environment is Shanghai, where he is harassed and propositioned by prostitutes on the street. He turns this struggle into his own physical attack against Ruyi. The lesson he learns is that if you want to win, you must fight, and what you must fight against is women. The past for Duanwu is servitude in the Pang family; the future is his power in the same locale. He is not traumatized by his past as is Zhongliang, who internalizes old wounds and can never get over them. Coming out of, accepting, and living the past as history—a narrative in which he will occupy a specific power position—rather than as psychological trauma, does Duanwu have a better chance of success, or minimally, can he avoid being shot by capitalist gangsters or destroyed by poisoned opium as are the other two characters?

Duanwu's allegorical rejection of the West's psychologized modern subjectivity appears to be the film's answer of "yes." Duanwu's character says, Forget psychological trauma, especially that associated with love. Throughout the film we hear women and men repeating the love phrases and demanding that others speak them: I love you, you love me, do you love me? do I love you? do you love her? you don't love him! As he becomes attracted to Ruyi and disgusted by her loyalty to Zhongliang, Duanwu at first appears to be sucked into the same sort of interaction. Like Zhongliang, Duanwu develops affection for a woman, but what does he do after she refuses to acknowledge his desire for her? He refuses traumatization, instead using rejection in love to gain power. After his experiences in Shanghai, he concludes that he must just grab power however possible, which is easiest if he takes it from Ruyi both in the rape and in his replacement of her, at the right opportunity, as head of the household. Duanwu's confident demeanor as he returns to the Pang household, his callous response to Zhongliang's needy sister, and his flagrant abuse of his servant's position as he tells Ruyi's fiancé that she has had sex with him and with Zhongliang all speak to the new power he has claimed. To be male is to have power, or to have power is to be male, as Zhengda tells us when forcing the young Zhongliang to kiss his own sister. Sexual politics merely carves out the road to power.

In some parts of her 1991 book *Woman and Chinese Modernity,* Rey Chow reads modern Chinese literature through Freudian psychology, analyzing both the characters and the writers. As for Ding Ling's "Sophia's Diary," Chow argues that instead of reading Sophia as a woman encompassed by her own trivial and boring emotions, oblivious to the larger social world around her and totally defined through the characteristics of bourgeois femininity, readers should view the alternately repressed and expressed sexuality in Sophia as one expression of female agency and subjectivity, a new and modern state of being for Chinese women. In Chow's analysis, "feminine self-sacrifice was the major support of traditional Chinese culture," and thus in times of cultural trauma, it is not unusual to find women centered as representative of change or of various kinds of ideologies.[20]

According to Chow's essay in this volume, Chen Kaige often constructs male subjectivity through a "fright-and-flight" paradigm, which we see in *Temptress Moon* as Zhongliang always on the run. I have argued that Chen's films generally feature a male character engaging a central narrative of modern China.[21] In *Yellow Earth,* the folk songs that Gu Qing collects from the People are to be rewritten as anti-Japanese Communist Party songs, thus embodying the concept of the Party going to the People for their inspiration and culture. Lao Gan takes over the role of teacher in *King of the Children,* a position from which he is supposed to influence the subjectivities and actions of his students. In *Big Parade,* several male characters attempt to ritualistically display the power and representational unity of the People's Liberation Army even as they question it. And in *Farewell My Concubine,* the first film by Chen in which the lead male role is split between two characters, Cheng Dieyi's role in Beijing opera represents and performs a quintessential Chinese cultural form.

This simple and direct action always fractures, however, as the film progresses. In each case, the male character is feminized, which in the films means that he is compromised with complex knowledge, a split subjectivity, and the inability to realize his goals through planned action. Chen's films construct this symbolic femininity as a means through which male subjectivity can be deepened and made aware of its own lack of, belief in, or control over the history that has been produced through central narratives. Although women embody the more primitive and pure

[20] *Woman and Chinese Modernity: The Politics of Reading between East and West* (Minneapolis: University of Minnesota Press, 1991), 162, 170.

[21] See my article "The Concubine and the Figure of History: Chen Kaige's *Farewell My Concubine,*" in *Transnational Chinese Cinemas: Identity, Nationhood, Gender,* ed. Sheldon Hsiao-peng Lu (Honolulu: University of Hawai'i Press, 1997), 334–46.

knowledge of lived experience, they cannot possess the deeply fractured consciousness of the central male characters. As is best shown in *Farewell My Concubine*, however, when male characters are feminized, they do not imitate woman's naturalness, but rather become the shattered victims of what was once a unified consciousness.[22]

What happens in *Temptress Moon*, and is Duanwu shattered and thus feminized as are the other male characters in Chen's films? By arguing that Duanwu presents an alternative to Zhongliang's embodiment of psychological angst as the basis of a modern life, I believe that the theme of psychologized experience is thematized within the film, and furthermore, that the Duanwu character represents a resolution to a problem theorized in several of Chen's earlier films. While refusing to give us any access to Duanwu's inner mind, *Temptress Moon* lovingly creates interior depth in the form of angst and passion in the character of Ruyi and especially in Zhongliang. In Leslie Cheung's finely tuned acting, we see Zhongliang disintegrate under the demands of love and its bonds. His traumatized mind leaves no positive road for him to take, and he ends up poisoning Ruyi much as he poisoned her brother before. Ruyi is almost equally traumatized by the love relationship, and even though she eventually rejects Zhongliang's declaration of love as coming too late and walks away while mumbling about her lifelong desire to be a bride, her tears and the blank look on her face belie any progression out of the damning love story into an actively and positively expressed future.

The gender difference underlies the power hierarchy and becomes a structure through which power is negotiated. Desiring and being desired, looking and being looked at are at the core of the love story; because they have national and international cultural implications and, especially in film, become the way in which one culture is viewed by another, issues of desire and the gaze also figure prominently in contemporary film criticism as well as postcolonial theoretical approaches to cultural analysis.[23]

---

[22] Ibid., 335.

[23] See Rey Chow, *Primitive Passions: Visuality, Sexuality, Ethnography, and Contemporary Chinese Cinema* (New York: Columbia University Press, 1995), 166–72, the section "The Oriental's Orientalism; or, Exhibitionism between Cultures." For theories of desire and the gaze, see Mary Ann Doane, *The Desire to Desire: The Woman's Film of the 1940s* (Bloomington: Indiana University Press, 1987); also idem, *Femme Fatales: Feminism, Film Theory, Psychoanalysis* (New York: Routledge, 1991). See also the work of Laura Mulvey, including *Visual and Other Pleasures* (Bloomington: Indiana University Press, 1989) and "Afterthoughts on 'Visual Pleasure and

To simplify the issue a bit, wanting to be gazed at and desired is a feminine position that indicates a lack of power. In the cross-cultural viewing of film, the presentation of unique cultural forms, especially from third-world cinema, has been criticized as a kind of look-at-me posturing that is aimed at gaining the respect and interest of the viewer from the first world.[24] By rejecting the love story and reducing it to a power struggle, Duanwu avoids the trap of wanting to be gazed on or desired and refuses to allow the mystification of power that love produces. To interpret Duanwu's stance in terms of cultural interaction, Duanwu's refusal of psychological trauma through love, or wanting to be desired, gives him a more powerful position from which to get what he wants. If Duanwu represents the new China, he has rejected the cultural inferiority that comes with wanting to be desired.

The film tells us very little about Duanwu's life after his enlightenment and his subsequent gaining of power within the Pang family. When Duanwu is called by family elders to become head of the estate, we see them with a sort of smile on their faces as they mention that although Zhengda is too sick, Ruyi should be present. She is wheeled in with the same blank, vegetative look on her face that Zhengda had when he was wheeled in at the film's beginning. The elders' apparent pleasure at Duanwu's new power is intriguing: will the future under his leadership simply be a continuation of life on the estate much as it was before Ruyi took over? As in Lu Xun's stories, the future is more a vague direction or abstraction than a clearly depicted set of ideas or actions. Yet although the film doesn't give us much to go on, we can draw some tentative conclusions from Duanwu's behavior throughout the film. Duanwu has rejected several narratives, including that of loyalty and obedience, subservience, inner traumatization resulting from what happens in daily life, and love as a basis of identity. He has accepted power as what underlies relationships, and also the gender hierarchy as the most basic and productive of power relations. Duanwu thus has rejected the Beijing narrative and its notions of equality and freedom, as well as the idea that knowledge leads to progress leads to a better life, and has chosen to fight it out within the down-to-earth Shanghai

---

Narrative Cinema' Inspired by *Duel in the Sun*," in *Psychoanalysis and Cinema*, ed. E. Ann Kaplan (New York: Routledge, 1990), 24–35.

[24] See E. Ann Kaplan, "Problematizing Cross-Cultural Analysis: The Case of Women in Recent Chinese Cinema," in *Perspectives on Chinese Cinema*, ed. Chris Berry (London: British Film Institute, 1991), 141–54.

story where money equals power. He also has chosen to do this while still residing at home. We perhaps can envision the concubines returning and Duanwu holding his own in any negotiations he has with Dada and his men. Duanwu's new regime will be based on a recognition of who has power and who does not; gaining and keeping power, rather than obsessing about wounds and the past and reliving over and over the circumstances in which they were endured, will be his goal.

THREE

Reading the Sky

STANLEY K. ABE

The following is an expanded version of an essay already submitted for publication at the time of the Berkeley workshop and distributed to the other speakers and discussants.[1] Rather than attempting to rewrite the original essay, I have made revisions and insertions, many inspired by the workshop. It should be noted that the essay opens with a Berkeley connection in that it involves Yang Buwei, the wife of Chao Yuen Ren, the noted linguist who taught for many years in the Department of Oriental Languages.

I

In his book *Brushes with Power,* Richard Kraus tells the story of Yang Buwei, the first female doctor of Western medicine in China, who as a child was unable to complete an examination essay that was to begin with the words, "Women are the mothers of the

I am grateful to the Center for Chinese Studies and Wen-hsin Yeh for the opportunity to present this material and to all of the participants, especially Rey Chow, for their comments and support. Parts of the essay were presented at the College Art Association Annual Meeting, Boston, February, 1996 (thanks to Richard Powell), and the "Gender, Visuality, Modernity in Twentieth-Century China" workshop, University of Pittsburgh, September 1997 (thanks to Kathy Linduff and Sheldon Lu). The original essay benefited from the comments of Kristine Stiles, Terry Smith, and Margaret Hattori. Jonathan Arac changed the shape of the essay by raising challenging questions regarding aesthetics, the sublime, and the work of art as "critical." A fortuitous meeting with Marie Aquilino introduced me to Louis Marin's *Utopics.* Special thanks to Yue Gang for urging me to open a space for the utopian in my reading of *A Book from the Sky.* The writing of this essay would not have been possible without the cooperation of Xu Bing as well as Amy Vanderhill, Massachusetts College of Art, and Zheng Hu, University Art Museum, Albany.

[1] The original essay, titled "No Questions, No Answers: 'China' and *A Book from the Sky,*" was published in *boundary* 2 25, 3 (Fall 1998): 169–92. Copyright 1998, Duke University Press.

race." The recognition of her gendered position and its relationship to the writing of Chinese was later played out as defiance of her father's insistence that she develop her skills in calligraphy: "But I never listened to my father's advice, so today I often write things which people cannot make out, in a true scrawl. Sometimes I even write characters which do not exist, with the result that my friends are puzzled, sometimes thinking me laughable."[2] Yang's deployment of nonexistent characters is reminiscent of *nüshu* (literally, "women's writing"), an invented script that was developed by women in an isolated area of southern Hunan province and used exclusively for their private communications.[3] The invention of scripts that are readable only by women or, as in the case of Yang, the refusal to participate in the conventional forms of writing suggest the significance of the Chinese written form within a patriarchal society and the gendered resistance that writing has inspired.

In a private communication, Richard Kraus made the observation that there is a fundamental difference between Yang's illegible characters, with no point to them, and the constructed system of writing that is *nüshu*. I would still maintain, however, that the two examples, while not performative equivalents, stage something of the range of ways in which writing has been transformed by women into a site of resistance.[4]

After emigrating to the United States, Yang in 1945 published a cookbook titled *How to Cook and Eat in Chinese*.[5] In anticipation of a book signing to benefit United China Relief of Boston, Yang was confronted with an unexpected request for calligraphy, as Kraus describes: "An American woman who had been in China enthusiastically suggested that Yang use a brush for signing the copies. Because she dared not say that she had not written with a brush for nearly twenty years, poor Yang was driven to practicing secretly at home. The day after a furtive trip to Chinatown to

---

[2] Richard Curt Kraus, *Brushes with Power* (Berkeley: University of California Press, 1991), 9. Translated from Yang Buwei, *Yige nüren de zizhuan* (Changsha: Yuelu shushe, 1987), 32–33 and 63.

[3] Thanks to Dorothy Ko for first suggesting the relevance of *nüshu*. For a full-length study of *nüshu* in English, see William Wei Chiang, *"We two know the script; we have become good friends": Linguistic and Social Aspects of the Women's Script Literacy in Southern Hunan, China* (Lanham, Md.: University Press of America, 1995).

[4] Thanks to Wendy Larson for providing Richard Kraus with a copy of my original essay.

[5] Pu-wei Yang Chao, *How to Cook and Eat in Chinese* (New York: John Day, 1945).

purchase a brush and ink for a night of practice, she signed three hundred copies."[6] For Kraus, the anecdote indicates the deep hold of calligraphy on Yang: "Yet so mighty is the emotional grip of this art that her calligraphic inadequacies haunted her decades after emigrating to the United States." While the power of the calligraphic tradition is undeniable, tradition is not where the demand made on Yang originates. In China, as an educated upper-class woman, Yang could display, even flaunt, her lack of calligraphic skill. It was only in the West and through the invocation of proper Chinese behavior by the "American woman," an "expert" whose knowledge and authority is based on personal experience in China, that Yang abandoned her resistance to calligraphic practice. Rather than the power of tradition, Yang was confronted with the power of Western representations that already knew what was properly "Chinese." She was, in a catachrestic moment, inadequate to the "authentic" Chinese subject anticipated in the West. Her capitulation can be understood not as individual weakness but as a desire to resolve the incommensurable demands on her subjectivity. The Chinese cause that the book signing supported should not be overlooked—it reminds us of the way in which the individual is subsumed by the nation-state in times of crisis. Yang is not the first to have the experience of learning what it means to be Asian upon arriving in the West, that is, the effect of encountering the foreknowledge of oneself in the Orientalist West.

II

> While it [*A Book from the Sky*] speaks in a national syntax, it disarticulates such a syntax and renders it completely garbled. While it constructs a symbolic national text, it evacuates all meaning from such a text. In this way, the work calls attention to the ongoing crisis of modern China and at the same time calls into question any easy resolution of such a crisis which might be afforded by simple allegiance to culture and tradition. In *A Book from the Sky*, language—a symbolic system fundamental to the integrity and perpetuation of a national culture—is endlessly reproduced but vitiated of any functional value and thus made curiously unproductive.[7]

---

[6] Kraus, *Brushes*, 9, after Yang, *Yige nüren*, 394.

[7] Alice Yang, "Xu Bing: Rewriting Culture," essay for the exhibition of *A Book*

Writing and the power of the written text are central for one of the best-known works of Chinese art from the 1980s, Xu Bing's installation (figure 1) titled *Tian shu* (in English, *A Book from the Sky*).[8] The work consists of books and hanging scrolls with text printed from woodblocks hand-carved over several years by the artist. The books carefully follow traditional conventions, from the bibliographic forms to the stitched bindings to the wooden storage boxes. All of this pays homage to the long history of Chinese learning and exegesis preserved in printed form but with an important twist: all of the characters (*hanzi*) are invented, composed of recognizable elements but illegible as conventional linguistic signs (figure 2). Xu Bing, tired by the endless philosophical discussions of modernism, pseudomodernism, and postmodernism that consumed young intellectuals in late 1980s Beijing, retreated to his studio to carve each of the several thousand invented characters onto individual woodblocks.[9] In the silence of that studio, *A Book from the Sky* was, to borrow the words of Louis Marin, the utopian figure of the neutral: "neither yes nor no, true nor false, one nor the other." For Marin, the utopian neutral is "not the neutral as neutrality" nor the "utopic figure that seems to be freed from society," but the "span between true and false," a theory that "would permit placeless contradiction in discourse to have limitless force."[10] Indeed, Xu Bing's careful re-creation of traditional forms on one hand and the denial of legibility on the other produced a powerfully contradictory work that refuses any singular reading. In the artist's words,

> My own interpretation is useless. This artwork is a very contradictory thing. One of the things I wanted to convey in *Tian shu* is that I feel that culture places too great a burden on people, it leaves people feeling exhausted. But by doing this work, I've brought up even more questions!...Art is helpless. The deepest

---

from the Sky, University Museum, The State University, Albany, New York, 1996, 3.

[8] The work is arguably the most oft-reproduced example of contemporary Chinese art in recent survey books. See, for example, Michael Sullivan, *Art and Artists of Twentieth-Century China* (Berkeley: University of California Press, 1996), 266, figs. 24.16–24.18; Craig Clunas, *Art in China* (New York: Oxford University Press, 1997), 221, fig. 124; and David G. Wilkins, Bernard Schultz, and Katheryn M. Linduff, *Art Past, Art Present* (New York: Harry N. Abrams, 1997), 593, fig. 10-134.

[9] Jonathan Goodman, "Bing Xu: 4,000 Characters in Search of a Meaning," *Art News* 93 (1994): 100.

[10] Louis Marin, *Utopics: Spatial Play* (Atlantic Highlands, N.J.: Humanities Press, 1984), 7.

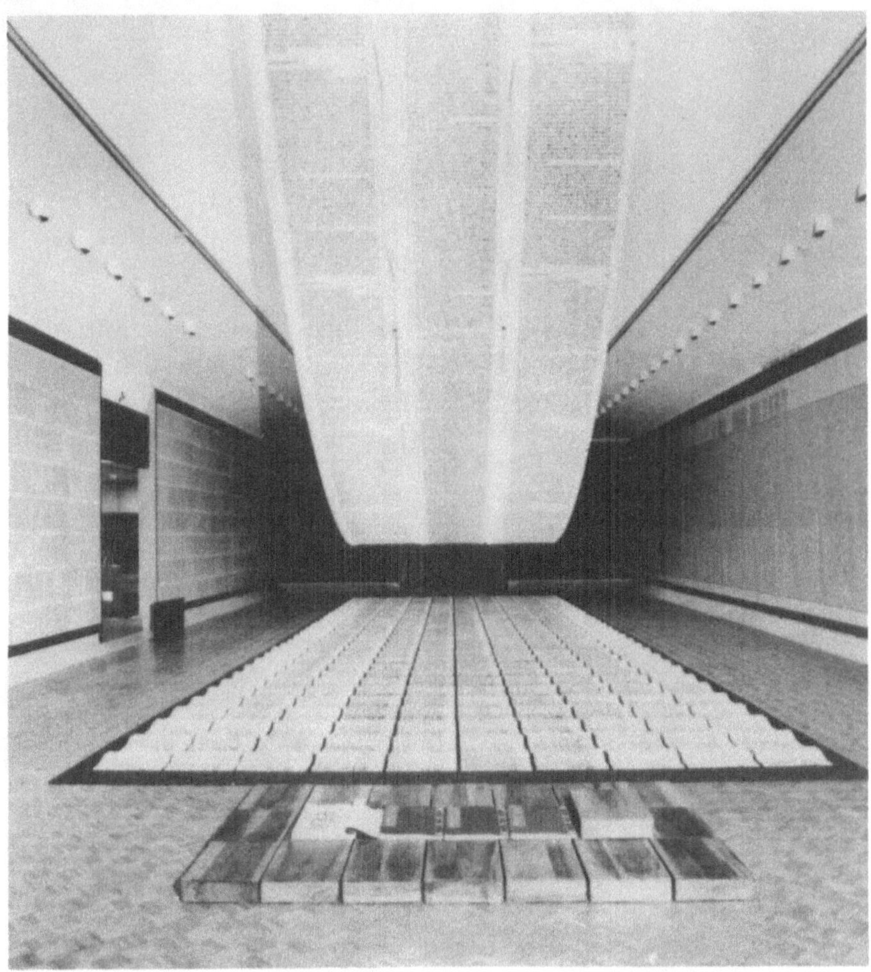

Figure 1. Xu Bing, *A Book from the Sky.* Installation at the Elvehjem Museum of Art, University of Wisconsin-Madison. November 30, 1991–January 19, 1992. Photograph provided by the Elvehjem Museum of Art.

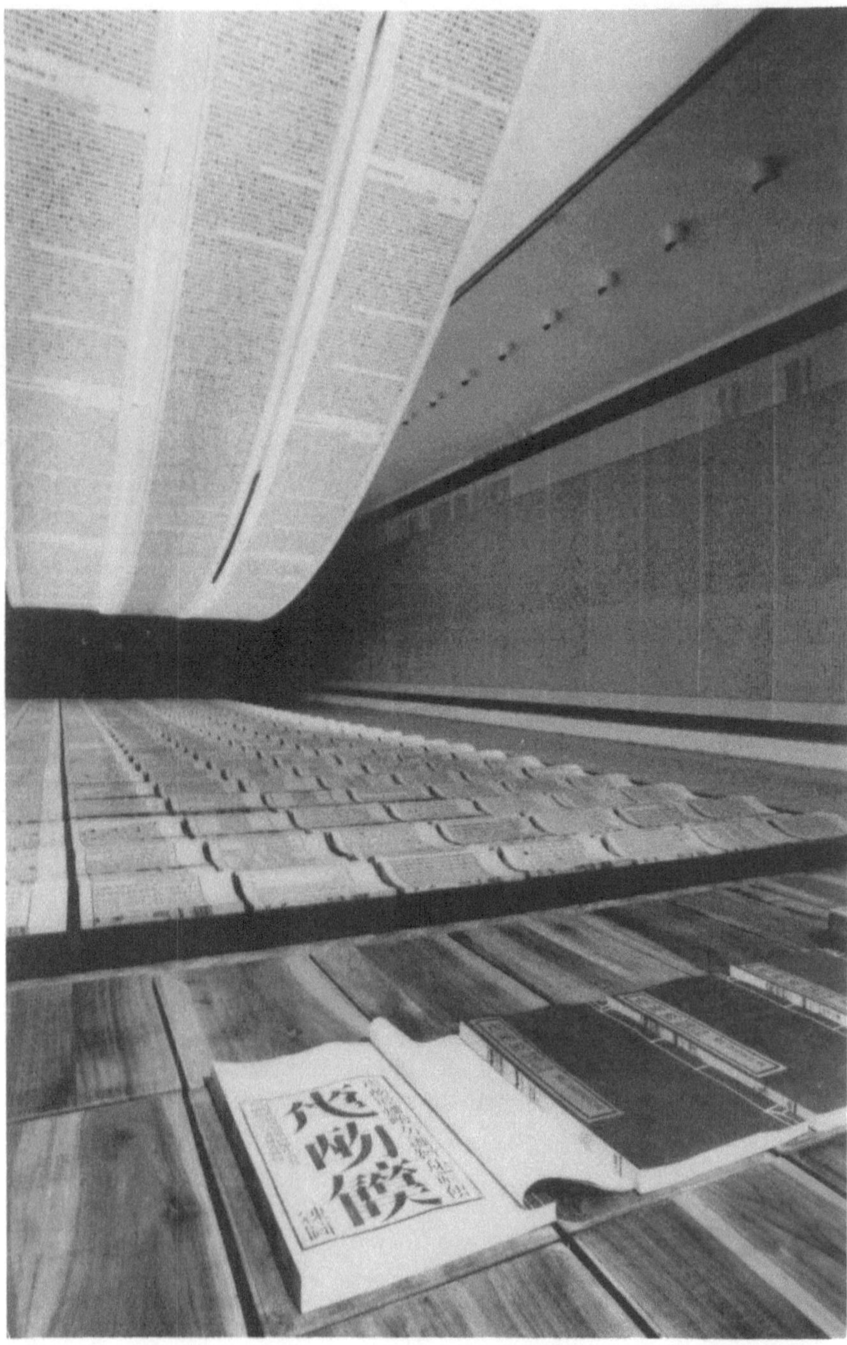

Figure 2. Xu Bing, *A Book from the Sky.* Installation at the Elvehjem Museum of Art, University of Wisconsin-Madison. November 30, 1991–January 19, 1992. Photograph provided by the Elvehjem Museum of Art.

human problems cannot ever be solved. But nevertheless we simply have to try to solve them; we must have things to do.[11]

When it was first exhibited in Beijing in October 1988, *A Book from the Sky* received considerable attention along with works of other New Wave (*xinchao*) artists such as Lü Shengzhong.[12] *A Book from the Sky* was shown again in early 1989 (figure 3) as part of the China/Avant-Garde exhibition (Zhongguo xiandai yishuzhan).[13] The imagination and beauty of the installation as well as Xu Bing's serious approach were often commended. But there was also considerable perplexity over whether to read the work as a critique or as an instantiation of Chinese culture or both; the debate reflected deep concerns and differences over the future direction of Chinese art.[14]

Xu Bing and *A Book from the Sky* left China in 1990, and the work was subsequently installed in Taiwan, Japan, South Korea, Australia, Spain, Italy, France, and England as well as multiple sites in the United States.[15] Demand for *A Book from the Sky*

---

[11] Janelle S. Taylor, "Non-Sense in Context: Xu Bing's Art and Its Publics," *Public Culture* 5, 2 (Winter 1993): 327. The idea that the work of art is helpless in the face of political crisis echoes Lu Xun, which came to my attention by reading the analysis of Lu Xun's well-known 1927 address to the Whampoa Military Academy by Liu Kang in his book manuscript "Aesthetics and Marxism," 99 (photocopy kindly provided by the author). Also see Wendy Larson, *Literary Authority and the Modern Chinese Writer* (Durham, N.C.: Duke University Press, 1991), 90–91.

[12] See, for example, the front-page coverage of the two artists in *Zhongguo meishubao*, no. 46 (1988): 1.

[13] Reviewed in Hang Jian and Chao Xiao'eo, "Zhongguo xiandai yishuzhan ceji" (Record of visiting the exhibition China/Avant-Garde), *Meishu*, no. 4 (April 1989): 5–9.

[14] In addition to the references in notes 12 and 13, see "'Xu Bing xianxiang' yifenfen" (Talking about the "Xu Bing phenomenon"), *Meishu*, no. 1 (1989): 20–22; Fan Di'an, "Zhuiqiu yongheng—Xu Bing chuangzuo xiansuo tanxun" (Seeking eternity—Xu Bing's art road), *Meishu yanjiu*, no. 1 (1989): 37–40; Yi Ying, "Xiandai zhuyi de kunjingyu women de xuanze" (The difficult position of modernism and our choices), *Meishu*, no. 4 (1989): 10–13.

[15] *A Book from the Sky*, complete or in part, has been exhibited at the National Fine Arts Museum, Beijing, 1988 and 1989; Lung Men Art Gallery, Taibei, 1990; Tokyo Gallery, Tokyo, 1991; Elvehjem Museum of Art, Madison, Wisconsin, 1991; North Dakota Museum of Art, Grand Forks, 1992; as part of "Post-Mao Product: New Art from China," an exhibition that toured the eastern states of Australia from September 1992 to June 1993; Bellefroid, Paris, 1993; Venice Biennale, 1993; Museo National Centro de Arte Reina Sofia, Madrid, 1994; Santa Monica Art Center, Barcelona, 1995; Massachusetts College of Art, Boston, 1995; Queensland Art Museum, Brisbane, 1996; University Art Museum, State University of New York, Albany, 1996; Institute of Contemporary Art, London, May 1997; Sonje Museum of Contemporary Art, Kyunju, South Korea, 1996; Prague Castle, 1997.

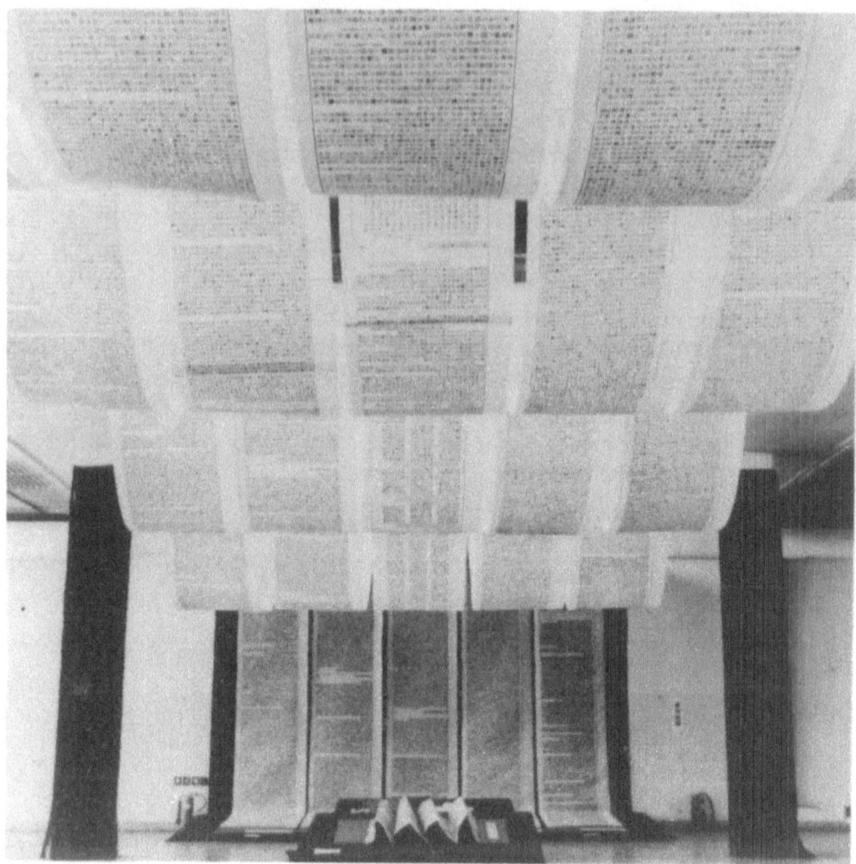

Figure 3. Xu Bing, *A Book from the Sky*. Installation at the National Fine Art Museum, Beijing. 1989. Photograph provided by Xu Bing.

continues to be strong, and exhibitions have been arranged well into the future.[16] A key question then is how a work such as *A Book from the Sky,* so powerfully engaging for Chinese viewers, might be received in the West. As Yang Buwei learned, knowledge of China and what is properly "Chinese" is firmly fixed in the imagination of the West. As a work from China, *A Book from the Sky* is both foreign and already known. As a work of art displayed in a museum, *A Book from the Sky* is made productive through its institutional setting and the language of critical

[16] In 1998 and 1999 the work is scheduled for the Museum of Far Eastern Antiquities, Stockholm; P.S. 1, New York; the Museum of Modern Art, San Francisco; and the National Gallery of Canada, Ottawa.

interpretation and contextualization produced from the site of the museum.[17] In what follows, I will be primarily concerned with how *A Book from the Sky* has been read, interpreted, and presented to the public in the United States, both the critical reception of the work and its (re)construction as a representative work of contemporary Chinese art.[18]

The first exhibition of *A Book from the Sky* in the United States was in 1991 at the Elvehjem Museum, University of Wisconsin (see figure 1).[19] At first glance, the formal qualities of *A Book from the Sky* might appear familiar to viewers acquainted with conceptual installations of the late 1960s and 1970s in Europe and the United States. The work, considerably expanded in comparison to its Beijing installations, now features long rows of neatly arranged open books in the central area of the floor. Printed sheets sweep down from overhead, and the side walls are draped with additional text. The manipulation of space, light, and shadow, the orderly arrangement of texts—all are stunningly evocative, even sublime.[20] What distinguishes this installation from works of conceptual art, however, is its heightened emphasis on visual effect and most crucially the complete illegibility of the text.[21] The unreadable signs of Chinese writing have fascinated the Western viewer for many centuries. While the form of the installation points toward modernist visual art practices, the text evokes the role of the Chinese written language in the development of modernist poetics, most closely associated with Fenollosa and Pound, and more recently the recuperation of their earlier move by Derrida.[22]

---

17 For a discussion of three museum exhibitions of "China," including *A Book from the Sky*, see my forthcoming "Exhibiting China" in *The Present, and the Discipline of Art History in Japan*, papers presented at the 21st International Symposium on the Preservation of Cultural Property (Tokyo: Tokyo National Research Institute of Cultural Properties).

18 For a primarily quantitative study, see Yan Ma, "A Reader-response Analysis of *A Book from the Sky*: A Postmodern Educational Enterprise" (Ph.D. diss., University of Wisconsin, Madison, 1993); and Yan Ma, "Reader-Response Theory: An Analysis of a Work of Chinese Post Modern Art," *Journal of Visual Literacy* 15, 1 (Spring 1995): 39–72.

19 From November 30, 1991, to January 19, 1992, as part of "Three Installations by Xu Bing."

20 For the sublime and its architectonic materiality, in the Kantian sense, see Paul de Man, "Phenomenality and Materiality in Kant," in *Aesthetic Ideology*, ed. Andrzej Warminsky (Minneapolis: University of Minnesota Press, 1996), 70–90. Thanks to Jonathan Arac for pointing out the relevance of Kant and de Man.

21 As discussed in Michael Peterson, "A Book That Resists Reading: The Enormous Signs of Xu Bing," *Fine Art Magazine*, January 1992, no pagination.

Fenollosa and Pound discovered in the Chinese character what they believed to be an alternative, ideogramic language to the phonological scripts of the West. Inspired by the Chinese ideogram, Pound and later poets such as William Carlos Williams sought to create new modernist forms of expressive language. Many scholars, however, have seized on the manner in which Fenollosa and Pound ignored the phonetic aspects of the Chinese character, and the issue of such a "misunderstanding," continued in Derrida, has generated a significant body of criticism over the last half century, one that is fascinating in its own right.[23] It should be noted, however, that while current-day scholars may find the orientalist fantasies of Fenollosa and Pound easy to dismiss, the sinologists' claim to a correct understanding of the Chinese writing system and its linguistic intricacies is only another side of orientalism, not its antidote, as we will see below.[24] Xiaomei Chen has made the point that appropriation is always also a creative reinterpretation that renders the charge of "misunderstanding" largely irrelevant.[25] This is a point that I would underscore in terms of a work such as *A Book from the Sky,* which operates not only at the juncture of visual and literary production, but tests the liminality of concepts such as "misunderstanding."

---

[22] For the formative texts and their continued recirculation, see Ernest F. Fenollosa, *The Chinese Written Character as a Medium for Poetry,* ed. Ezra Pound (San Francisco: City Lights Books, 1936); Jacques Derrida, *Of Grammatology,* trans. Gayatri Chakravorty Spivak (Baltimore: John Hopkins University Press, 1976); Zhang Longxi, *The Tao and the Logos: Literary Hermeneutics, East and West* (Durham, N.C.: Duke University Press, 1992); Zhaoming Qian, *Orientalism and Modernism: The Legacy of China in Pound and Williams* (Durham, N.C.: Duke University Press, 1995).

[23] For example, see George Kennedy, "Fenollosa, Pound, and the Chinese Character," *Yale Literary Magazine* 126 (1958): 24–36; Hwa Yol Jung, "Misreading the Ideogram: From Fenollosa to Derrida and McLuhan," *Paideuma* 13, 2 (Fall 1984): 211–27; Guiyou Huang, "Ezra Pound: (Mis)Translation and (Re)Creation," *Paideuma* 22, 1–2 (Spring–Fall 1993): 99–114; Jiewei Cheng, "Derrida and Ideographic Poetics," *British Journal of Aesthetics* 35, 2 (April 1995): 134–44.

[24] This sentence was added in response to a question by Richard Kraus about why I was "so defensive" about the orientalism of Fenollosa and Pound.

[25] Xiaomei Chen, "'Misunderstanding' Western Modernism: The Menglong Movement in Post-Mao China," *Representations* 35 (Summer 1991): 143–63; idem, "Rediscovering Ezra Pound: A Post-Postcolonial 'Misreading' of a Western Legacy," *Paideuma* 23 (Fall–Winter 1994): 81–106.

III

The most important attribute of *A Book from the Sky* is the manner in which it offers itself for inscription by viewers. Gao Minglu put it this way: "When he establishes a space without meaning in his work, Xu believes, viewers will fill it with their own readings of the confrontations that occur between different cultures and eras."[26] Even the title of the work is slippery, an attribute that Xu encouraged from the beginning: "The name of this artwork, *Tian shu,* originally refers to the pattern left on the skin of a person who had been struck dead by lightning. People looked at these patterns, which were like words written by the sky, and they couldn't understand them. My original title for the piece was *Fenxi shijie de shu* [A book that analyzes the world], but everyone called it *Tian shu.*"[27] Discussions in the Chinese media, however, almost always refer to the work by a third title: *Xishi jian,* sometimes followed by *shijimo juan.* The first part of the title has been translated in a number of ways: *An Analyzed Reflection of the World, A Mirror That Analyzes the World,* and *Analytical Mirrors of the World.* Another alternative translation would be *An Analyzed Warning to the World.*[28] The second section of the title is similarly ambiguous and has been translated as both *The Final Volume of the Century* and *Fin-de-siècle Volumes.*[29] Xu Bing has chosen to use the popular title, *Tian shu,* as the basis for the English title of the work, *A Book from the Sky.* But even this name has not gone unchallenged. Wu Hung argues that in colloquial Chinese, *tianshu* means "abstruse or illegible writing that makes no sense to its reader" and, considering the contents of the work, the English title would be better rendered as *Nonsense Writing.*[30] Interestingly, this translation would bring us close to the disdainful sense of *Tian shu*

---

[26] Gao Minglu, "Meaninglessness and Confrontation in Xu Bing's Art," in *Fragmented Memory: The Chinese Avant-Garde in Exile,* ed. Julia F. Andrews and Gao Minglu (Columbus: Wexner Center for the Arts, Ohio State University, 1993), 28–31.

[27] Taylor, "Non-Sense," 324.

[28] Britta Erickson, "Process and Meaning in the Art of Xu Bing," in *Three Installations* (Madison: Elvehjem Museum of Art, 1992), 15. Wu Hung, "A 'Ghost Rebellion': Notes on Xu Bing's 'Nonsense Writing' and Other Works," *Public Culture* 6, 2 (Winter 1994): 411. Eugene Yuejin Wang, "Of Text and Texture: The Cultural Relevance of Xu Bing's Art," in *Language Lost* (Boston: Massachusetts College of Art, 1995), 10. Erickson, "Process and Meaning," 15.

[29] Respectively in Erickson, "Process and Meaning," 15, and Wang, "Of Text and Textures," 10.

[30] Wu Hung, "'Ghost Rebellion,'" 411.

that was invoked by some critics of the work.[31] The unstable litany of names and translations for the work suggests the manner in which it is able to elicit a multiplicity of readings, something like a Rorschach test, revealing the interests and politics of the viewer.[32]

In its initial exhibitions in the United States, the openness of the work to a variety of interpretations contributed to a series of politically charged readings. The Tiananmen Square crackdown was still a powerful memory in the United States when the Elvehjem Museum exhibition opened, and *A Book from the Sky* was positioned as symbolic of both pre–June 4 freedom and post–June 4 repression.[33] The catalogue of the exhibition, which featured a detailed expository essay by Britta Erickson, clearly arose in the midst of this emotional and difficult moment. Erickson's essay on *A Book from the Sky* reports that the work was initially "hailed as the definitive work of the New Wave and as a sign that artists could, indeed, find a valid means of expressing themselves in a new China."[34] Soon, however, "as part of the reversal of the temporary freedom of expression in China, just two days before the massacre in Tiananmen Square," *A Book from the Sky* was vilified in an official publication.[35] In its rush to join "vilified" with "massacre," the essay is blind to its own footnote, which shows that the attack on *A Book from the Sky* was published on June 2, 1990, two days before the first anniversary of the June 4 incident.[36] The slip in the catalogue essay points to a widespread desire to reduce *A Book from the Sky* and the events of 1989 to a simple political allegory of good and evil. The 1990 attack was certainly political and purposefully timed, but its target was continued support for the New Wave as much as *A Book from the Sky*.[37] Unmentioned in any reports is the muted but no less clear defense of the New Wave, Xu Bing, and *A Book from the Sky* in a reply to the negative

---

31 Yang Chengyin, "'Xin chao' meishu lun gang" (A discussion of the main principles of "New Wave fine arts)," *Wenyibao*, June 2, 1990, 5.

32 The work as a mirror is emphasized by Wu Hung, "'Ghost Rebellion,'" 411.

33 See, for example, Ina Pasch, "Chinese Printmaker's Work Illustrates Futility," *Wisconsin State Journal*, December 8, 1991, Showcase section, 1I.

34 Erickson, "Process and Meaning," 11.

35 Ibid., 15.

36 Yang, "'Xin chao,'" 5.

37 It should be noted that intense displeasure with the New Wave had been expressed for a number of years, and indeed Xu Bing was a target for attack as early as December 1989. See John Clark, "Official Reactions to Modern Art in China since the Beijing Massacre," *Pacific Affairs* 65, 3 (Fall 1992): 334–52.

article in the same official publication.[38] Certainly the events of June 4 had a profound negative effect on Chinese artists associated with the New Wave, but Xu Bing continued in his position at the Central Academy of Art in Beijing, and in May and June 1990 he was able to organize his project to make a monumental rubbing of the Great Wall.[39] There was clearly less and less room for works of modern art in China, however, and Xu Bing accepted an invitation to be an honorary fellow at the University of Wisconsin; he has been resident in the United States since that time, although he continues to visit China and produce work there.[40]

Despite the immense complexities and contradictions of the 1989 democracy movement, it is telling that the U.S. print and electronic media representation of the demonstrations—that they were wholly antigovernment and anti–Communist Party—was shared by the hard-line Party leaders who suppressed the movement.[41] The goal of the democracy movement was understood by most in this country as the desire for U.S.-style liberal democratic institutions such as one person, one vote. This form of projection as political analysis also informed early interpretations of *A Book from the Sky*. The Elvehjem catalogue states that the set of ten characters for numbering pages and volumes in *A Book from the Sky* was derived from a special set of numbers used in small-scale Chinese elections. From the fact that these are the only intelligible characters among the thousands created by Xu Bing, the Elvehjem Museum catalogue suggests the following interpretation:

> [A]ll is meaningless except for the opportunity to vote. The Chinese government may make whatever lengthy pronouncements it wishes, but only an announcement that democracy would be enacted would have any meaning: all else is excess verbiage. *Xu denies that this is his intended meaning,* but admits that it is a possible interpretation. It would be an audacious statement for an artist to make, but it is entirely in keeping with the *general desire*

---

38 Du Jian, "Dui 'Xin chao' meishu lun gang de yijiang" (A discussion of the main principles of the "New Wave" of fine arts)," *Wenyibao*, December 29, 1990, 5.

39 This work would be exhibited along with *A Book from the Sky* at the Elvehjem Museum.

40 For example, in Beijing in January 1994 he organized and produced *A Case Study of Transference*, a performance/installation that featured two pigs mating in a pen filled with books of invented characters.

41 As emphasized in Kay Ann Johnson, "The Revolutionary Tradition of Pro-Democracy Students," *Radical America* 22, 4 (July-August 1988): 7–12; also, see "Documents from the Chinese Democratic Movement," ibid., 13–21. Despite the earlier date, these articles were published soon after the June 4 events.

> for democracy expressed by the young intelligentsia during the later 1980s. Such a reading of *A Book from the Sky* has not been discussed in the Chinese media [emphasis added].[42]

This is an interesting passage in the way a liberal ideology is instantiated even as it is forced to disavow the artist's intention and acknowledge the lack of such a reading in China. As the first explanation of *A Book from the Sky* in English, the Elvehjem catalogue was often referred to in later writings, and, not surprisingly, this line of thinking was reiterated in later commentaries on the numbering system—for example, "This aspect of the work might lead one to *speculate* that an underlying theme of the work is that all of the sometimes venerated and ancient Chinese culture based upon written language is meaningless if one cannot vote [emphasis added]."[43]

Interpretations such as these are not fanciful; rather, they are overdetermined in the United States, where China has been historically understood as rich in cultural tradition but lacking in modern institutions of civilization such as liberal democracy. Tiananmen and June 4 are only the latest examples of "oriental despotism" and the traditional Chinese disregard for human rights. Here one can recall after June 4 the recitation on television by sinologists of the litany of abusive Chinese despots from Mao back to Qin Shi Huangdi.[44] It seems as though "oriental despotism" can never be sufficiently fixed and must therefore be reiterated over and over.[45] A recent example is an article by Robert Drexler, former U.S. consul to Hong Kong, on how "in addition to opening up trade with China, the first visit ever by an American ship to the port of Canton in 1784 also led to the first human-rights struggle between the Asian giant and the United States."[46] The article describes the idealist opposition of a young American against Chinese demands for the execution of a British gunner who was responsible for accidentally killing a Chinese

[42] Erickson, "Process and Meaning," 12.

[43] Laurel Reuter, "Into the Dark Sings the Nightingale: The Work of Xu Bing," in *Xu Bing* (Grand Forks: North Dakota Museum of Art, 1992), 2.

[44] One of the few exceptions was Rey Chow's courageous essay "Violence in the Other Country: Preliminary Remarks on the 'China Crisis,' June 1989," *Radical America* 22, 4 (July–August 1988): 23–32. For a vituperative response, see Longxi Zhang, "Western Theory and Chinese Reality," *Critical Inquiry* 19, 1 (1992): 105–30.

[45] Reminiscent of the racial stereotype as described in Homi K. Bhabha, "The Other Question: The Stereotype and Colonial Discourse," *Screen* 24, 6 (1983): 18.

[46] Robert W. Drexler, "The Canton War," *American History* 32, 1 (April 1997): 42.

fisherman with a ceremonial salute in Canton in 1784. Such dominant representations of incomprehensible Chinese illiberalism—wholly narcissistic, self-congratulatory, and orientalist—immensely complicate the field from which to advance criticism of current Chinese government political policies. Orientalism and liberalism combine today to produce the alliance of high-profile dissidents such as Harry Wu with the most right-wing think tanks or the strange bedfellows of the Dalai Lama and Jesse Helms.[47] In a situation where opportunism is rampant, how does one maintain a principled opposition to injustice that does not simply play into the hands of the most cynical political elements in the United States?

In her response to this essay at the workshop, Pat Berger suggested that the Dalai Lama's embrace of Senator Helms was not difficult to understand—after all, the Dalai Lama is a bodhisattva, a Buddhist deity of compassion, acting out of unconditional love and charity. This might be taken as a measure of the success of the Dalai Lama's self-promotion, that his alliance with arguably the most vile, hateful, and defiantly racist living politician in the United States can be characterized as an act of grace without a murmur of dissent from the workshop audience or participants including myself. In 1996, when a faculty member suggested inviting the Dalai Lama to speak at Duke University and giving him an award, I told a colleague that the Dalai Lama should be required to bring his friend Jesse along. My colleague's response was that I must be a supporter of China's position on Tibet since I was following the PRC "line" on boycotting the Dalai Lama. These may be inconsequential anecdotes; they indicate, however, something of the outlines of the "legitimate" in political positions today no less than in 1991.[48]

The representation of *A Book from the Sky* as critical of the Chinese government was a product of many historical factors galvanized by the sensational and narrowly polemical media

[47] The Dalai Lama was hosted and embraced by Helms at his North Carolina alma mater, Wingate University, in 1995. See feature photo and article by Yonat Shimron, "Karma Can Make Strange Bedfellows," *News and Observer* (Raleigh, N.C.), September 6, 1995, A1.

[48] Situations change, however, and a welcome indication that there might be room for sustained critical discussion of Tibetan Buddhism and the Dalai Lama in relation to orientalist constructions and self-constructions is Donald S. Lopez, *Prisoners of Shangri-La: Tibetan Buddhism and the West* (Chicago: University of Chicago Press, 1998).

coverage of the June 4 incident.[49] The weight placed on a political reading of *A Book from the Sky* was in the historical context inevitable and involved not only museums and curators but Xu Bing himself, who would certify such political readings as much by silence as by positive affirmation. It was usually enough for him to simply state that the work had been praised by critics before June 4 and not liked by some after.[50] Interestingly, the characterization of *A Book from the Sky* as an antigovernment work was pursued in China just as the Elvehjem installation was being prepared.[51] Xu Bing's U.S. friends and Chinese critics were in complete agreement about the nature of his highly ambiguous work, and this kind of unexpectedly symmetrical political consensus should once again alert us to the continued shared stakes of strange political bedfellows.

IV

The aesthetic qualities of the work, heightened by dramatic installations and the exotic subject matter, have made an important contribution to the consistently favorable reception of *A Book from the Sky* over nearly a decade of exhibition. It is natural then that recently, when "China" is more likely to summon up visions of a billion potential consumers rather than Tiananmen, interpretative readings have concerned themselves more with the form of the work than with politics. The eulogy for the earlier political readings of *A Book from the Sky* as representative of dissident politics was delivered by Eugene Wang in 1995: "There is a tendency

[49] An important corrective, though not without its own controversial issues, is the documentary film *The Gate of Heavenly Peace* (Brookline, Mass.: Long Bow Group, 1996).

[50] See, for example, Xu Bing's statement in Taylor, "Non-Sense," 324. He was uncharacteristically direct in agreeing that the work was a political critique in Christina Davidson, "Words from Heaven," *Art and Asia Pacific* 1, 2 (April 1994): 52. Britta Erickson, who has been very helpful to me in this research project and was present at the Berkeley workshop, made a strong case for Xu Bing's role in the political reading of *A Book from the Sky* by pointing out that, as an inexperienced graduate student, she very much depended on the artist's lead—for example, in pointing out the original function of the numbering system. In addition, Erickson mentioned the way in which Xu Bing's openness to various readings of his work can be interpreted as disingenuous when it encourages a (mis)reading of his work.

[51] Li Qun, "Dui yu 'Xin chao' meishu zhi wo jian—jiu shang yu Du Jian tongzhi" (My opinions of "New Wave" fine arts: A discussion with comrade Du Jian), *Wenyibao*, March 30, 1991, 6.

to pseudocontextualize him by subjugating him to the procrustean bed of facile sociopolitical terms." Instead, Wang adroitly sketches the complex relationship between works of New Wave artists and the politics of the pre- and post-Tiananmen periods, for example the way in which Xu Bing was made "an easy pawn because there are signs in his works that could be everything to everyone."[52]

The aesthetic value of *A Book from the Sky* was never separate from the political, and the unity of the two elements was crucial for its reception in the United States. For example, one of the most compelling arguments for the success of *A Book from the Sky* places emphasis on the excess of labor and concentrated effort that is represented in the work.[53] The representation of oppressive human toil in China—forced (child, women, prison) labor, cheap workers—has a powerful and alluring aesthetic counterpart: "There is also much to be said for the accumulation of labor, the repetition of simple acts, over and over, for years even, that give both an authority and a reservoir of meaning to Xu Bing's art that would be difficult to achieve with the quick execution usual to western artists."[54] Against ample examples of Chinese artists who have used "quick execution" with spectacular results or Western artists who work quite deliberately, cultural difference is reduced to a matter of tempo, a familiar move for those who have followed the discussion of the relationship between "fast" and "slow" economies, where speed marks the modern from the traditional. There is simultaneously, however, another direction in which the logic of repetitious labor moves. Xu Bing himself has likened the laborious process of creating *A Book from the Sky* to the practice of Zen Buddhism.[55] That a Chinese artist, as opposed to a Western critic, interjects Oriental philosophy into his work adds a touch of authenticity that is indeed impossible for many to resist. It is also significant that Xu Bing has consistently used the Japanese term "Zen" for its Chinese equivalent, "Chan," a recognition that "Zen" is by far the more widely known term in the West and that the two terms are commonly conflated. By deploying Zen around *A Book from the Sky,* Xu Bing calls up a panoply of cultural traits that represent "ancient China" to the West: solitude, quiet, meditation, wisdom and in the visual arts, surface, repetition, pattern.[56]

---

52 Wang, "Of Text and Texture," 14.

53 Wu, "'Ghost Rebellion,'" 417.

54 Reuter, "Into the Dark ," 4.

55 Jonathan Hay, "Ambivalent Icons," *Orientations* 23, 7 (July 1992): 38.

56 Parallel examples are reiterated in popular conceptions of Chinese painting

This is not to suggest that the idea of Chan or Zen was not a part of Xu Bing's explanatory vocabulary in China as it certainly was, but to be reminded that value production is not the sole prerogative of the critic.

At the workshop, Richard Vinograd made the correct observation that Zen/Chan in ink painting connotes qualities of quickness and spontaneity; but I had in mind the wavelike pattern of books in *A Book from the Sky,* which suggests the still surface of a Zen garden. What is of course indicated here is the multivalence of Zen/Chan, a quality that is very attractive to Xu Bing.

Xu Bing has described *A Book from the Sky* as a kind of teasing or joke.[57] The tension produced through the repeated frustration of the desire to read meaning in the text, however, is a strategy limited to those who are literate in Chinese. For the Beijing audience who experienced *A Book from the Sky* in 1988 and 1989, there was much force to his no-sense characters. A non-Chinese-reading audience, however, cannot be seduced into the game of searching the text for readable forms, and therefore there is no impulse to read and no shock of illegibility. Rather, there is a doubled alienation from the written forms that makes the joke irrelevant, at least in Xu Bing's original terms. What then could be the point to Xu Bing's joke for the non-Chinese-reader? The Elvehjem catalogue provides a clue in its masterful recuperation of *A Book from the Sky* for the Western viewer: "*A Book from the Sky* frustrates the viewer's inescapable urge to decode the written word, and this frustrated act of viewing ties the viewer in with the work, making his passage through it a part of the work of art."[58] This is the effect on the Chinese-reading viewer. The catalogue continues, "Once the viewer can let go of the urge to read, the urge to act upon the work of art, then he can accept and appreciate its beauty." That is, to release oneself from the act of reading is the path to beauty. And finally, "The viewer who does not read Chinese is free to absorb the work's beauty without having to confront its unintelligibility." That is, the non-Chinese-reading viewer, free of the necessity of moving through unintelligibility, is the privileged viewer who can most unproblematically absorb the

---

and cinema as grounded in Chan Buddhism, the Dao, or other Oriental philosophies. See, for example, Linda C. Ehrlich and David Desser, eds., *Cinematic Landscapes: Observations on the Visual Arts and Cinema of China and Japan* (Austin: University of Texas Press, 1994).

[57] Xu Bing, "Sight, Text, Vision," lecture at Duke University, November 6, 1995.

[58] Erickson, "Process and Meaning," 12.

beauty of *A Book from the Sky*. A lack—the inability to read Chinese—is transformed into a site from which the Western audience can generate singular enjoyment and aesthetic pleasure.

At the same time, Jonathan Arac has pointed out that "unintelligibility need not be avoided for the aesthetic power to operate."[59] That is, the frustration of intelligibility can also be productive for the non-Chinese-reading viewer. The productivity of incomprehension has a long history in the West, passing back from Fenollosa and Pound to Leibniz to Kircher and the seventeenth-century fascination with the Chinese written form in the context of the search for an original human language and the construction of a universal written script.[60] In this project, desire and frustration produced a surplus of fantasy in which Chinese writing "functioned as a sort of European hallucination."[61] The alterity of Chinese writing in relation to romanized scripts is, of course, central, but it is the visuality of the character—the manner in which it is made manifest in highly abstract forms—that most contributes to its enduring effectiveness as a symbol of China.[62] That Yang Buwei was required to produce writing as a sign of China or that *A Book from the Sky* would provide so gripping a spectacle in the West should be considered in light of this venerable tradition of Western fantasy production and willful misrecognition.

The installation of *A Book from the Sky* at the Massachusetts College of Art in 1995 (figure 4) might be taken as a visual allegory for the privileged, aestheticized site of the viewer in the West. In a departure from other exhibitions, Xu Bing did not place text on the walls. The effect was to open the claustrophobic space of the installation which in turn released the viewer to move around the periphery of the work—there is even a view from above. The shift in the positioning of the audience was subtle but profound. No longer physically enclosed by the work, the viewer now faced *A Book from the Sky* from the exterior, an observer always on the outside. This arrangement manifests in visual terms a fundamental aspect of the exhibition of *A Book from the Sky*

[59] Jonathan Arac, discussant's remarks, "Gender, Visuality, Modernity in Twentieth-Century China" workshop, University of Pittsburgh, September 13, 1997.

[60] David E. Mungello, *Curious Land: Jesuit Accommodation and the Origins of Sinology* (Stuttgart: F. Steiner Verlag Wiesbaden, 1985), 34, 174ff.

[61] Derrida, *Of Grammatology*, 80.

[62] A spectacular example of the visual allure of Chinese writing can be found on the cover of the paperback version of Derrida's *Grammatology*.

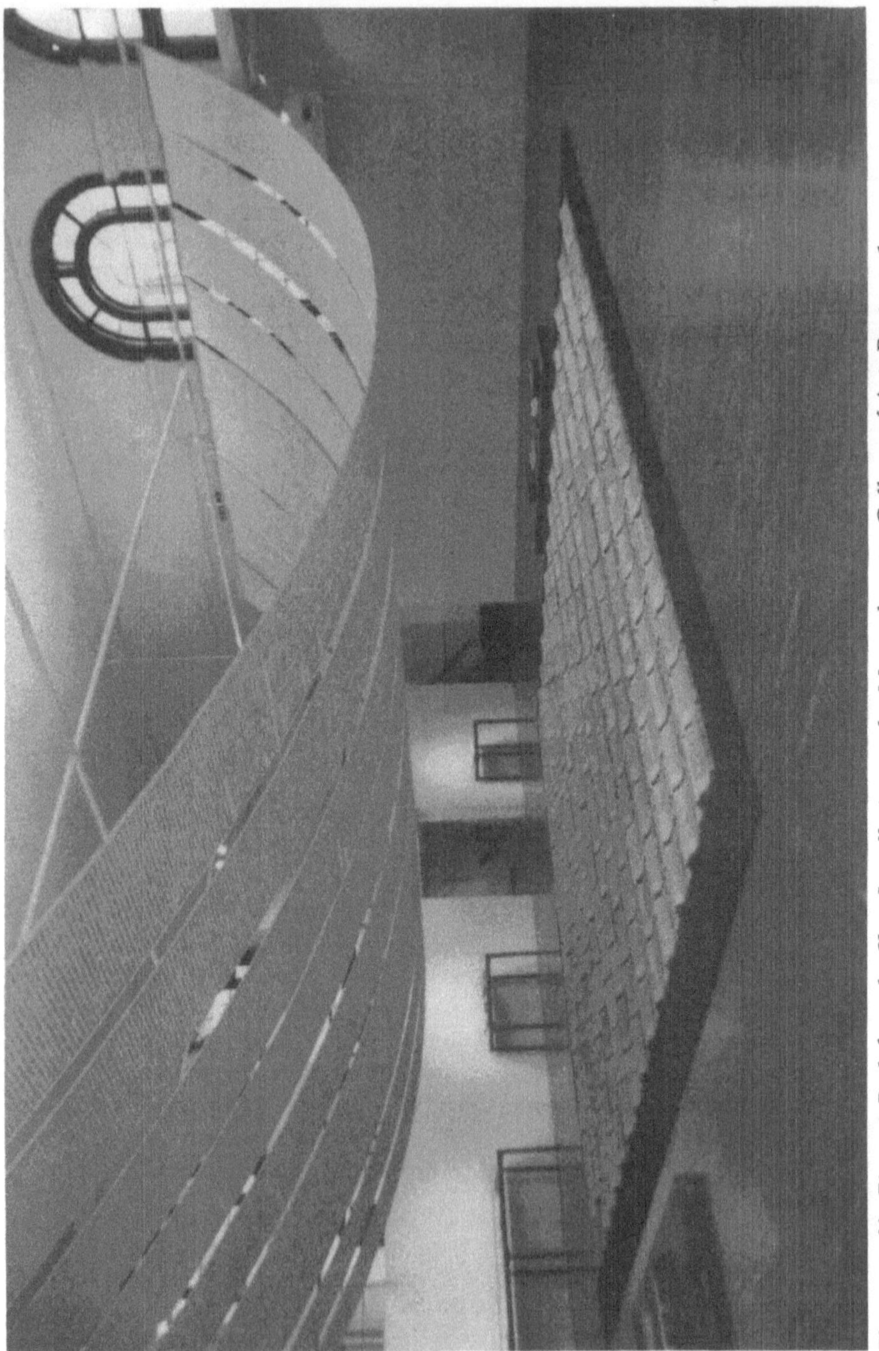

Figure 4. Xu Bing, *A Book from the Sky*. Installation at the Massachusetts College of Art, Boston. 1

in the West where the non-Chinese-reading audience is literally on the "outside" of the point.[63] To be outside of comprehension, however, is where the privilege of the non-Chinese-reading audience is located—a site at which enjoyment of the aesthetic might be substituted for considerations of the political.

The freedom to not engage the difficult issues raised by *A Book from the Sky* for a Chinese audience is a large part of its allure in the West. It is important that the problematic of Xu Bing's work be directed at the Chinese language, Chinese tradition, Chinese culture, or Chinese modernity. And it is equally important that critical commentary on the work confine this critique to China and not allow it to open onto the problematic implications of the role of the West in the very formation of Chinese problems of tradition or modernization.[64] For the typical viewer in the United States, *A Book from the Sky* is not only beautiful; it signifies, through the artist's critique, a problem not for us but for the other country out there.

V

While writing this essay I happened to look in on a World Wide Web site that some readers may be familiar with—the Han-Shan Tang booksellers in London—and found that works by Xu Bing were featured items in a recent book list.[65] Four hand-printed and -bound volumes from *A Book from the Sky* in a wooden case were offered in a limited edition of a hundred sets for £10,000 or roughly US$16,000. The sale immediately follows the exhibition of *A Book from the Sky* as part of a series of installations and performances of Chinese and British Chinese artists titled "Fortune Cookies" at the Institute of Contemporary Arts in London.[66] This is not the first sale of part of the work. In 1994 the Queensland

[63] Wang, "Of Text and Texture," 15.

[64] One exception is Peterson, "Book That Resists Reading": "[*A Book from the Sky*] is a challenge not only to ancient Chinese writing, the contemporary Chinese art establishment, or the state power of the People's Republic, but also of the discourses of Western art criticism, the 'free communication' of Western democracies, and the meanings encoded in capitalist systems of exchange."

[65] Han-Shan Tang Books, list 82 (June 1997) at <http://www.hanshan.com/>.

[66] The "Fortune Cookies" series was two years in planning and coordinated with the July 1 return of Hong Kong to China. Three works by Xu Bing were exhibited May 24–26, 1997: *A Book from the Sky, Square Word,* and the video of *A Case of Transference.* See the Web site of the Institute of Contemporary Art <http://www.illumin.co.uk/ica/Bulletin/livearts/fortunecookies/index.html>.

Art Museum in Australia purchased scrolls and sets of books from *A Book from the Sky* for $75,000;[67] other portions have been sold to private collectors and museums. Although it remains unclear how many of the books will be sold by Han-Shan Tang, the dispersement of books and scrolls from *A Book from the Sky* will undoubtedly continue. Over the past decade, *A Book from the Sky*, through its insertion into a transnational circuit of exhibition, has been transformed from a limited work responding to primarily local concerns into a commodified, aesthetic spectacle of contemplation and collection. In this sense, the career of *A Book from the Sky* marks the trajectory of contemporary Chinese visual arts from an engagement with the cultural debates characteristic of the mid-1980s New Era to the "postmodernity with Chinese characteristics" of the post-1989 period.[68]

The public offering of books from *A Book from the Sky* marks an important new development in the career of the work. With the sale by Han-Shan Tang, it slips from the category of high art with its attendant exclusivity, marked by limited sales to art dealers, collectors, or museums, to the status of something closer to an ordinary commodity, albeit a high-priced one, available to the general public. There is also a shift in emphasis in the representation of the work from a monumental installation to an example of print and book arts in which the value of *A Book from the Sky* lies not in its potential critique of traditional Chinese written culture but in the way "it lovingly adheres to all the material-cultural conventions and forms of traditional Chinese book-making and bibliography." The Han-Shan Tang text dwells on the meticulous attention to detail, the extraordinary production of the books from hand-carved movable type, the faithfulness to traditional Chinese bibliographic forms; it touts the book as having the form of "a 'Classic' or 'Collectanea' of Heaven, a work with a long exegetical history which has deserved and received the close attentions of many scholars for a millennium or more."[69] The advertisement targets a consumer who would most appreciate the antiquarian qualities of *A Book from the Sky* and, though there is appended an explanation of the critical potential in the invented characters, it is

[67] Goodman, "Bing Xu," 101.

[68] As outlined in Sheldon Hsiao-peng Lu, "Art, Culture, and Cultural Criticism in Post-New China," *New Literary History* 28, 1 (Winter 1997): 111–24.

[69] Han-Shan Tang Books, list 82 (June 1997), at <http://www.hanshan.com/x1.html#XU0TS2>.

the book's traditional aesthetic qualities that have been moved to the foreground.

The conversion of *A Book from the Sky* into a celebration of Chinese tradition highlights the continued importance of the orientalist interest in traditional exotica and the role of sinological expertise in making *A Book from the Sky* an authentic and valuable work of traditional Chinese culture. It is not surprising that the marketing strategy of Han-Shan Tang brings sinological exegesis, fundamental to producing "China" in the West, to bear on *A Book from the Sky*. In fact, the central claim of the work—that its characters were not readable—was taken to be a professional challenge by sinologists. Charles Stone, a doctoral candidate in Chinese literature, was one of the first to respond. Referring to the cover of a 1993 issue of *Public Culture,* Stone reports, "Undaunted, it took me no more than five minutes of leafing through an unabridged four-corner index of Chinese characters to turn up two real characters.... True, they are obsolete orthographies, and no normal person would care to know them, but they are still real characters. I imagine that a careful examination of the whole work would turn up many more." Stone asserts the authority of sinology by claiming a mastery of the Chinese language superior to that of the natives, those Chinese scholars who are said to have spent "hours, even days, at the Beijing exhibition searching in vain for a readable character."[70] However, it has been noted that one of the characters identified by Stone was an invention of the ninth century with no meaning or pronunciation, which indicates something of the difficulty of fixing a "real" or "fake" character in the Chinese language.[71] While the point of sinology remains the debunking of the myths of the natives, sinology's deep investment in the traditional is reproduced in Stone's assessment of *A Book from the Sky* as

> a study of the layer upon layer of tradition which Xu Bing evidently finds stifling. I do not understand how it is related to the

[70] Charles Stone, "Xu Bing and the Printed Word," *Public Culture* 6, 2 (Winter 1994): 407.

[71] Wu Hung, "'Ghost Rebellion,'" 417. The subject of nonstandard Chinese characters is complex and would need to include ancient mistakes that became canonical (see Bai Qianshen, "The Irony of Copying the Elite: A Preliminary Study of the Poetry, Calligraphy, and Painting on 17th-century Jindezhen Porcelain," *Oriental Art* 41, 3 [Autumn 1995]: 10–21) and contemporary invented orthographies such as the previously mentioned *nüshu*. For more, see Pat Berger's contribution to this volume.

> politicization of the meaningless, the prestidigitation of the deconstructed, or the denial of culture. What I see is a hyperaesthetic investigation of Chinese culture, and many many words I don't know, except for those two I found in the dictionary.[72]

Here one can discern the essentialized, traditional China that sinology insists on—the very same China that rose up to so unexpectedly confront Yang Buwei in the West.

VI

A fundamental structural element of *A Book from the Sky* is its juxtaposition of the past and present: "its reliance on traditional forms to express profound contemporary ideas."[73] The figures of time that constantly recur in interpretations of the work are not surprising considering the crucial role of temporality for the construction of China as an Other of the West.[74] The traditional elements of *A Book from the Sky* ensure that old lines of opposition—China/tradition/past versus West/modern/present—continue to operate as a powerful framework for our appropriation of the work.[75]

A Book from the Sky was created to resist easy interpretation, yet it has been relentlessly inscribed with political and aesthetic significance. In February 1989 in Beijing, Xu Bing wrote the following about the work:

> Nowadays the art world has become an arena. What do I want from it? Handing one's work to society is just like driving living animals into a slaughterhouse. The work no longer belongs to me; it has become the property of all the people who have touched it. It is now concrete and filthy. I hope to depart from it, looking for something different in a quiet place.[76]

There is a stunning clarity with which Xu Bing sees what the

[72] Stone, "Xu Bing," 410.

[73] Erickson, "Process and Meaning," 11.

[74] For a critique of the denial of coevalness in the construction of the Other, see Johannes Fabian, *Time and the Other* (New York: Columbia University Press, 1983), 31.

[75] For an example of the continued operation of the traditional/modern binary, see Jonathan Spence, *The Search for Modern China* (New York: W. W. Norton, 1990), and the critical review by Arif Dirlik, "Sisyphus in China," *Transition* 55 (1992): 94–104.

[76] Xu Bing, "Looking for Something Different in a Quiet Place," *Beijing qingnianbao*, February 10, 1989, as translated and quoted in Wu Hung, "'Ghost Rebellion,'" 418.

future holds in store for his work, but what is of interest here is the past that has been lost—a time when *A Book from the Sky* belonged only to the artist, before it was claimed by the "touch" of others, which turned it "concrete and filthy." This is a poignant moment because we know that circumstances have refused to allow Xu Bing to leave his work behind, that in the West nearly a decade later *A Book from the Sky* continues to hold its creator suspended in the past, trapped in our desire to see his "concrete" art reinstalled, again and again.

But even as the "filthy" books and scrolls are sold, the work has begun to regenerate. The exhibition of *A Book from the Sky* at the University Art Museum, Albany, New York (figure 5), in early 1996 was the largest installation of the work yet. Because of the size of the hall (80 × 60 × 35 feet), the work required hundreds of new books from China and several thousand feet of additional scrolls printed locally by Xu Bing and two assistants. Lacking enough individual woodblocks to produce the scrolls, Xu Bing had his characters digitally scanned into a computer and transferred onto photosensitive polymer "blocks" for printing.[77] In addition, one new text was added to the installation on a downstairs wall: "In the continual trauma that is 'modernity,' the question that returns to haunt the Chinese intellectual is that of continuity and (re)production of Chinese culture.... How is culture—in ruins—to be passed on, by whom and with what means."[78] The insertion of the quote is still another attempt, of course, to recuperate in legible language exactly what is omitted, left as a blank, in *A Book from the Sky*. Yet even as the quote returns us to familiar images of "ruin" and "trauma," the crucial role of "tradition" in the work has been undercut, displaced by the material introduction of the computer-generated, polymer-imprinted characters. Seamlessly inserted into the installation, these characters corrupt the purity of the traditional means of production so beloved in the West. No longer able to represent the "reliance on traditional forms to express profound contemporary ideas," *A Book from the Sky* is given a new life, a second chance to claim a utopic space,

[77] Personal communication, October 27, 1997, from Zheng Hu, exhibition designer at the University Museum and curator of the installation.

[78] Rey Chow, *Writing Diaspora* (Bloomington: Indiana University, 1993), 74, as quoted in Peg Churchill Wright, "Xu Bing Art Reveals Persistence of Spirit," *Daily Gazette*, February 1, 1996, Arts and Entertainment, 1. Also reproduced on the Web page of the exhibition <http://www.albany.edu/museum/www.museum/xb/xubing2.html>.

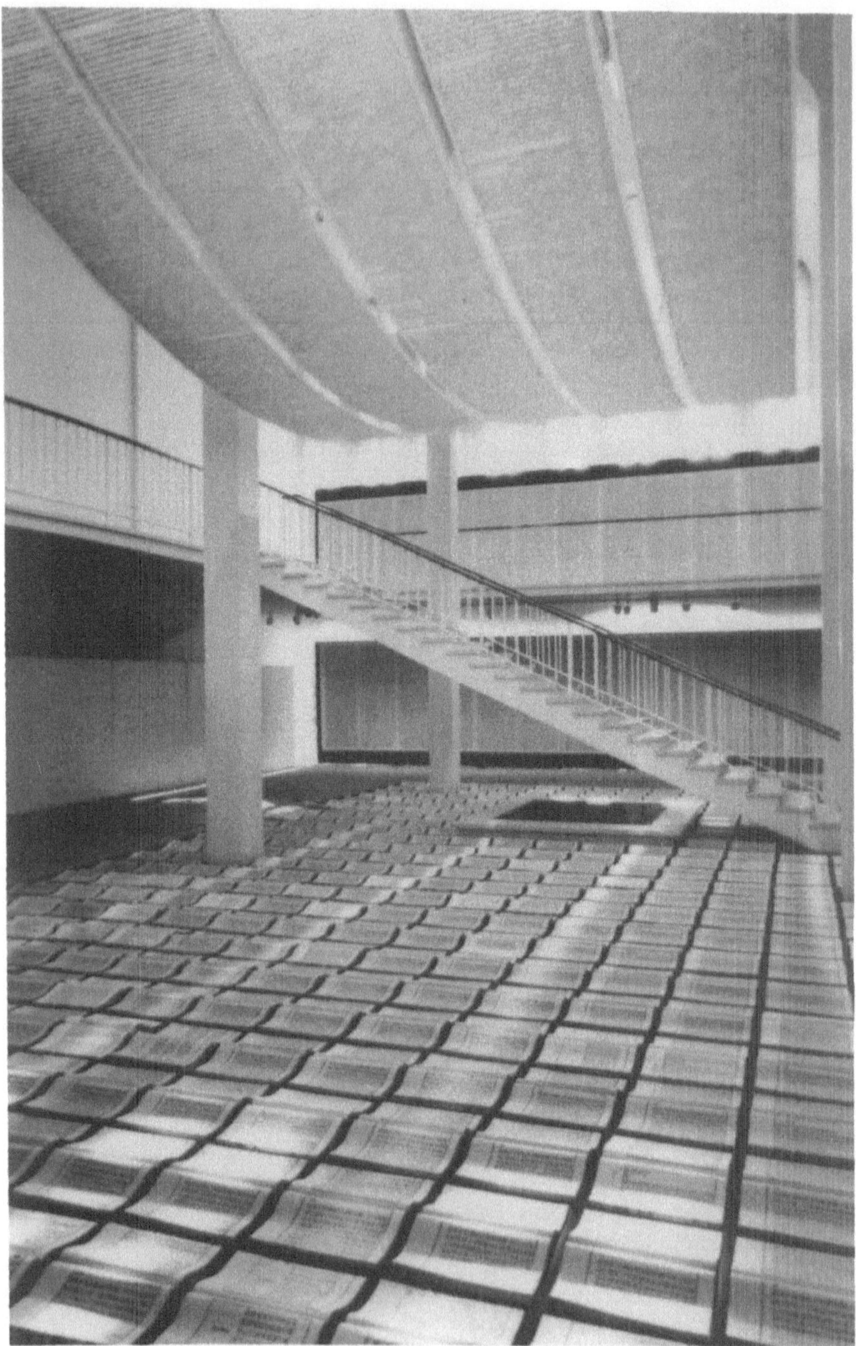

Figure 5. Xu Bing, *A Book from the Sky.* Installation at the University Art Museum, State University of New York, Albany. 1996. Photograph by Gary David Gold. © Gary David Gold, 1997.

"introducing into narrative history and geography the sudden distance that breaks apart closely held spatial and temporal surfaces. Lightninglike, before coming to a hard and fixed image in the utopic figure and 'ideal' representation, the *other* appears: limitless contradiction."[79] It is no coincidence that it was at this lightninglike instant of material and conceptual disjuncture that the figure of the modern Chinese intellectual appeared in the quotation to confront the wearying dilemma of Chinese culture and modernity.[80] This is the point, after all, from which the work began, and it seems that in Albany, *A Book from the Sky* turned briefly back to a moment in Beijing when its conception offered nothing more than a utopic space without questions or answers.

Glossary

shijimo juan 世紀末卷
Xishi jian 析世鑒

[79] Marin, *Utopics*, 7.

[80] One might argue that the "difference" in the Albany installation is also in part due to the Chinese background of the curator of the exhibition, Zheng Hu, and the author of the never-published catalogue, Alice Yang, but this fact is both relevant and inadequate.

FOUR

Pun Intended: A Response to Stanley Abe, "Reading the Sky"

PATRICIA BERGER

> I never thought that [my Nonsense Writing] would also get entangled within [this literary process], making a quite simple point chaotic, obscure, and troublesome.[1]
>
> Xu Bing, 1991

Xu Bing's *Tian shu,* as Stanley Abe explains in his "Reading the Sky," is an ever-changing monumental installation of bound and unfurled pages printed with more than 4,000 meaningless characters[2] invented by the artist himself and arranged into a visually convincing, but unreadable, traditional format of text and commentary. A work conceived as an alternative to traditional language, as a piece of antiverbiage, *Tian shu* has ironically generated more artspeak than any other single work of contemporary Chinese art, both in China and in the United States (most prominently in *Public Culture,* but also in *Art News,* the Chicago-based *New Art Examiner,* and elsewhere).

Abe, however, notably shifts the focus of previous criticism to take a look at the remarkable reception in the West of Xu Bing's *Tian shu* since the artist's move here in 1990. Beginning with Xu's first solo exhibition in the United States in 1991–92,[3] American commentary has been directed at the intentional unintelligibility of

---

[1] Wu Hung, "A 'Ghost Rebellion': Notes on Xu Bing's 'Nonsense Writing' and Other Works," *Public Culture* 6 (1994): 414.

[2] Xu Bing has said he created 4,000 characters "because Chinese government publications often use about 4,000 words. This is the number of commonly used words in Chinese newspapers and official texts." See Christina Davidson, "Word from Heaven," *Art and Asia Pacific* 1, 2 (1994): 48–55.

[3] At the Elvehjem Museum, University of Wisconsin, *Tian shu* was first shown together with *Ghosts Pounding a Wall* and *Five Series of Repetitions.*

Tian shu, its extraordinary display of diligence and traditional aesthetic values (toward which its Chinese and Western critics all stand in awe), and, at the opposite end of the critical spectrum, its easy fit with issues of interest to many postmodern artists in the West (fluidity of meaning, multivalence). Is it simply, as Charles Stone has said, "a luxuriant display of futility," or is it, as in Eugene Wang's view, "everything to everyone"?[4]

Abe argues that Xu Bing's *Tian shu* can only be appreciated in the West via an orientalist perspective, which is either "hyper-aesthetic" (Stone's term), or, if at all enmeshed in a cultural or political matrix, "narcissistic and self-congratulatory."[5] His analysis follows a number of lines; a potent one has to do with the Chinese language and the (mis)understanding and reinvention of it in the West. But Abe is also wary of the slant of political readings that *Tian shu* has been given both here and in China; his prime target is the catalogue written for Xu Bing's exhibition at the Elvehjem Museum, University of Wisconsin, from November 1, 1991, to January 19, 1992.

At the Elvehjem, *Tian shu* was shown for the first time in a solo exhibition to an American audience (it's not the first time, however, that it was staged for a non-Chinese audience; the artist had already taken it to South Korea, Spain, France, and England, among other venues). Catalogue author Britta Erickson connected *Tian shu* to recent events, namely, the rise and fall of the student democracy movement at Tiananmen a year and a half earlier, in June 1989. This interpretation, tenuous only at first glance, was built on Xu Bing's incorporation in his otherwise illegible "text" of real Chinese numbers enclosed in boxes, a form exclusively used on election ballots and an anomaly in a text of pure neologisms that he pointedly brought to Erickson's attention.[6]

Abe's argument against this reading attacks the liberal Western assumption that American-style democracy was the desideratum of the democracy movement and the paired, deeply held notion that Asian political systems are inevitably despotic. Curiously, as Abe points out, Chinese critics also eventually found a way to

---

[4] Charles Stone, "Xu Bing and the Printed Word," *Public Culture* 6 (Winter 1994): 407. Eugene Wang, "Of Text and Texture: The Cultural Relevance of Xu Bing's Art," in *Language Lost* (Boston: Massachusetts College of Art), 15.

[5] See Stanley K. Abe's essay in this volume, "Reading the Sky," 61.

[6] Britta Erickson, personal communication, January 30, 1998.

construe *Tian shu* as politically subversive, thereby making the Chinese government-controlled press the "unlikely bedfellows" of our own liberal third estate.[7]

Xu's own intentions and sources have been somewhat overshadowed and mystified by the sheer amount of discourse his work has generated. This is not surprising, given his genius for reacting to and incorporating the responses of others into his thinking, a practice that ultimately both reveals and veils his original intentions (and seems to serve him admirably). In fact, Xu Bing himself hasn't contradicted anyone's interpretation of *Tian shu,* generally acquiescing in response to suggestions of all kinds and thus revealing a roomy, postmodern view of how (and by whom) meaning is generated. When Erickson questioned Xu about whether *Tian shu* bore any relationship to China's democracy movement, he denied it was his original intention but amiably said that such an interpretation was possible.[8] He has, in fact, been notably swayed by critics to redirect his work toward new audiences on more than one occasion. It is because of this spacious attitude that *Tian shu* is still alive and in its second, third, or even fourth incarnation. It is not a static piece but seems intentionally situated to adumbrate the fluidity of meaning that, in the postmodern view, is inherent in art, text, and language.

Xu Bing's *Tian shu,* in his own description, was born of an alienation brought on by overindulgence in New Wave (*xinchao*) gabble on the modern, postmodern, and pseudomodern. "Thinking so much made me so tired," he says.[9] He conspicuously retreated from the heated discourse in late 1980s Beijing and began to work on the project that would come to be known as *Tian shu,* inventing about 4,000 characters in all, rendering them into superbly carved woodblocks, and then printing them into an

[7] Abe also says that "orientalism and liberalism combine today to produce the alliance of high-profile dissidents such as Harry Wu with the most right-wing think-tanks" and makes it possible for the Dalai Lama to be photographed embracing North Carolina senator Jesse Helms. "Reading the Sky," 61. These sorts of alliances, it seems to me, cross the categories of liberal and conservative that define American politics so easily only because they have no meaning outside the Western world. Is the Dalai Lama, for example, a liberal?

[8] Britta Erickson, *Three Installations by Xu Bing* (Madison, Wisc.: Elvehjem Museum of Art, 1991), 12.

[9] Jonathan Goodman, "Bing Xu: 4,000 Characters in Search of a Meaning," *Art News* 99, 2 (September 1994): 100.

accordion-book format. After four years of this, his friends feared for his sanity.

But when Xu Bing showed his work at the China Art Gallery in Beijing in 1988 and again in 1989 in a privately funded group show of New Wave art,[10] he was greeted by enthusiastic critical response. The writing of his hagiography began then, abetted by his own laconic, provocative comments. Here was a young man who came from an educated, elite, academic family (his father was chair of the history department at Beijing University), persecuted and sent to the country like so many others during the Cultural Revolution but, in the end, trained at the prestigious Central Academy of Art in Beijing. His work, therefore, came from within the intellectual establishment, and it is not surprising that it attracted a roomful of Beijing's best text editors, who stood confounded for days on end in front of the wall-like displays of unbound pages, curiously reminiscent of the scene at the subversive 1978 Democracy Wall, trying to find a single readable character. They failed—but in 1993, American sinologist Charles Stone quickly, in fact, immediately, in his own account, succeeded in finding two, presumably in addition to the election numerals detailed in the Elvehjem catalogue.[11] How could this be so? In Abe's opinion Stone's find is just one more symptom of American orientalism—the Western expert explaining Asian culture to benighted Asians. In any case, Stone's triumph was short-lived. In the same issue of *Public Culture,* Wu Hung revealed that one of Stone's discoveries, Morohashi 7061, was a Tang-dynasty fake character promulgated by Tang Wuzong (r. 841–47), thereby further complicating Xu Bing's motives.[12] Or was Xu's replication of an intentional falseness simply accidental?

As Abe suggests, Xu Bing's own complex and ongoing process of conceptualization is revealed in his vacillation over what to call his project. First named *Fenxie shijie de shu* (A book to analyze the world), some critics preferred *Xishi jian* (A mirror that analyzes the world), often followed by the phrase *shijimo juan* (fin-de-siècle

---

10 This second exhibition was quickly shut down through no fault of Xu Bing's after another artist, Xiao Lu, fired a pistol to shatter a mirror in her piece, *Dialogue.* The show was reopened, however, after participants assured the government that the performance pieces would not be restaged. Meg Maggio, review of *Desire for Words: Installation Works by Xu Bing and Gu Wenda* (Hong Kong Arts Centre and Hanart TZ Gallery), *Orientations* 23, 7 (July 1992): 68.

11 Stone, "Xu Bing and the Printed Word," 407.

12 Wu Hung, "'Ghost Rebellion,'" 417.

volumes). Ultimately, it was Xu's critical public that named (and nailed) the work for him. When one writer referred to it as *tian shu* (literally, "heavenly writing" or "book from the sky," but also used idiomatically to mean "nonsense writing" and to describe the marks left on the body of someone struck by lightning), Xu Bing quickly adopted the phrase as his new official title, proclaiming his project nonsense, a thing ultimately empty of meaning or, at best, like burns on the skin, susceptible only to general interpretation as symptoms of a previous, horrific event. Xu's intoxication with this new name opened up his ability to think in the broadest terms about the implications of his work—on the one hand, a piece that would fit in Wonderland, and on the other, one that resonates with a sense of catastrophe.

Intertextuality

Xu Bing continued to work uninterruptedly even as the protests at Tiananmen unfolded, engaged in another project, a rubbing of the Great Wall undertaken with the help of fifteen assistants. (Xu's Christo-like ability to mobilize a group effort of this size, especially at the time, to reproduce the inarticulate surface of the monument that best draws the line between what is Chinese and what is not begs to be read politically.) Like *Tian shu,* the Great Wall rubbing had no fixed title until an article by Yang Chengyin appeared in the official organ, *Wenyibao,* in 1990, on the first anniversary of the events at Tiananmen. Yang criticized Xu's *Tian shu* as being like "a ghost building a wall around travelers in the night" (Chinese: *gui da qiang*), rendering them immobile and ineffectual.[13] Yang's attempt to gut Xu Bing's work resembles an almost Platonic attack on art as epiphenomenal and unattached to the real world. Deny the ability of art to influence events, claim that it can function only aesthetically, and its power to sway opinion is effectively vitiated.[14] But with characteristic wit, Xu Bing turned Yang's critique on its head. With his interest in promoting multiple readings of his work already established, Xu changed the

[13] Yang Chengyin, "'Xinchao' meishu lungang" (On the principles of "New Wave" fine arts), *Wenyibao,* June 2, 1990, 5. Abe also points out another article, which has been much ignored, that appeared in the same issue of *Wenyibao* and that took a much more positive view of Xu Bing's work.

[14] See, e.g., Arthur C. Danto, *The Philosophical Disenfranchisement of Art* (New York: Columbia University Press, 1986).

Great Wall project's name to the same three-character phrase, *gui da qiang* (ghosts pounding a wall), emphasizing the alternative reading of *da* (build) as "pound," or "to make a rubbing." In one fell swoop, he had identified himself as a "ghost," literally a dead man incapable of fruitful action, but, idiomatically, as someone in exile from the political arena.

The question of *where* Xu Bing and his colleagues pounded—from inside the wall or outside—is further complicated, however, by stories of the original Qin-dynasty builders of the wall being thrown dead or half-dead into it and added to the rubble. The funerary and political components of *Ghosts Pounding a Wall* were thus underlined and linked, not just by Xu's pounding, but by his willingness to incorporate critical responses into his title, just as the reading of the earlier *Tian shu* was inevitably nuanced by its newly clarified, intertextual tie to *Ghosts.* And, even better, one of Xu Bing's harshest critics suddenly found himself complicit in a work he had publicly railed against.

In 1990, shortly after this neat inversion of criticism into entitlement, Xu Bing left China, ostensibly to take *Tian shu* on tour and to take up a post as an honorary fellow at the University of Wisconsin, where his first show opened at the Elvehjem Museum in November 1991 with the by-now familiar politicized reading of *Tian shu.* At the same time, however, American audiences, unlike their Chinese counterparts, were forced to confront the work with a distinct disadvantage, their inability to "get the joke," to distinguish between *hanzi* (proper Chinese characters) and Xu Bing's characters, or between what is readable and what is not, between what is meaningful and what is not.

Stanley Abe points out that, despite the attempt at the Elvehjem to fill the work with a new political content with which Americans could sympathize (however incorrectly, in his view), viewers were also told in the catalogue essay that they were liberated, rightfully or wrongfully, by their very illiteracy to pass to a purely aesthetic appreciation of *Tian shu* and revel in its exquisite execution and immense scale. This criticism overlooks the fact that, in deference to his "illiterate" audience, Xu Bing also included a section (admittedly small) of nonsense text constructed with roman letters.[15] But Abe nonetheless argues that the cultural gap between East and West lays bare the inadequacy of Western conceptions of Chinese culture, which are inevitably orientalizing,

15 Erickson, *Three Installations by Xu Bing,* 12.

built on ill-conceived, false ideas of what it means to be Chinese. I would like to demur, however slightly, from this correctly outraged perspective to suggest that the Chinese have hardly been immune to the plagues of aestheticization either, whenever they have decontextualized bits of their own material past and erected them as monuments of communal memory or recycled fragments of partially understood religious or philosophical systems into a theory of art (a particularly complex example is the Song-dynasty reutilization of Chan Buddhist ideas by literati devotees in their poetry and painting, which led to their eventual creation of a curiously oxymoronic and hyperaestheticized *wenzi* or "lettered" Chan in the face of Chan's fundamental rejection of the value of written text).[16] By a similar process of aestheticization, Abe points out that *Tian shu* was both undermined and fetishized, as U.S. audiences emphasized the traditional, handmade aspect of the work, a quality associated in the Western mind with diligent Oriental production.[17] Fetishization of *Tian shu* accelerated when Xu Bing began to sell individual volumes of the work and the famed London dealers of rare Chinese books, Han Shan Tang, advertised volumes for sale at the equivalent of U.S. $16,000 on their World Wide Web site, complete with antiquarian commentary.

Thus we must ask whether Xu Bing is a willing participant in the American art scene, a victim of orientalist critics, or intent on exoticizing himself and his audiences. After producing his Elvehjem exhibition, and seemingly not at all fazed by his new prominence, whether politically charged or hyperaestheticized, the artist moved to New York City, where he began to study contemporary life, in particular "its social excesses,"[18] and managed to

[16] See, e.g., Robert Gimello, "Marga and Culture: Learning, Letters, and Liberation in Northern Sung Ch'an," in *Paths to Liberation: The Marga and Its Transformation in Buddhist Thought*, ed. Robert Buswell, Jr., and Robert Gimello, 371–438. (Honolulu: University of Hawai'i Press, 1992).

[17] Never has Chinese script been quite so fetishized as in Peter Greenaway's film *Pillow Book* (1997), in which a beautiful young Japanese woman named Nagiko, daughter of a famous calligrapher, searches for a calligrapher-lover who will write on her body. She finds Jerome, a man who wants her to record her innermost thoughts on his body, which he will literally carry to her publisher. The plot takes a bizarre turn when Jerome commits suicide out of jealousy and Nagiko writes an erotic poem on his skin, then buries him. The publisher exhumes him and flays his skin, crafting it into a "pillow book." Nagiko retrieves the pillow book by sending the publisher a series of beautifully calligraphed young men, the last of whom kills him.

[18] Goodman, "Bing Xu," 101.

arrange several new exhibitions of *Tian shu,* all without the aid of a dealer or agent. And, far from being in exile from his native China, Xu has continued to return periodically to stage new work. He has also deployed more changes in the original installation of *Tian shu,* both to accommodate his new audiences and to respond to the installation-oriented aesthetic of his new milieu (site-specific works are not easily commodifiable, are difficult to store or collect, and therefore somehow appear to escape the financial excesses of the art market, so Xu Bing's meteoric rise has not necessarily corresponded to a rapid increase in wealth).

In an installation in Albany, New York, involving a much-expanded version of *Tian shu,* Abe says Xu went so far as to include sections of text that were digitally scanned and printed by computer. Abe sees this alteration in Xu Bing's otherwise impeccably handcrafted aesthetic as effectively restating the "utopian neutral," in the sense described by Louis Marin, that had informed the work in its earliest stages, when it was "neither yes nor no, true nor false, one nor the other." Now divorced from "the purity of traditional means so beloved in the West"[19] (but not in the East?), *Tian shu* is thrust forcibly into a placeless postmodern world (a positioning that has been embraced by Hong Kong and Singapore in their role as new world masters of fine, computer-generated, omnilingual printing).

Xu Bing's latest work is even more multicultural and multimedia, indicating a willingness on his part to reach new and, more and more often, non-Chinese audiences. For instance, his *Wenhua dongwu* (literally, "cultured animals," but titled in English *A Case Study of Transference*), staged in Beijing in January 1994, involved printing a pair of pigs with nonsense words, the female with Xu Bing's own characters and the male with nonsense words written in roman letters.[20] The idea was to present the pair together in a pen and wait until they copulated (which they obligingly did, much to the embarrassment of the gathered crowd. Xu Bing says that throughout, "[t]he pigs were very cool, very focused, and when the piece was finished, the pigs were just the same, but not so the people."[21]). In her essay "Lost and Found,"

---

[19] Abe, "Reading the Sky," 71.

[20] See, for example, Bill Stamets, review of Xu Bing, *Randolph Street Gallery, The New Art Examiner* (February 1996): 43; and Ann Wilson Lloyd, "Lost and Found," in *Xu Bing: Language Lost,* 20–24.

[21] Lloyd, "Lost and Found," 21. Xu Bing clearly does not subscribe to the Platonic view that art never made anything happen. See Danto, *The Philosophical Disenfranchisement of Art,* 2–4.

included in the catalogue of Xu's exhibition at the Massachusetts College of Art in 1995, Ann Wilson Lloyd raised the level of hilarity in Xu Bing criticism to a new high when she wrote, "While the pig farmers likely thought all this was just quizzical, it's a good bet the art intellectuals were obsessing about metaphoric meanings, references to Dadaist irony, tradition versus postmodernism, cultural hierarchies, and who's screwing whom, culturally speaking." She went on to point out that Xu Bing's own choice of the word "fornicating" to describe what the pigs did is not quite accurate. It is a term "with a definite gloss of morality, meaning lust outside of marriage. Since it's not possible for pigs to marry or be immoral, it's not possible for them to fornicate either."[22]

A Case Study of Transference was followed in 1994–95 by *Parrot,* featuring a bird who had learned to say, "Why are you holding me prisoner?" and "Humans are so boring! Modern art is crap."[23] Then in 1996 came Xu Bing's most wide-ranging effort yet, the *Tsan* (Silkworm) *Book,* in which he installed silkworms (called "larval terrorists" by one critic[24]) in a case containing print material of all sorts—traditional Chinese books, Western leather-bound books, computer printouts, and even computer screens glowing with text. The silkworms' task was to weave filaments of silk over the entire array, spotting and obliterating the pages with larval droppings and enmeshing everything equally in a natural web[25] (but one, nonetheless, with inevitable Chinese associations; silk, or Seres, was the name by which the Chinese people were first known in the West; only later were they associated with another wondrous invention, porcelain or china).

But we might as equally see printing as one of China's greatest inventions, and this is one element that has characterized the majority of Xu Bing's pieces. He is essentially a printer and a printmaker, interested in multiple repetitions of certain forms—especially, but not exclusively, culturally fixed forms, like writing—and their reception and manipulation by a wide audience.

Xu Bing's early reputation was based on his Master of Fine Arts thesis project, a series of xylographs, called *Five Series of Repetitions* (*Wuge fushu xilie,* 1987), in which he began with a print of a plain block (resulting in an image of wood grain), then cut the

22 Lloyd, "Lost and Found," 21–2.

23 *Xu Bing: Language Lost,* 5.

24 Stamets, review of *Xu Bing,* 43.

25 For *Tsan,* see *Xu Bing: Language Lost.*

same block down into a series of images (rice fields, tadpoles in pools), ending up with a blank hole in the middle of the last variation.[26] A comparison to the *Ten Ox-herding Pictures* of Chan Buddhist fame is hard to resist.[27] In that often-repeated series, a bull, standing in for the unenlightened, wayward mind, is slowly brought under control by a small herdboy, who catches him, tames him, and leads him quietly home. The tenth image is an empty circle, susceptible, like Xu Bing's carved-away block, to multiple interpretations.

Writing and Meaning

Stanley Abe raises an important issue when he asks "whether to read *Tian shu* as a critique or as an instantiation of traditional Chinese culture or both."[28] This is an excellent question, because Xu Bing's characters not only superficially resemble traditional Chinese writing in form, they are also curiously like Chinese characters because they are, in essence, hollow; they do not directly represent the phonetic value of spoken words, the way an alphabet or syllabary does, and would be able to take on a flexible range of grammatical function and meaning if only Xu Bing wanted them to. But in Xu Bing's writing, this range of meaning and function is still unlimited because his graphs are just script, not lexicon, a group of arbitrary signs whose meaning has not yet been culturally brokered. Therefore, when Xu denies his characters have any meaning at all, most of us feel we are in no position to contradict him; like Wittgenstein, he recognizes that there is no such thing as a personal language. His graphs are not *hanzi* or "Chinese characters," as Abe calls them,[29] but Xu Bing *zi*, unique to him but supralinguistic, open to infinite interpretation.

Yet there is something else at play here. Wu Hung, for example, referring to one of Xu Bing's early names for *Tian shu*, *Xishi jian* (A mirror that analyzes the world), has said that the reversal implied in Xu's writing, from sense to nonsense, "does not destroy meaning....It only destroys the signified (i.e., content), not the signifier." This is true on the level of one kind of signification, but

[26] See *Three Installations by Xu Bing*, 3–8.

[27] For a history of the ox-herding theme, see Scarlett Ju-yu Jang, "Ox-Herding Painting in the Sung Dynasty," *Artibus Asiae* 52, 1–2 (1992): 54–93.

[28] Abe, "Reading the Sky," 53.

[29] Ibid., 50 and elsewhere.

it ignores the culturally embedded meaning of style in Chinese culture, which Xu maintains so rigorously, even lovingly, and which inexorably aligns him with centuries of scholarship. Here we see texts produced in brilliantly carved characters, like those used in printing the classics ("I am after a Classical goal," Xu has said[30]) or the Buddhist canon, complete with "commentaries" printed in smaller scale.

Xu Bing is therefore clearly more than aware of the slipperiness of language, both in its verbal and written form, and it is to the details of this aspect of Abe's critique that I wish to return now.

Abe cites two cases of opposition to traditional Chinese language, both of them gendered: the curious *nüshu* (women's writing) of Hunan province and a series of anecdotes told by Yang Buwei, physician, gourmet chef, writer, and wife of the irrepressible, linguistically playful professor Chao Yuanren. These examples represent two quite different types of resistance, the one generated by a group, the other personal.

The comparison to women's writing has also been made by Yao Souchou, who has (erroneously, in my view) called *nüshu* a type of "nonsense writing," "an esoteric script [used] by women to express their inner world of feminine friendship, patriarchal repression and domestic practicalities," something they apparently were not free to do in *hanzi*.[31] Used particularly for "telling bitterness" (*sheku*), especially by older widows trying to find an outlet to express grief and loss, it is difficult for me, at least, to see *nüshu* as nonsense, even if such autobiographies are unusual, if not absent, in Chinese literature written in *hanzi*. *Nüshu* is, moreover, legible to those who have learned it (i.e., it is not intentionally meaningless), even if it excludes half the reading public by definition. It should be noted, however, that writers of the script appear to sign their names in *hanzi*, which is therefore still the medium of their social identities. For our purposes, however, the comparison of *nüshu* to *Tian shu* urges a tragic reading of Xu

[30] Wu, "'Ghost Rebellion,'" 411; 415. Wu Hung counterposes this latter statement against Xu's comment that he hopes his work will "expose and criticize Cang Jie's towering crimes" (he refers to Cang Jie's legendary invention of writing, after which "all the ghosts wailed in the night"; 414).

[31] Yao Souchou, "Books from Heaven: Literary Pleasure, Chinese Cultural Text and the 'Struggle Against Forgetting,'" *Australian Journal of Anthropology* 8, 2 (1997): 190–207. Yao also demonstrates the extreme range of interpretive possibility Xu Bing's work presents by using *Tian shu* as a medium of criticism of policies set by the government of Singapore.

Bing's work, a sense of the artist also noted by Wu Hung in his comment that the ghosts inhabiting Xu's Great Wall rubbing are tragic—"part of sadness of *Ghosts* is because of what happened at Tiananmen," Xu Bing says.[32]

In a second, very different example, Abe cites the experiences of Yang Buwei, who, though highly educated, was nonetheless a terrible calligrapher, so bad, in fact, that even her most intimate friends could not read her writing. Evidently reveling in the misconstructions placed on her meaning, she even invented her own characters, simultaneously confusing and appalling her friends. By the time she came to the United States on a book tour for her newly published *How to Cook and Eat in Chinese* about 1945, she had not written with brush and ink for twenty years. But when her American hostess insisted she sign her books with a brush, Yang capitulated, because, as Abe says, "It was only in the West and through the invocation of proper Chinese behavior by the 'American woman,' an 'expert' whose knowledge and authority [was] based on personal experience in China, that Yang abandoned her resistance to calligraphic practice.... She was, in a catachrestic moment, inadequate to the 'authentic' Chinese subject anticipated in the West." And so, panicked, Yang rushed out to find brush and ink, staying up all night to practice. Apparently, her American fans did not notice her lack of ability (how could they?) but, as Abe says, by assuming that she would be able to perform as any Chinese must, they displayed their essentialized, orientalist attitude toward her, causing her to recall all her ambivalences about Chinese script, "making incommensurable demands on her subjectivity."[33]

Abe goes on to describe one of the most egregious examples of the appropriation of Chinese script in the West, that of Ezra Pound and his source on all things East Asian, Ernest Fenollosa. Pound didn't particularly care about the visual qualities of characters, beyond his misunderstanding that they were ideograms; he was interested in appropriating them for his modernist agenda because of their semantic fluidity, especially as seen against their neat, modular form (they were neat nuggets of infinite possibility, in his view, just like Xu Bing's characters). This comparison of *Tian shu* to Pound is not really exact; however, the Beat fascination with characters, and a similar interest among action-painters of the

[32] Goodman, "Bing Xu," 101.

[33] Abe, "Reading the Sky," 49.

1950s (e.g., Franz Kline) comes a bit closer. Here figure versus field issues were fundamental; the graph clearly was written on an empty page, and with this came recognition that Chinese-style calligraphy is indeed a form of writing, and one unusually engaged in the physical, muscular process of making marks. Thus Kline and his colleagues could join hands, even if superficially, with the great calligraphers of China, who attenuated the shapes of characters to the point of near unreadability, their reason for being written almost entirely a question of style.[34] Yet despite, or perhaps because of, this recognition (could he have been so insightful?), Kline's titles are somehow subtly detached from the purely verbal (*Figure 8, Accent Grave*); his graphs cannot be "read" as phonemes or words but are designed to direct the viewer's attention back to the process of writing or painting itself.

All of this sets the stage for one of Abe's main points: that American audiences of *Tian shu* were reduced to (or freed to enjoy, depending on who's talking) an aesthetic reading of the work because of their illiteracy, which led to a complete misconstruction of what Chinese writing and culture are about (we have already seen how this was not completely true after Xu incorporated ABCs in the work beginning at the Elvehjem). But Abe does not consider if or how American illiteracy differs from reverent, Chinese illiteracy. The illiteracy rate in historical times past in China was high, but even the illiterate maintained an inculcated regard for scholars and the characters they wrote, to the point of believing them to possess magical qualities. *Tian shu,* however, powerfully reveals the elitism of literati culture to another exclusive group, the art-viewing public, by leaving them literally wordless.

The other side of reverence is mistrust, an attitude toward language that is also far from new in China. Chan Buddhists, in particular, distanced themselves, theoretically if not in practice, from text-based study of the Dharma, claiming a special mind-to-mind transmission outside the sutras from Śakyamuni Buddha to his disciples, and so on all the way down to masters of the present day. In their view language, spoken or written, was inadequate to describe or substitute for a personal experience of the prelinguistic, unsullied, original mind. Could this strangely postmod-

[34] This level of unintelligibility, which Charles Stone explores, is somewhat different from the inherent meaninglessness of *Tian shu,* however. See Stone, "Xu Bing and the Printed Word," esp. 409.

ern attitude toward language have developed because of the very nature of Chinese—phonetically spare, loaded with homophones in its oral form and famously allusive in its written form, designed, as it were, with pun, spoken and visual, intended?[35]

Indeed, Xu Bing's public presentation of himself seems to owe something to the culturally sanctioned role of the oracular, word-shy eccentric, some of the most entertaining and enlightening examples of whom have emerged in Chan Buddhist or Daoist contexts. Witness the zany Chan duo Hanshan and Shide, the one a poet whose poems, one suspects, were read off a blank page (and later "compiled" by a suspiciously obscure official), the other illiterate (figure 1). Far from tragic, these two embody the comic, wide-open aspect of original mind and recall Xu Bing's comment about *Tian shu*: "I'm willing to wait years to make a joke."[36]

On a more serious note Xu Bing himself has characterized his work as a kind of inner cultivation (*qigong*). In an article on *Tian shu* he wrote for *Beijing Youth Newspaper* in February 1989, he says:

> One of my painter friends once told me about a crazy guy in his village, who always went out to collect wastepaper at a certain hour, washing these papers in a river, carefully mounting them piece by piece, and then storing them under his bed after they had become dry and flat. I thought quite a long time about this person's behavior—a kind of cultivation of the Dao. It was indeed a very powerful kind of *qigong*. It exemplifies an Eastern way of achieving true knowledge—obtaining sudden enlightenment and correspondence with Nature by endlessly experiencing a fixed point.[37]

---

[35] Abe quibbles with Xu Bing's use of the Japanese word "Zen" to mean "Chan"—Zen, of course, being a term well known to Americans, if perhaps misused. He says, "By deploying Zen around *A Book from the Sky*, Xu Bing calls up a panoply of cultural traits that represent 'ancient China' to the West: solitude, quiet, meditation, wisdom and in the visual arts, surface, repetition, pattern" (63). But Xu's use of the word "Zen" only demonstrates how new his English is; in his *Art News* interview in September 1994, he was still using a translator (see Goodman, "Bing Xu," 99). "Zen" is in most contemporary English dictionaries and is a commonly accepted way to render "Chan" in English. So it seems unreasonable that Xu should be dragged into the debate, so eloquently stated by Bernard Faure and others, that focuses on the differences between Chan and Zen historically. See, e.g., Bernard Faure, *Chan Insights and Oversights* (Princeton, N.J.: Princeton University Press, 1993).

[36] Goodman, "Bing Xu," 99.

[37] Translated by Wu Hung, "'Ghost Rebellion,'" 418. The quote originally appeared in *Beijing qingnian bao* (Beijing youth newspaper), February 10, 1989.

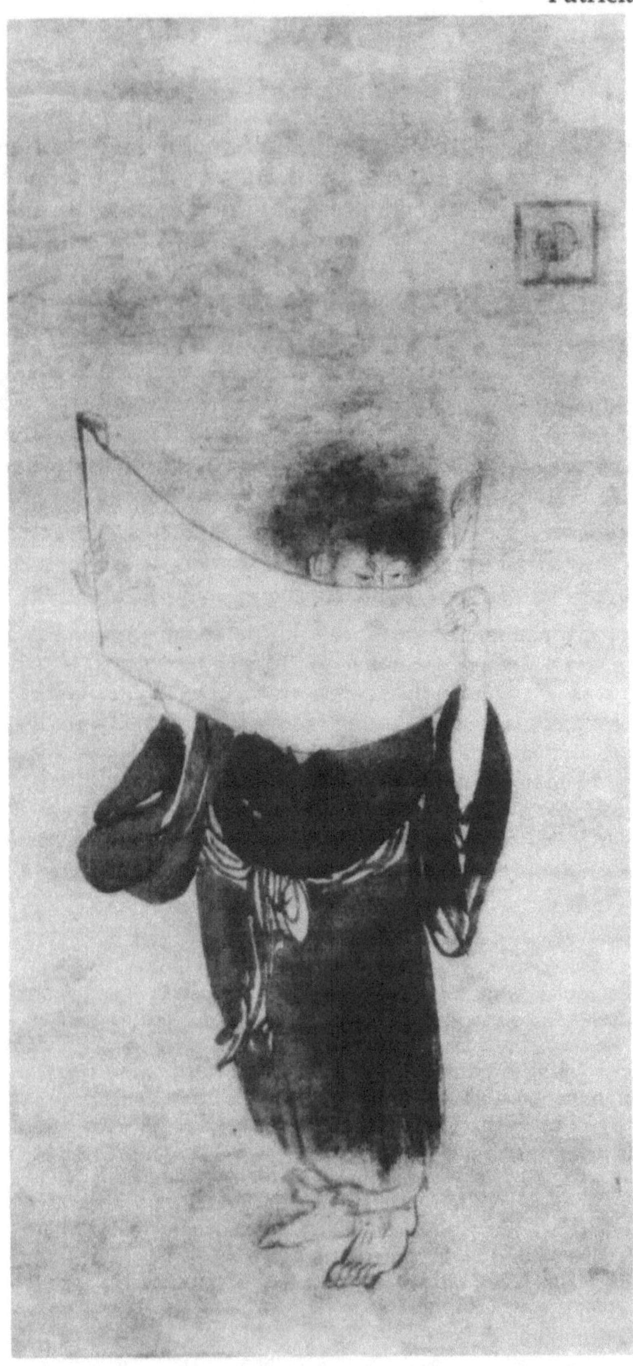

Figure 1. Luochuang (*ca.* 13th century), "Hanshan Reading a Scroll," Yuan dynasty, hanging scroll, ink on paper. University of California, Berkeley Art Museum.

If part of Xu Bing's agenda has been to make his viewers and even himself feel like outsiders from beyond the Great Wall, the situation in which they find themselves has ample precedent in East Asian history. A number of relevant examples come to mind in the context of the promulgation of the Buddhist canon, originally Indian and Central Asian. For example, Xu Bing's characters bear a certain relationship to Chinese translations of sutras incorporating unintelligible *dharani*, incantations that, even in the original Sanskrit, are composed of strings of enticingly wordlike phonemes generally without clear (or at least standard) grammatical syntax or semantic content.[38] *Dharani* are offered up in Chinese versions as series of characters, usually all with the "mouth" (*kou*) radical, which are meant to be chanted rather than taken literally (which, indeed, it would be impossible to do). The "mouth" radical clues the reader in to the fact that their meaning is linked to their orality and to the notion of pure sound.

Xu Bing's work has had other resonances beyond the Great Wall, the surface of which, as we have seen, was the mute subject of his *Ghosts Pounding the Wall*. *Tian shu* must have had an effect on its Chinese viewers similar to that produced by such languages as Tangut and Khitan, in use in written form from the tenth to at least the thirteenth century (figure 2) and, in the case of Tangut, reproduced as "fakes" for the antiquarian market even into the early twentieth century, presumably by Chinese carvers as avant-garde as Xu Bing. Both Tangut and Khitan were nonsinitic tongues, the one related to Tibetan, the other to Mongolian, and both appropriated the externals of Chinese characters in their written forms, but used them in very different ways, such as phonetically. Tangut characters are not, for example, hollow vessels waiting to be filled with sound and meaning depending on context, but spell out the spoken language in a systematic way.

Like Tangut and Khitan, Xu's characters represent some completely unknown Other, meant to ape Chinese characters, and, I would hazard in Xu Bing's case, to create the same sharp sense in the viewer as something familiar but disturbingly unreadable, like writing seen in the mind's eye, in a dream (or, for Western viewers, like seeing a page of Chinese). And like Tangut and Khitan, languages of two Chinese-inspired frontier empires, Xixia and Liao, Xu Bing's writing is the ultimate act of homage to the power

---

38 See, e.g., Frits Staal, *Rules without Meaning: Ritual, Mantras, and the Human Sciences* (New York: P. Lang, 1989).

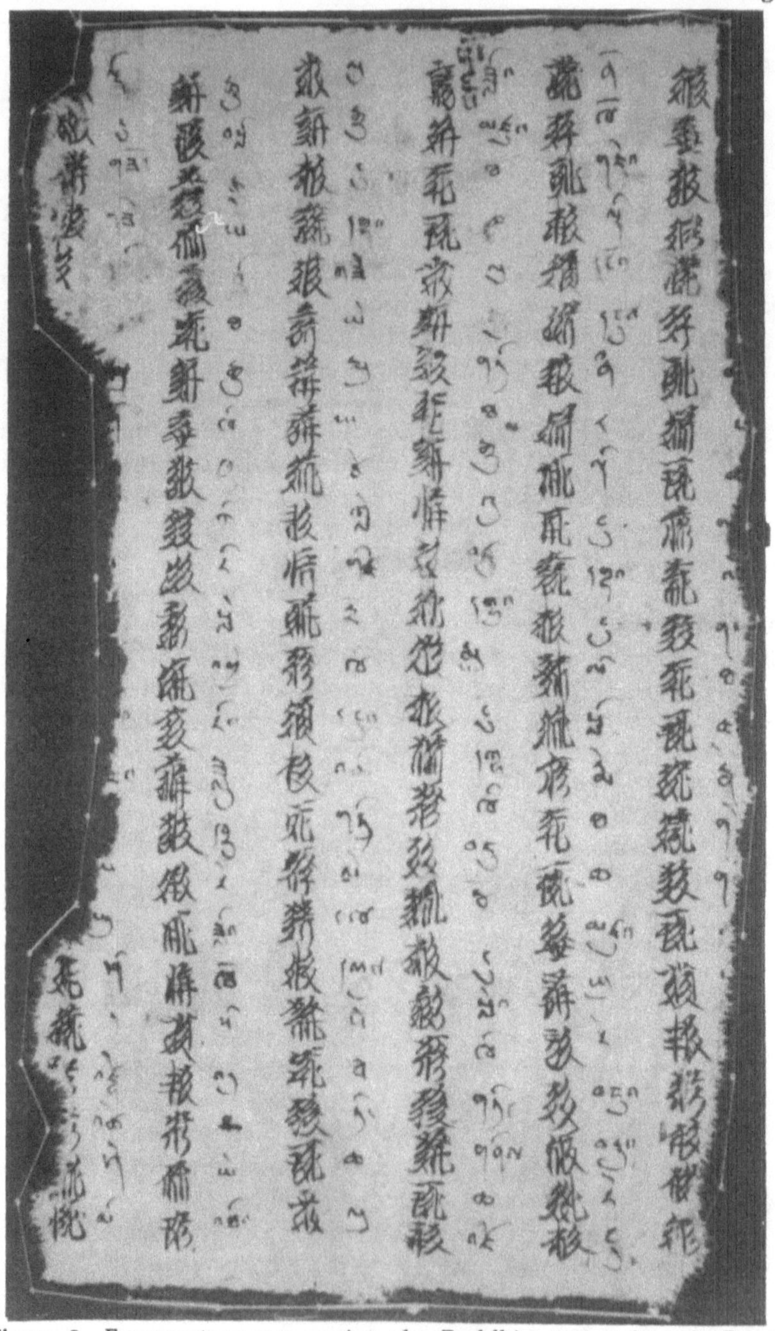

Figure 2. Fragmentary manuscript of a Buddhist text written in Tangut (Xixia), ink on paper, 13th century (Institute of Oriental Studies, Russian Academy of Sciences, St. Petersburg. Inventory No. 8363). After Mikhail Piotrovsky, ed., *Lost Empire of the Silk Road: Buddhist Art from Khara Khoto* (Milano: Electa and the Thyssen-Bornemisza Foundation and Electa, 1993), catalogue no. 75.

of writing, both troubled instantiation and reverent critique, just as Abe has suggested. The joke Xu has waited so long to see unfold is multipart, and part of it, as he had hoped, is on him. His writing is a self-encrypted system but, ironically or not, one that is slowly being filled with meaning. Since his first American exhibitions, Xu has received fan mail written in his odd characters—resonances of the Klingon clubs that flourish on the Web[39]—and he now says that meanings have begun to stick to them, to the point that he's teaching people how to read them. The process of cultural brokerage has thus begun. In deference to his new American audience, the always-enterprising Xu has even developed a new "square" script, reminiscent of Phagpa Lama's writing system, which the Tibetan Sakyapa guru invented to render Mongolian in the thirteenth century for his imperial patron Khubilai Khan (figure 3). Xu Bing's square script allows English speakers to write words in English that have the formal properties of characters—neat, self-contained, uniformly sized modules of meaning or nonmeaning, depending on who's doing the writing and who the reading.[40]

[39] Wu, "'Ghost Rebellion,'" 417. Xu Bing has plans to legitimate his writing, like Klingon, which is recognized by the Modern Language Association, by publishing volumes of his *Tian shu* as ordinary paperbacks, complete with ISBNs.

[40] I am grateful to Ingrid Dudek for this information, which she gleaned in an interview with Xu Bing in his Queens, New York, studio in March 1998, when Xu also gave her photos of the classes he holds in Xu Bing *zi* and square ABCs. Dudek is writing an honor's thesis on the artist for the Department of the History of Art, University of California, Berkeley. The work was recently shown at Art Beatus Gallery, in Vancouver, British Columbia, who generously supplied the photograph shown here.

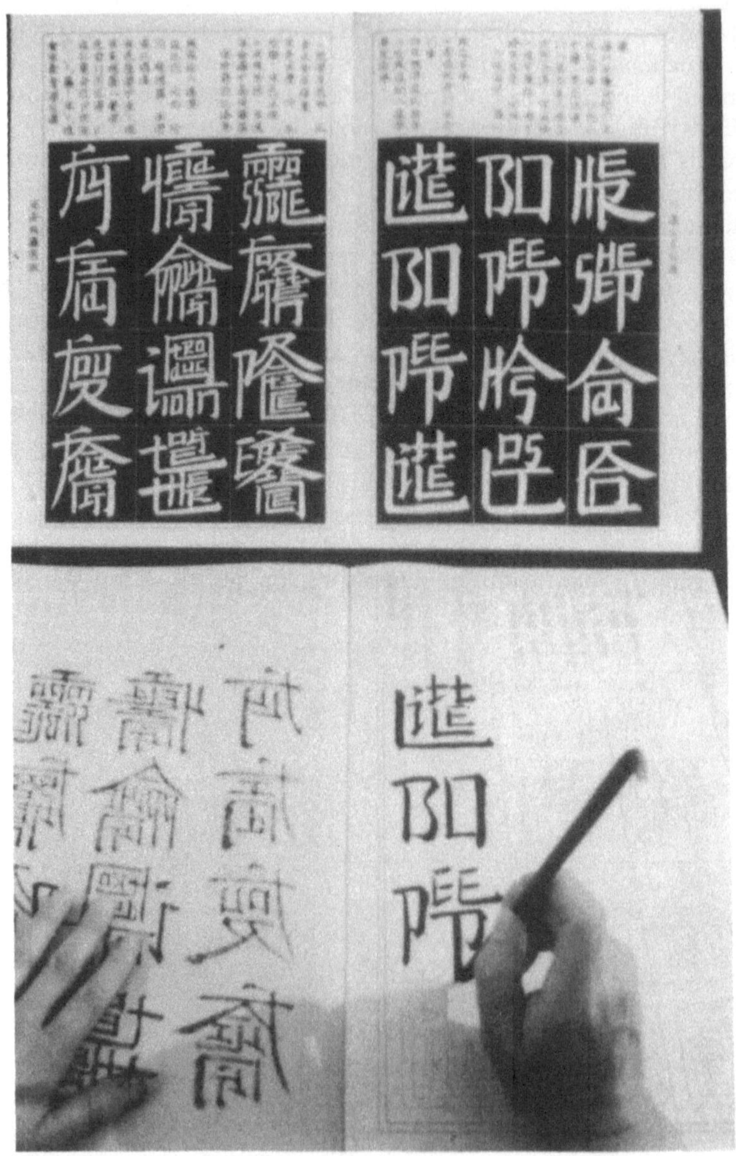

Figure 3. Xu Bing, "Introduction to New English Calligraphy." 1994–95.

Glossary

Chan 禪
Fenxie shijiede shu 分析世界的書
gui da qiang 鬼打牆
Hanshan 寒山
hanzi 漢字
kou 口
nüshu 女書
qigong 氣功
sheku 舍哭
Shide 拾得
Shijimojian 世紀末鑑
Tian shu 天書
Tiananmen 天安門
Wenhua dongwu 文化動物
Wenyi bao 文藝報
Wuge fushu de xilie 五個復數的系列
Xinchao 新潮
Xishijian 析世鑑
Xu Bing 徐冰
Xu Bing zi 徐冰字
Yang Chengyin 楊成寅

FIVE

Chinese Postmodernism and the Cultural Politics of Modern Chinese Poetry

MICHELLE YEH

If we were to choose one word to describe modern Chinese poetry, it would have to be "revolution." Modern Chinese poetry is an aesthetic revolution in the full sense of the word, encompassing all poetic conventions, including form, prosody, subject matter, and, above all, language. The advocacy of the modern vernacular to replace the literary classical Chinese struck the fatal blow to the formidable, seemingly indestructible edifice of traditional poetry. The use of the vernacular also distinguishes the literary revolution of 1917 from its predecessor in the late Qing known as the "revolution in the poetic realm" (*shijie geming*), led by Huang Zunxian, Xia Zengyou, and Tan Sitong. Although Hu Shi did not actually use "revolution" (*geming*) in the published version of "A Preliminary Proposal for Literary Reform" (Wenxue gailiang chuyi), generally regarded as the first manifesto of modern Chinese poetry, the word was in fact used in the drafts and appeared frequently both before and after January 1917,[1] not to mention the equally famous battle cry raised by Chen Duxiu: "On Literary Revolution" (Wenxue geming lun).

My sincere thanks to Rey Chow for her helpful comments and to the audience at the Center for Chinese Studies, University of California, Berkeley.

[1] See relevant writings collected in Hu Shi, *Hu Shi shihua* (Discourses on poetry by Hu Shi) (Chengdu: Sichuan wenyi chubanshe, 1991).

The Literary Revolution of 1917

The notion of a literary revolution—spearheaded and epitomized by poetry—was articulated as early as September 1915, when Hu Shi wrote a long farewell poem for his friend Mei Guangdi when Mei was headed for Harvard and Hu himself for Columbia University for graduate studies. The poem contains these lines:

The literature of China has long withered;
No leader was born in the last hundred years.
One cannot stop the new waves;
Now is the time for a literary revolution![2]

Hu did not expect that, for using eleven transliterations of foreign words, including ten proper nouns (names of places and writers) and one common noun (*yanshipilichun* for "inspiration"), his poem would invite a sharp response from Ren Shuyong, also a dear friend, in which he mocked the "literary revolution" that Hu envisioned:

Newton, Edison,
Bacon, Calvin,
Thoreau and Hawthorne,
"Inspiration."
Whip the ghosts filling a cart load
To bring you, Sir, fine jade.
Now that literature is undergoing a revolution,
I write this song to bid Mr. Hu farewell.[3]

All the images and names are taken from Hu's poem. In the original context, however, "ghosts" refers to those traditional poets whom Hu aims to overthrow to bring in the "new century." But Ren turns it around and uses it to refer to the foreign thinkers and writers whom Hu invokes. By saying that Hu looks to those "foreign ghosts" (*yangguizi;* a derogatory name by which the Chinese call Westerners) for inspiration, Ren also implies that Hu rejects China in favor of the West, thus providing an antecedent of the dichotomy of China versus the West that is to dominate most debates in the history of modern Chinese poetry.

---

[2] Hu Shi, "Song Mei Jinzhuang wang Hafo daxue" (Poem for Mei Jinzhuang leaving for Harvard University), cited from *Hu Shi shihua*, 59–61.

[3] Cited ibid., 21.

One important, perhaps inevitable consequence of polarizing China and the West is the politicization of the issue of language. The dichotomy of China versus the West is invariably replicated in the dichotomy of classical Chinese versus the modern vernacular. If the former is identified with China, the latter is always treated as evidence of being influenced by and imitating the West. In his letter of July 24, 1916, after dismissing Hu's poem "Reply to Guangdi: On Vernacular Poetry" as a "beggars' jingle" (*lianhualao*), Mei sees a parallel between Hu's revolution and the literary scene in the West: "In the world of Western poetry today, there are many who, like you, Sir, hoist the banner of revolution." The tone grows more acrimonious as Mei continues, "I have heard so much about the so-called new waves and new trends in contemporary Europe and America. A man of will must stand steadfast and not be swayed. I sincerely hope you, Sir, will not plagiarize (*piaoqie*) those worthless new waves to dupe our compatriots."[4]

Even if we accept the historical reality that the avant-garde in literature and art is, by definition, "ahead of its time," the harshness with which Mei rejects Hu's proposal for vernacular poetry goes beyond a mistrust or misunderstanding of the new. His rejection stems from a deeper cause, which has to do with Hu's supposedly uncritical acceptance of the West as superior. (On the list of new waves of the West are futurism, imagism, and free verse under literature, and symbolism, cubism, and impressionism under art.) In other words, underlying the contention between classical and vernacular Chinese as the poetic medium for Chinese poetry is the subtext of China versus the West. Once vernacular Chinese is perceived as non-Chinese and the literary revolution as an imitation of the West, the plane of discussion shifts from aesthetics to cultural identity. This explains why Mei simply ignores Hu's reasoning that vernacular literature has a long indigenous tradition, from the *Book of Songs* to the Music Bureau poetry beginning in Han times, to Song lyrics and Yuan dramatic arias, to the epistles and analects of Song and Ming philosophers and literati, and to Ming and Qing vernacular fiction. Neither is he open to Hu's explanation that the literary revolution that he advocates "is based only on the status quo of Chinese literature" and "has nothing to do with new trends in Anglo-European literature." "When from time to time I refer to Western literary history for examples, I only cite how 'national literature' of European

[4] Ibid., 99.

countries was born three or four centuries ago, because today China's need for a vernacular literature is very similar to that of Europe at that time."[5]

Whether one believes Hu or not in this exchange is beside the point. What is noteworthy is that both Mei and Hu find it necessary to discuss China's literary reform in an international context, especially in reference to the Anglo-European part of the world. It is no longer possible to discuss China solely in terms of China; any such discussion must take into account a worldview that is both broader (geographically) and deeper (historically). If, as evident from Hu's writings in the 1910s (including diaries and correspondence with friends), the adoption of the modern vernacular as the new poetic medium invited vehement opposition from some intellectuals, I would argue that, as the episodes of Ren Shuyong and Mei Guangdi suggest, such opposition arose because the issue of language was inextricable from broader cultural issues, especially those related to China's cultural identity as a modern nation.

When seen from this perspective, the theorizing of language in modern Chinese poetry takes on far-reaching significance in that it reveals one of the deep-rooted tensions that China has yet to resolve since the late nineteenth century, namely, the tension between China's dependence on the West for modernization and its simultaneous resistance to the West in its effort to establish a distinct self-identity as a modern nation. The early debate on the poetic language in many ways epitomizes the tug-of-war between these two opposite forces, and it is no wonder that language has remained a thorny issue since Hu Shi's time. In other words, the ramifications of discourses on modern Chinese poetry point to the intricate relationship between the aesthetic and the political.

To explore some of these ramifications, in what follows I focus on the debate in the 1990s that revolves around Zheng Min's essay "Retrospect at the End of the Century: Chinese Language Reform and Modern Chinese Poetry" (Shijimo de huigu: Hanyu yuyan biange yu Zhongguo xinshi chuangzuo). First published in the March 1993 issue of *Wenxue pinglun* (Literary criticism), Zheng's critique, directed not only at modern Chinese poetry but also at the modern Chinese language in general, has triggered a debate

[5] Hu Shi, "Bishang Liangshan" (Driven to rebellion), cited from *Hu Shi gudian wenxue yanjiu lunji* (Essays on classical literature by Hu Shi) (Shanghai: Shanghai guji chubanshe, 1986), 213.

among scholars in China in the ensuing years. The debate is worth investigating for several reasons. First, Zheng's essay calls into question the use of modern vernacular Chinese as the dominant literary medium in the twentieth century. To the extent that it criticizes the theoretical polarization of classical and modern Chinese, it belongs to a long line of reevaluations of the May Fourth legacy throughout the modern period. It differs, however, from earlier critiques in that it draws almost exclusively upon contemporary critical theory, in particular Saussure, Derrida, and Lacan, hence providing a good example of Chinese appropriation of Western theory in the 1990s. Finally, some of the points of view emerging in the debate, including Zheng's own follow-up essays, are symptomatic of recent trends in the literary and cultural scene in mainland China, especially those subsumed under the rubric of postmodernism. By analyzing Zheng's polemical essay, hereafter referred to as "Retrospect," and other related pieces, I address these issues from a critical perspective.

Summary and Critique of Zheng's Argument

Let me begin by examining the logic by which "Retrospect" presents its argument. It goes like this: modern Chinese poetry written in the vernacular has severed itself from the classical linguistic and literary tradition and therefore has deprived itself of that valuable cultural resource. As a result, modern Chinese poetry to date has not produced world-class poets and world-acclaimed masterpieces. Finally, this deplorable state has come about because the leaders of the literary revolution of 1917, Hu Shi and Chen Duxiu in particular, committed two fundamental mistakes: they fell into an extremist, dualistic mode of thinking, and they were ignorant of modern theories of language. To prove the point of extremism, "Retrospect" cites Chen's statement that the literary revolution "will not allow room for discussion with the opponents."[6] By dualistic mode of thinking, Zheng refers to the binary oppositions that underscore Hu and Chen's position, which she summarizes as follows:[7]

---

[6] Zheng Min, "Shijimo de huigu: Hanyu yuyan biange yu Zhongguo xinshi chuangzuo" (Retrospect at the end of the century: Chinese language reform and modern Chinese poetry), *Wenxue pinglun* 3 (1993): 5.

[7] Zheng Min, "Guanyu 'Ruhe pingjjia "Wusi" baihuawen yundong' shangque zhi shangque" (A rejoinder to the rejoinder "How to evaluate the May Fourth vernacular movement"), *Wenxue pinglun* 2 (1994): 118.

cultural reform	inheritance of the tradition
vernacular Chinese	classical Chinese
spoken language	written language
Ming-Qing vernacular literature	earlier classical literature
new culture	old culture

Instead of seeing the two sides as complementary, Hu and Chen pitched one against the other and brought harm to both. Rather than carrying out language reform based on classical Chinese, which was proposed, for instance, by the Xueheng School, Hu and Chen tried to do away with classical Chinese once and for all. In a 1994 rejoinder, Zheng reiterates her point that "tradition can be inherited in a critical spirit...but it cannot be overthrown" and holds that compared to modern Chinese, classical Chinese is a better "vehicle of culture."[8] The other mistake, according to "Retrospect," is that Hu and Chen did not understand that language is "a system of signs which are arbitrary, inherited, and not open to choice." Their attempt to "completely erase" classical Chinese from modern Chinese violates the "nature and rules of language itself" as theorized by Saussure, Lacan, and Derrida.[9]

Zheng's argument contains some gross generalizations and serious distortions. First, it equates the literary revolution of Hu and Chen of the 1910s–20s with the political revolution of Chinese communism throughout the twentieth century and equates the struggle between the vernacular and the classical language with that between "proletarian culture" and "bourgeois culture." If for Chen the distinction between literary and political aspirations was never clear, the same cannot be said of Hu. As to the claim that Hu and Chen's dualism has been the "orthodox logic and has enjoyed indisputable authority"[10] in China since the May Fourth period, it contradicts Zheng's main argument in that at the beginning of "Retrospect" she lists other viewpoints on language reform during the May Fourth period and faults Hu and Chen for not listening to them. Further, as Xu Ming has pointed out, the 1920s were indeed a time of diverse voices and multiple positions when it came to linguistic and literary reform.[11] Hu and Chen

[8] Ibid., 118, 119.

[9] Zheng Min, "Shijimo de huigu," 5, 7.

[10] Ibid., 6.

[11] Xu Ming, "Wenhua jijin zhuyi lishi weidu" (Historical dimensions of cultural radicalism), *Wenxue pinglun* 4 (1994): 115.

came out the winners not because they possessed any coercive, political power to impose their view on society but because it struck a sympathetic chord in the younger generation, who saw classical Chinese as both a cause and product of China's backwardness. Thus, Zhang Yiwu emphasizes the connection between the literary revolution and China's modernization discourse, between the triumph of the vernacular and China's drive toward modernity.[12] Although I agree that the literary reform was inextricably related to China's modernization project, modernization is not to be understood solely in political, economic, and social terms; it embodies, above all, significant aesthetic considerations, to which I will return.

Zheng's equating the literary revolution with the political revolution also leads her to associate the former with the Anti-rightist Literature, Great Leap Forward Literature of the People's Commune, and Anti-imperialist, Anti-revisionist Literature of the 1950s–60s and the literature of the Cultural Revolution later on. Further, Zheng identifies the polarity between classical and vernacular Chinese with that between Misty Poetry and "popular poetry."[13] Despite its ideal of making poetry more accessible to an increasingly literate population, the new poetry launched by the 1917 literary revolution was not directed by political decisions. Not only is it mystifying to subsume Misty Poetry under classical Chinese, which it plainly is not, but to pit it against "popular poetry" is to espouse the official line against the experimental spirit that Misty Poetry embodies. When Misty Poetry was under attack by the cultural establishment in the early 1980s, one of the criticisms was that it exhibited characteristics of Western modernism and was therefore undesirable. Misty Poetry shares such modernist themes as alienation and social critique and employs such modernist techniques as stream of consciousness, ambiguity, and personal symbolism. Besides acknowledged, albeit limited, Western influences, its native genealogy can be traced through the modernist poetry of the pre-Communist era, especially the School of Nine Leaves (Jiuyepai) of the 1940s, the works of Bian Zhilin and He Qifang of the 1930s, and the early Ai Qing, to the New Poetry of the May Fourth period.

---

[12] Zhang Yiwu, "Chonggu 'xiandaixing' yu Hanyu shumianyu lunzheng" (A reevaluation of "modernity" and the debate on written Chinese), *Wenxue pinglun* 4 (1994): 107–13, 120.

[13] Zheng Min, "Shijimo de huigu," 14.

These distortions and fallacies stem from Zheng's failure to grasp fully the historical context. Chen Pingyuan points out in *The Establishment of Modern Chinese Scholarship* that "it was the vogue of the time for late Qing intellectuals to advocate the vernacular." Whether as a vehicle for enlightenment or as a means of literary expression, "the promotion of the vernacular did not begin with Hu Shi; Hu's invention lies in his giving 'classical Chinese' a death sentence."[14]

Namely, Zheng overlooks the historical fact that the so-called extremism was a strategy rather than praxis, in view of the traditional elite culture still dominant at the time. In "Chinese Literature of the Past Fifty Years" (Wushi nian lai Zhongguo zhi wenxue), Hu Shi recalls that in naming the first individual collection of modern Chinese poetry "Experiments" (Changshi ji), he adopted a more moderate attitude than Chen Duxiu. Expressing admiration for Chen's "courage," Hu regards Chen's extremist position as a necessary complement to his own, because "if we had followed my way, the literary revolution would have taken at least ten more years of discussion and trials" and "had we not had Chen's spirit of 'not allowing any room for discussion with the opponents,' the literary revolution would not have attracted that much attention."[15]

The failure to distinguish theory from practice accounts for another contradiction in "Retrospect." That is, although Zheng claims that Hu and Chen's negation of the classical tradition is total and complete, she nevertheless cites Hu's poems "Two Butterflies" and "Dream and Poetry" as revealing "traces" of classical poetry. In fact, the common criticism and *self*-criticism of early modern poets is that they are overly indebted to traditional poetry. Almost all the pioneers of modern poetry were well versed in classical Chinese literature. Hu Shi made fun of his own work as "bound feet unbound," admitting a marked influence by Song lyrics. Liu Dabai (1890–1932) was a degree-holder under the late Qing and, in the preface to his first collection of modern poetry, *Old Dreams* (*Jiumeng*), describes himself as "steeped in old poetry for almost thirty years." Zong Baihua (b. 1897) tells us that his miniature poems, which led the trend in the early 1920s, are

[14] Chen Pingyuan, *Zhongguo xiandai xueshu zhi jianli—yi Zhang Taiyan Hu Shizhi wei zhongxin* (The establishment of modern Chinese scholarship centered on Zhang Taiyan and Hu Shizhi) (Beijing: Beijing daxue chubanshe, 1998), 195–96.

[15] Cited from Hu Shi, *Hu Shi gudian wenxue yanjiu lunji*, 156, 157.

directly influenced by Tang *jueju* (quatrain) and have nothing to do with Tagore, Goethe, or Japanese haiku, as some critics have suggested.[16] Elements of classical literature, whether it's late-Tang poetry or Taoism-Buddhism, are clearly discernible in such poets as different as Zhou Zuoren (1885–1968), Yu Pingbo (b. 1900), Li Jinfa (1900–76), Fei Ming (1901–67), and Dai Wangshu (1905–50). What is also true is that Zhou, Yu, Wen, and many other early modern poets turned to writing classical poetry exclusively after a short while, and some even became scholars of classics. Rather than accusing them of "forgetting and abandoning" classical literature, as Zheng does, it is more accurate to say that exactly *because* the pioneers knew the resources as well as the limitations of the classical tradition they deemed it necessary to emphasize difference over continuity, radical departure over inheritance.

More important than the strategic iconoclasm that I defend, however, is that in reacting against the classical tradition, the literary revolution is always already a reinterpretation, even reinvention, of that tradition. "Retrospect" is predicated on the unexamined assumption that the Chinese classical tradition is a permanent, immutable, universally accepted entity, but historically it has never been such. Each generation of writers and scholars redefines tradition to carve out its own position, whether for creative or intellectual purposes. It is true that the pioneers of modern Chinese poetry rejected certain strands of classical literature and culture, but they differed widely in their emphasis on what was culturally and artistically useful. The literary revolution of 1917 was an overall effort to radically revise the tradition by challenging the canon, elevating thitherto neglected authors and works, and creating a vernacular poetry free from all poetic and aesthetic conventions. One of my favorite quotations about modern Chinese poetry is from Ye Gongchao, who said in 1937, "Although there are conspicuous differences between old and new poetry, our ultimate hope is that we will add the voice of our time to Chinese poetry as a whole, making it necessary to reevaluate once again all that has come before."[17] The seeming anachronism

---

[16] Liu Dabai, "'Jiumeng' fuyin ziji" (Preface to *Old Dreams*) (1922), cited from *Zhongguo xinshi ji xu ba xuan* (Selected prefaces and postscripts to collections of modern Chinese poetry), ed. Chen Shaowei (Changsha: Hunan wenyi chubanshe, 1986), 104. Zong Baihua, "Wo he shi—'Liuyun xiaoshi' houji" (Poetry and me: Postscript to "Floating Clouds") (1923), cited from *Zhongguo xinshiji xu ba*, 122.

[17] Ye Gongchao, *Ye Gongchao sanwen ji* (Collected essays of Ye Gongchao) (Taipei: Hongfan shudian, 1982), 81.

points to the paradox inherent in any literary tradition: it is in the emergence of the new that tradition gets defined over and over again. We always go "back to the future."

This also brings us to the greatest significance of the literary revolution. Early modern Chinese poets were not content with merely changing the diction, imagery, subject matter, or formal conventions—changes that had already been attempted to some degree in the late Qing—but aimed to establish the vernacular language as a new, viable poetic medium on which a new poetics could be developed. In 1922 Hu Shi himself made a clear distinction between the call for "the vernacular" in the earlier era and the call for "vernacular literature" that he and Chen advocated. In the 1920s–30s such poets as Liang Shiqiu, Xu Zhimo, and Yu Pingbo expressed their awareness of the necessary but difficult process of transition from "the vernacular" to "vernacular poetry." Modern Chinese poetry is arguably the boldest experiment in Chinese literary history inasmuch as it raises fundamental questions about the nature and purpose of poetry that have never been raised before. Coupled with simultaneous, profound transformations of China's political, economic, educational, and cultural conditions, the literary revolution compelled poets and readers to ask themselves What is poetry? Whom does poetry address? Why poetry? The literary revolution is both a cause of and a response to the new cultural context of modern China, and its most original contribution lies in effecting a paradigm shift through the invention of a new poetic medium and explorations of new poetics.[18]

Ironically, although her criticism of the logocentrism of Hu and Chen is valid, Zheng cannot escape from the rigid dichotomy of the written language versus the spoken, classical versus modern Chinese. She insists on seeing the two terms as discrete and, in fact, opposed to each other, rather than as forming a continuum. Even a cursory observation of how modern Chinese is spoken and written suffices to show how much classical Chinese is very much part of modern Chinese, not so much in terms of grammar as in terms of idioms and phrases, proverbs, sayings, oft-quoted verses, and the like, many of which are traceable to Confucian, Buddhist, or Taoist traditions. Contrary to the rigid dichotomy on which "Retrospect" bases its argument, I see modern and classical Chinese as forming a wide spectrum of formality and erudition.

---

[18] See Michelle Yeh, *Modern Chinese Poetry: Theory and Practice since 1917* (New Haven, Conn.: Yale University Press, 1991), esp. chap. 1.

In modern Chinese poetry there is a similar range of language use, from the elegant and classically flavored to the colloquial and even slangy.

Neither in theory nor in practice does modern Chinese poetry define the vernacular exclusively as the spoken language in an attempt, as Zheng claims, to "replace both the spoken and written language" with the spoken. The insistence with which she holds on to such a dichotomy, I submit, is inseparable from the theoretical model that she employs, namely, structuralist and poststructural theory. Her understanding of poststructuralism in particular leads to the following pronouncement: "Another major mistake of Hu and Chen was that they only emphasized *parole* and did not consider *langue* carefully, they only knew synchronicity but neglected diachronicity."[19] Based on such evidence, she criticizes Hu and Chen as logocentric.

Saussure's contribution lies in his original approach to language as a self-contained system of relationally defined signs (each further divided into the signifier and the signified). Unlike historical linguists of his time, he was interested not in the evolution of language over time—the diachronic view—but in the state of the system at any one point in time—the synchronic view. Whereas he calls the system of discursive possibilities *langue*, *parole* is the actualization, particular utterance, or speech event whose meaning is made possible by the system. The former is likened to the structure and rules of the chess game, the latter to individual games actually played. Although each actualized game is different, it is understood as a chess game because of the structure and rules behind it. Thus, meaning derives from structure.

Many Euro-American scholars interpret *parole* as the spoken language. However, Zheng's equating the vernacular with the spoken language and then criticizing Hu and Chen as logocentric is farfetched. By constructing a genealogy of vernacular literature throughout Chinese history and emphasizing that "the vernacular is capable of producing first-rate literature," Hu became a seminal figure in rewriting Chinese literary history. The vernacular that he advocated is by no means limited to the spoken language but includes a large amount of vernacular poetry and prose. Wang Hui sums up the situation clearly: "The issue at hand is one in which one system of written Chinese replaces another system of written Chinese.... As a system of written language, the replace-

[19] Zheng Min, "Shijimo de huigu," 17, 10.

ment of the classical language with the vernacular cannot be described as logocentrism."[20]

Both Lacan and Derrida drew upon Saussure's structural linguistics, especially his theory of language as a system of differences, which they carry to a radical conclusion in psychoanalysis and philosophy, respectively. Both deny the necessary link between the signifier and the signified, and both emphasize the absolute autonomy of the signifier. For Lacan, language as a symbolic order defines the nature of human psychology. His famous formulation that "the unconscious is structured like a language" suggests that desire functions much like the signifier. Just as the signifier "always anticipates meaning by unfolding its dimension before it"[21] and is always situated in "the signifying chain" that, through metonym (displacement) and metaphor (substitution), produces the effect of the signified, desire always points to an absent Other (the object of desire) and marks the symbolic differentiation and relationships that govern human activity. Similarly for Derrida, the signifier leads not to the signified but only to other signifiers, just as metaphor as a "transference" is not a detour to the literal "truth" but leads to more metaphors. The infinite play of the signifier debunks such Western metaphysical notions as presence, Being, origin, and Logos, which are constituted by the play of the signifier, also denoted by notions of *differance,* trace, and supplement.

In refuting Hu and Chen's claim that a new poetry written in the modern vernacular would be more accessible, Zheng invokes Lacan's notion that the bar separating the signifier from the signified cannot be crossed; the signified, she argues, remains inaccessible whether it is in classical or modern Chinese. She also turns to Derrida's notion of trace to make a point about how futile it was for Hu and Chen to try to erase classical Chinese because its traces are everywhere in modern Chinese.

Zheng's appropriation of poststructuralism is questionable on several counts. First, she accepts it uncritically, treating it as if it were a newly discovered, absolute truth rather than an interpreta-

---

[20] Hu Shi, "Bishang Liangshan," 212. Wang Hui, "Difang xingshi, fangyan tuyu yu kangri zhanzheng shiqi 'minzu xingshi' de lunzheng" (Local form, dialect, and the debate on "national form" during the anti-Japanese war), in *Wang Hui zixuan ji* (Self-selected work by Wang Hui) (Guangxi: Guangxi shifan daxue chubanshe, 1997), 342.

[21] Jacques Lacan, *Ecrits,* trans. Alan Sheridan (New York: W. W. Norton, 1977), 153.

tion, however illuminating it may be, that challenges earlier interpretations. (For instance, Lacan's theory of desire as lack or absence is vastly different from Deleuze and Guattari's, in which desire is a creative, productive force.) Her confidence in the infallibility of poststructuralism comes across clearly when she chastises Hu and Chen "from the height of contemporary linguistic theories."[22] Ironically, on one hand, Zheng repeatedly emphasizes the ideographic nature of Chinese characters in sharp contrast to Western alphabetic languages, attributing the unique qualities of classical Chinese poetry to the former; on the other hand, she does not hesitate in imposing a Western theory about the signifier and the signified, *parole* and *langue*, on the Chinese language.

Second, Lacan's opaque, idiosyncratic style notwithstanding, Zheng reads him too simplistically and too literally. For Lacan, language is a metaphor for human psychology. To the extent that he deconstructs the one-to-one correspondence between the signifier and the signified, he does not deny the existence of meaning (i.e., signification) but only radically redefines how meaning comes about. To say that modern Chinese is just as inaccessible as classical Chinese because the signifier never leads to the signified is missing the point.

Third, Zheng's use of Derrida is self-contradictory in that if indeed there are "numerous 'traces' of classical literature... in the so-called vernacular poetry and prose,"[23] can one still claim that the vernacular has "toppled," "smashed," and "erased" the classical tradition? Why then worry about classical Chinese not being part of modern Chinese if it is always already there?

Finally, Zheng's appropriation of poststructuralism fails to take into account that its production and significance are inseparable from the Western philosophical tradition. Neither Lacan nor Derrida holds the only universal truth; to treat them as such is to misunderstand and misuse them. The other side of the irony is that "Retrospect" also neglects the historical context of modern Chinese poetry. Tradition—with a capital T—is upheld as if it were a self-contained, stable, unchanging entity. In doing so, Zheng postulates an originary presence, a concept that again violates the deconstructive spirit. Let us recall what Derrida says about *trace:* "The trace is not only the disappearance of origin... it means that the origin did not even disappear, that it was never

[22] Zheng Min, "Shijimo de huigu," 7, 8.

[23] Ibid., 10.

constituted except reciprocally by a non-origin, the trace, which thus becomes the origin of the origin."[24] By polarizing classical and modern, written and spoken Chinese, by insisting on tradition as an originary presence that has somehow been obscured and awaits restoration to its original fullness, "Retrospect" exhibits the same logocentric tendency that Derrida seeks to deconstruct. "Retrospect" merely reverses the hierarchy of modern and classical Chinese, leaving the logocentric structure intact. To the extent that classical Chinese has never disappeared from modern Chinese, it has never existed as pure and complete-in-itself either.

The Subtext: A Chinese Alternative to Postmodernism?

In light of the critical analysis of Zheng Min's essay presented above, we cannot help asking why a veteran poet—and a modernist poet at that—would engage in a violent assault on modern Chinese poetry. Why would a senior literary scholar seem so lacking in critical self-awareness and self-reflexivity that she would commit as many logical and intellectual blunders as she does? Finally, given the wholesale attack on modern Chinese language and poetry, why has the essay not been subjected to more critical responses than what has been published thus far? Is it because the essay is beneath countering? Or is the dearth of criticism the result of other factors? In other words, I am interested in investigating the issue further as a cultural phenomenon whose ramifications, as I suggested at the beginning, go beyond literary history and provide some clues toward answering the above questions.

To understand the cultural significance of the controversy, we need to revisit the "Retrospect" essay, which opens with these remarks: "Modern Chinese poetry has a history of nearly one century. Recently international sinology has raised this question in the mass media: Why has Chinese literature, with a tradition of millennia of poetry, not produced masterpieces that garner the recognition of the international literary community?"[25] Zheng's critique is motivated by the allegation that modern Chinese poetry has not lived up to the glory of its classical counterpart, which has won universal praise. Besides well-known social and political

---

[24] Jacques Derrida, *Of Grammatology*, trans. Gayatri Chakravorty Spivak (Baltimore, Md.: Johns Hopkins University Press, 1976), 61.

[25] Ibid., 5.

forces that have severely impeded the free and natural development of literature, she attributes the situation to the fact that modern Chinese poetry has willfully severed itself from the classical linguistic and literary tradition. Modern poetry is not part of that tradition because, first, it is iconoclastic, and, second, it borrows extensively from the West. These interrelated factors account for the loss of Chineseness. And Chineseness is China's only admission ticket to the international cultural community.

My reading is further supported by Zheng's rejoinder to Fan Qinlin, in which she proclaims, "When an ancient nation enters the forest of world culture, the possession that it needs most to bring with it is its own cultural tradition. If it goes empty-handed, it will not be a partner of...world culture."[26] For Zheng, world culture is like a multinational corporation; one must own sufficient capital to become a partner. The capital in this case is Chinese culture, for it is the only attribute that distinguishes China from all other nations in the world. Without it, China would be "empty-handed" and would not be accepted into partnership.

That modern Chinese is influenced significantly by Western languages and literature through translation is seen as a negative phenomenon on the ground that it has brought about the loss of Chineseness. Referring to Mu Dan (1918–77), a fellow-poet and fellow-student at the Southwest Associated University in Kunming in the early 1940s, Zheng acknowledges the artistic accomplishment of his work but still finds it unsatisfactory because it reveals a "modern consciousness" whose "main source is Western languages and literature" and is thus even "farther off from classical Chinese literature" than May Fourth poetry. The other side of losing touch with the indigenous tradition is that modern Chinese poetry borrows extensively from foreign cultures, especially those of the West. Zheng deplores the situation: "We have been forced to borrow vocabulary, syntax, grammar from Western languages."[27] The implication is clear: modern Chinese poetry, influenced more by Western than by classical Chinese literature, is not Chinese, or at least not Chinese enough. Zheng's series of essays amounts to a lament that modern Chinese poetry embodies

---

[26] Zheng Min, "Guanyu 'Ruhe pingjjia "Wusi" baihuawen yundong,'" 120.

[27] Zheng Min, "Shijimo de huigu," 13. Zheng Min, "Guanyu 'Ruhe pingjjia "Wusi" baihuawen yundong,'" 120.

the "loss of language" and the concomitant "loss of personality and culture" of modern China.

However, Zheng is neither alone nor even the first in voicing this concern in the 1990s. At the beginning of her essay she appeals to "international sinology" as an authoritative source of evidence. We do not know which sinologists she is thinking of, but two come to mind.

William J. F. Jenner, a prolific translator and scholar of modern Chinese literature at the Australian National University, published a review in the January 1990 issue of the *Australian Journal of Chinese Affairs.* The short essay begins with a supposedly factual statement: "Great poetry can no longer be written in Chinese.... No really memorable Chinese verse has been written for the last forty years, and not so very much was created in the half century before that." He goes on to describe the poetry under review as "rarely ha[ving] the inevitability, the weight, the structure, the authority of real poetry." Further, the low quality of the poetry under review is symptomatic of a general "cultural decline" during the Cultural Revolution when "the resources of China's literary tradition were out of reach"; what *was* available to the poet was "the politically degraded language of the Mao era."[28]

I agree with Jenner (and Zheng Min, for that matter) that the Cultural Revolution wrought a massive destruction on Chinese culture from which it is still struggling to recover. I also agree that most, if not all, of the modern poetry produced during the Mao era is of little literary worth. However, I find it problematic when Jenner, like Zheng, goes beyond the historicity of Mao's China and makes a blanket statement about modern Chinese poetry in general.

Jenner holds that there is an unbridgeable gulf between the classical tradition and modern poetry. "While purporting to reflect living speech," the vernacular "could in fact only be used to its full effect by people soaked in the concise but daunting written code of the past."[29] Both the wording and the argument bear a striking similarity to Zheng's.

Jenner goes on to say, "Even the classically educated have found it almost impossible to create poetry in the vernacular that

---

[28] William J. F. Jenner, Review of *The August Sleepwalker*, by Bei Dao, translated and introduced by Bonnie S. McDougall, *Australian Journal of Chinese Affairs* 23 (January 1990): 193, 194.

[29] Ibid.

is better than quite good. Wen Yiduo and Xu Zhimo are not up there with Auden and Yeats."[30] The statement is not convincing because although most of us would probably agree that Auden and Yeats made a greater contribution in poetry than Xu and Wen, let us not forget that Xu (1896–1931), who started writing poetry at the age of twenty-four, died in a plane crash at the age of thirty-five, and Wen (1899–1946) stopped writing modern poetry by the end of the 1920s and devoted himself exclusively to the study of classics until he was assassinated at the age of forty-seven. Each poet had a brilliant but brief career of a decade whereas, in contrast, Auden and Yeats continued writing poetry for half a century. Jenner's statement that even classically trained poets like Xu and Wen "found it almost impossible to create poetry in the vernacular" only attests to the immense challenge that modern Chinese poetry faces in establishing a new poetic tradition, a goal all pioneers strove toward through experiments that were not always successful even by their own accounts.

Incidentally, in dismissing modern Chinese poetry in toto as a failure, neither Jenner nor Zheng pays much attention to the poetry that has come out of Taiwan, Hong Kong, and Chinese communities in Southeast Asia and other parts of the world for decades. It is no surprise, then, that when they deal with a limited number of samples they find few to be any good. Jenner and Zheng complain that modern Chinese poetry has nothing to show while at the same time ignoring its robust development outside mainland China especially during the period when poetry was stifled under Mao. The elision not only smacks of sinocentrism but weakens their argument against modern Chinese poetry.

Another likely source of authority that Zheng has in mind may be Stephen Owen at Harvard University. Interestingly, Owen's reflection on modern Chinese poetry was prompted by the same book of poetry that Jenner reviewed, and both essays were published in 1990, only ten months apart. In his review article Owen makes basically the same argument that modern Chinese poetry has lost its Chineseness, although he provides a more nuanced analysis as to how it came about. Implicitly referring to the literary revolution of 1917, Owen describes modern Chinese poetry as originating from "that first hope for a poetry free of history, for words that could be transparent vehicles of the liberated imagination and pure human feeling."[31] The result was a poetry in-

30 Ibid., 194–95.

31 Stephen Owen, "What Is World Poetry?" *New Republic*, November 19, 1990.

distinguishable from "world poetry," which is modeled primarily on the Anglo-European traditions of Romantic and modernist poetry.

In Owen's view, modern Chinese poetry suffers from a double lack: it fails to measure up to traditional Chinese poetry on the one hand, to Western poetry on the other. Cut off from its roots, modern Chinese poetry is doomed to mimic the Western original, becoming an inferior hybrid that is neither Chinese nor Western. He concludes, "We, the Anglo-American or European part of the international audience, are reading translations of a poetry that originally grew out of reading translations of our own poetic heritage."[32] Hence, the question "Is this Chinese literature, or literature that began in the Chinese language?" For him, the answer is definitely the latter.

I appreciate Owen's insight that international recognition has become the most coveted form of capital for many contemporary Chinese poets. Such a desire underscores much of the politics in the transnational circles of contemporary Chinese literature and sinology. The inordinate amount of attention to the so-called international reception and recognition is an issue I will come back to at the end of the essay. But international reception per se is irrelevant to our present discussion on cultural identity. Without repeating the various responses to Owen's essay that have come from Gregory B. Lee (1996), Andrew F. Jones (1994), Rey Chow (1993), and me (1991), I would like to address briefly Jones's defense as presented in his 1994 essay "Chinese Literature in the 'World' Literary Economy."[33]

Jones praises Owen's essay for "pinpointing the *structural inequalities* that underlie the creation and consumption of world literature" and for "rais[ing] questions of vital importance to anyone interested in deconstructing the orientalist discourse that continues to plague the translation, reception, and marketing of Chinese literature in the American context." "Owen's contribution," according to Jones, "lies in the way in which he situates

---

[32] Ibid., 29.

[33] Gregory B. Lee, *Troubadours, Trumpeters, Troubled Makers: Lyricism, Nationalism and Hybridity in China and Its Others* (Durham, N.C.: Duke University Press, 1995), chap. 4; Andrew F. Jones, "Chinese Literature in the 'World' Literary Economy," *Modern Chinese Literature* 8 (1994): 171–90; Rey Chow, *Writing Diaspora: Tactics of Intervention in Contemporary Cultural Studies* (Bloomington: Indiana University Press, 1993), Introduction; and Michelle Yeh, "Chayi de youlu: yige huixiang" (The anxiety of difference: A rejoinder), *Jintian* (Today) 1 (1991): 94–96.

'world poetry' within the larger problem of Western cultural hegemony vis-à-vis the so-called 'third world.'" Whereas an earlier response to Owen from Rey Chow critiques sinology for its "valorization of China's traditional heritage and concomitant 'disdain' for contemporary Chinese culture," Jones employs the same strategy but directs his criticism not at the institution of sinology but at the institution of "world literature"—"the system in which the distribution of international (i.e., Western) recognition, literary prizes, and lucrative book contracts are awarded."[34]

Jones mounts a forceful attack on the Orientalist underpinnings of the concept and praxis of "world literature." But whereas he criticizes Goethe's notion of *Weltliteratur* as projecting an essentialized difference "onto a passive East for the narcissistic benefit of the Western spectator," he does not tell us how Owen's essentialism differs from Goethe's. He remarks further, "Despite Goethe's universalizing rhetoric, it rapidly becomes clear that world literature is, for the most part, a European phenomenon."[35] What he does not say is that "national literature," which he and Owen both defend, is just as European in its origin and conceptualization. The crux of the problem is how to define "national literature," specifically, how to define "Chineseness" when it comes to modern China. For Jenner, Owen, and Zheng, classical Chinese literature is the sole depository of Chineseness, and their disappointment with and disdain for modern Chinese poetry stems from this conscious or unconscious assumption and a common subscription to what I would call "the myth of purity," "the myth of authenticity," or, borrowing from Julia Kristeva, "the cult of origin."[36] In the foregoing analysis of Zheng's "Retrospect" essay, I have already pointed out its inherent logocentrism in ignoring the fact that tradition itself undergoes constant transformation and is always subject to negotiation and reinterpretation. However radical it may seem, modern Chinese poetry is very much part of Chinese tradition, which is going through its latest phase of transformation and being subjected to the latest round of reinterpretations. As such, it is integral to any discussion of Chineseness in the modern context.

---

34 Jones, "Chinese Literature," 176, 175, 176.

35 Ibid., 180, 179.

36 See discussion in Michelle Yeh, "International Theory and the Transnational Critic: China in the Age of Multiculturalism," *Boundary 2* 25.3 (Fall 1998): 193–222.

I believe that the critics under discussion have a genuine respect and love for Chinese literature, nor do I doubt their honorable intentions in speaking against Western cultural hegemony in an attempt to rescue China from being "trapped in a 'secondary position.'"[37] I would further characterize the "secondary position" that Jones talks about as a twofold crisis: a temporal crisis (of always falling behind the West) as well as a normative crisis (of never measuring up to the Western original). This is a perception shared by many critics and writers alike. For Zheng, the solution to the problem is to reassert Chineseness by reconnecting modern literature with the classical tradition. I find this solution problematic—and ultimately ineffective—because the reification of China versus the West is exactly the problem. Equating Chineseness only with China's past, with Tradition, she traps herself in a vicious circle created by her own logic: modern Chinese poetry is not Chinese enough, so we go back to Tradition to look for Chineseness, which nevertheless has nothing to do with modern Chinese poetry. Modern Chinese poetry remains hopelessly in a double bind, suffering from an acute anxiety of belatedness on one hand and of inauthenticity on the other. To put it in a different way, the defense of tradition against modernity, of Chineseness against Westernness, is itself an articulation of the structural inequalities that Owen and Jones critique since it is the reverse side of Orientalism.

Orientalism goes both ways. To the extent that the critics in question essentialize Chineseness, they also essentialize Westernness. The predominantly modern Anglo-European literary traditions that the critics oppose to the classical Chinese tradition do not embody "pure" Westernness but are similarly the result of continuing processes of transformation, contestation, and revision. We tend to forget that "the works of neither Dante nor Shakespeare nor Cervantes were considered classics...until well after the beginning of the nineteenth century,"[38] that romantic and modernist poetry in the West was regarded as foreign and strange when it first emerged, and that poets such as William Blake, Wordsworth, Baudelaire, Rimbaud, Ezra Pound, and E. E. Cummings were all notoriously iconoclastic but were eventually canonized in the literary tradition that they helped shape.

---

37 Jones, "Chinese Literature," 188.

38 Claudio Guillén, *The Challenge of Comparative Literature* (Cambridge and London: Harvard University Press, 1993), 39.

Is modern Chinese poetry the product of imitating Anglo-European originals, hence doomed to forever lag behind? Or is it, in responding to internal needs for change, predisposed to certain influences—mainly coming from Anglo-European cultures—because they deal with similar problems and answer similar questions? In other words, is modern Chinese poetry a passive receiver of Western imperial culture? Or is it an agent of self-transformation? I have argued—and will continue to argue—for the latter in view of the documented painstaking efforts of the pioneers of modern Chinese poetry. But unfortunately, all too often critics—both in and outside China—and sometimes even poets themselves adhere to the former assumption, hence accepting a priori Western norms and standards and leaving China with no choice but to fall back on cultural nationalism. Reification of Chineseness becomes the only way to *out-original* the West, thus setting in motion the vicious circle that we see in Zheng Min's argument.

In an essay appropriately titled "The World Language of Modern Poetry," Hans Magnus Enzensberger reminds us that twentieth-century poetry is aptly characterized by its cosmopolitanism in view of the multicultural backgrounds and international aspirations of poets everywhere: "In most disparate areas of the world, writers who have never heard of each other are simultaneously and independently encountering the same problems and finding the same solutions.... Poetry no longer is nationalistic. The great masters of modern poetry, from Chile to Japan, have more in common than do all those who parade their national origin." Citing examples as diverse as Apollinaire, Aimé Cesaire, Vallejo, Hikmet, Pound, Neruda, and Kavafis, Enzensberger concludes,

> The list can be continued almost indefinitely. A person setting out to claim poets such as these for any one country would find himself in no small dilemma. Today it is less possible than ever to demand of poetry a passport. Such biographical details deserve to be recorded because their significance is more than just superficial and they serve to show how little can be achieved, in the face of modern poetry, by the concept of autonomous national literature.[39]

[39] Hans Magnus Enzensberger, "The World Language of Modern Poetry," in *The Consciousness Industry: On Literature, Politics, and the Media* (New York: Seabury Press, 1974), 50, 51.

That some of the leading modern poets are committed Marxists and that the international community of poets that Enzensberger celebrates may be as much political as cultural does not detract from the validity of his observation. In fact it accentuates the changing connotations of "international" along the divide of the Cold War era. Whereas internationalism symbolized a transcendence of political and ideological conflicts in an earlier time, in the 1990s it takes on the new meaning of sweeping capitalist globalization, which is sometimes perceived as threatening to national cultural distinctness. Enzensberger's point still stands, however, in that national identity is a conceptual straitjacket especially when it comes to modern poetry. To Owen's despair that there is only "world poetry" but very little authentic "national poetry" in this day and age, Enzensberger's answer would be that the issue of national identity is irrelevant.

Which brings us to this central question: Why do the critics focus on cultural identity when they read modern Chinese poetry? To elaborate, why is it that for them the fact that a poem is written in modern Chinese is insufficient evidence of its "Chinese" identity? What other kinds of cultural-literary evidence besides the linguistic indicator would satisfy them? And, finally, what would or should a modern Chinese poem look like? Would it satisfy the critics if modern Chinese poetry were more like classical Chinese poetry? But, then, wouldn't that be classical Chinese poetry even though it is written in the twentieth century, something that in fact does exist and is alive and well in China, Taiwan, and other Chinese communities? But that wouldn't be modern Chinese poetry, only classical Chinese poetry of the twentieth century. So we must look elsewhere for the answer.

I don't pretend to know what modern Chinese poetry should be like. But I do wonder why it is the first and foremost question asked about modern Chinese poetry. Perhaps it has something to do with the longevity of the poetic tradition and the pride China takes in being a nation of poetry. Perhaps it has something to do with the high prestige that poetry traditionally enjoys in Chinese culture and society. More than any other literary genre, poetry, along with calligraphy and literati painting, defines the "essence" of cultural China. When the foundation of that poetic tradition was shaken by the literary revolution of 1917, concurring with the equally fundamental changes in the political, social, and educational spheres, there was bound to be a culture shock, an identity crisis. This also explains why the question of cultural identity is raised far less often with regard to modern Chinese fiction or drama.

It is a universal human need to have a sense of belonging, to establish and hold on to an identity whether at the individual or collective level. However, I have argued so far that the exclusive focus on cultural identity in relation to modern Chinese poetry often leads to a cultural essentialism that merely replicates rather than successfully deconstructs Orientalism. As a result, there is little attention to the actual works produced in modern Chinese and little recognition of the original artistic innovations that modern poets have made through an individualistic, imaginative transformation of both Chinese and foreign linguistic and literary elements.

It is ironic that one argument for a return to the classical Chinese tradition that Zheng Min makes is that it has inspired a number of Western poets, most notably Ezra Pound: "Western Modernism...was inspired by the pictographic nature of the Chinese character and the rich imagery of classical poetry," yet "in its ancestral home it has been mocked, cursed, even banned."[40] In both logic and rhetoric, Zheng parallels Owen so closely that we can rephrase Zheng with Owen's own sentence, changing only the reference to the cultural tradition: "We, the *Chinese* part of the international audience, are reading translations of a poetry that originally grew out of reading translations of our own poetic heritage"! If Pound's indebtedness is used as a testimony to the beauty and power of classical Chinese poetry, the fact is no critic has ever suspected, much less declared, that in drawing on classical Chinese poetry for his imagist poetics, Pound lost his cultural identity as an American poet. If we follow the same logic, why does Zheng regard modern Chinese poets as un-Chinese when they are inspired by Western poetry? More important, she seems to discount the fact that the classical Chinese poetry that inspired Pound (via Ernest Fenellosa) is not the classical Chinese poetry that Zheng or Owen or Jenner has in mind because it is a radical, idiosyncratic interpretation and invention of "China."[41] Why can't the same creative process be recognized with regard to modern Chinese poets in relation to Western traditions? Describing modern Chinese poetry as a mere imitation of

[40] Zheng Min, "Shijimo de huigu," 9.

[41] Longxi Zhang, *The Tao and the Logos: Literary Hermeneutics, East and West* (Durham, N.C.: Duke University Press, 1994), 22–33.

Western models, Zheng and the other critics in effect deny it the capacity of agency—the problem that Jones addresses and tries to solve.

The discussion on the cultural identity of modern Chinese poetry dramatizes a tension that has been at work throughout modern Chinese history and inherent in China's twofold objective of modernization from the late Qing onward—namely, the tension between enlightenment (by learning from the West) and national salvation (by resisting the West), between particularism and universalism, and finally, between nationalism and internationalism.

The last form of tension comes to the fore in the recent round of discussion about modern Chinese poetry in that it reveals a profound desire for self-validation, an eagerness for affirmation of Chinese values in a global context—on the basis of the classical literary tradition for Jenner, Owen, and Zheng, contemporary avant-garde fiction for Jones. But in all of these cases self-validation is ultimately inextricable from validation by the West—whether it is the "international literary community," "international sinology," or the "world literature" market. Although each critic presents his or her notion of Chineseness as an explicit critique of the West, that notion is inseparable from international reception and would be meaningless without it.

As a solution to Western cultural domination, Jones proposes that we "pay consistent and meticulous attention to what Chinese critics have to say" and "promote dialogue and even 'communal action' directed against the perpetuation of a system mired in unidirectionality." The danger, however, is a return to the simplistic binarism of the foreign and the indigenous, "Western" audiences and "Chinese" writers and critics. Especially in the 1990s the "contact zone" where Chinese and Western cultures encounter each other is no longer limited to geographical locations defined by national boundaries. Much of "what Chinese critics have to say" is often dictated by Western agendas and based, implicitly or explicitly, on a Western frame of reference. The West, in other words, remains the perennial "preferred Other" of China.[42]

---

[42] Jones, "Chinese Literature," 189. Arif Dirlik, "Chinese History and the Question of Orientalism," in *The Postcolonial Aura: Third World Criticism in the Age of Global Capitalism,* ed. Arif Dirlik (Boulder, Colo.: Westview Press, 1997), 105–28. Rey Chow, "Can One Say No to China?" *New Literary History* 28.1 (Winter 1997): 147–51.

This is evident in the postmodern slant to how the issue of modern Chinese poetry resurfaces in the 1990s. If Zheng Min invokes semiotics and poststructuralism, Stephen Owen and Andrew F. Jones couch their arguments in the language of postcolonial theory. In his response to Zheng's "Retrospect" essay, Zhang Yiwu also invokes postmodern and postcolonial theory to critique the West-dominated modernization discourse. And he does this not without self-awareness: "Although these two kinds of new 'knowledge' obviously also come from a Western academic background, our appropriation and elaboration can no doubt stimulate our ability of self-reflection and self-reevaluation." Zhang goes on to quote Homi K. Bhabha's concept of "mimicry" as a means to "expose the contradiction and unease of Western discourses."[43] Zhang's subscription to postmodernism is complete with his newly coined term "postvernacular" (*hou baihua*), which supposedly transcends the old binary opposition of classical versus modern that underscores China's modernization discourse.

In recent years there has been much talk about Chinese alternatives to Western paradigms. Can postmodernism offer a viable Chinese alternative to the hegemonic West? Can China finally be free from the dominance of Western norms and standards? The attractiveness of postmodernism comes from several interrelated factors. At one level, postmodernism lends itself to empowering the marginalized non-West. Compared to modernism, postmodernism seems to be a more affirmative, liberatory discourse with regard to the non-West in that it espouses an aesthetics that emphasizes imitation over originality, fragmentation over organic unity, return of the repressed over perpetuating the authority of the center. Postmodernism may be seen as the cultural counterpart of the fragmentation and decentralization that is unfolding in the global political and economic order, and it is an eloquent articulation of the ideal of multiculturalism.

However, postmodernism is empowering largely through a logic of reductionism. According to this logic, the West is identified with modernization or the Enlightenment project, and any critique of modernization discourse is seen as a critique of the West. Thus, as a critique of modernization, postmodernism, with its aforementioned aesthetics, becomes a de facto ally of the non-West. I believe that the eagerness with which some Chinese critics embrace postmodernism in the 1990s can be partly explained by

[43] Zhang Yiwu, "Chonggu 'xiandaixing,'" 112.

this *perception* of postmodernism as anti-West and pro-China. In this respect, postmodernism is certainly "politically correct" in terms of the official nationalist ideology of the Chinese Communist Party, however unintended it may be.[44]

To give an example, Zhang Yiwu describes the poetry of the 1990s as postmodern and postcolonial (in addition to "post–New Era" [*hou xinshiqi*] and "post-allegory" [*hou yuyan*]) and as seeking to "redefine Chineseness" (*Zhonghuaxing*). This new poetry is distinguished from earlier poetry in that it does not self-orientalize to cater to the West. Zhang's reference to Owen in support of his argument gives an interesting twist to the issue under discussion. Both have a negative view of modern Chinese poetry because it is dependent on and submissive to the hegemonic West. Both criticize modern Chinese poetry as inauthentic. However, whereas for Owen inauthenticity stems from a departure from the Chinese tradition, for Zhang the problem is one of overt Chineseness or "national allegory." Whereas for Owen (as well as for Zheng and Jenner) the remedy is to return to the classical tradition, Zhang advocates a poetry "based on the current situation of Chinese language and reality to establish...a dialogue with other cultures and poetry."[45] The so-called Chinese postmodernism—including its strands of postcolonialism and multiculturalism—is thus underscored by cultural nationalism.

Postmodernism also provides a way of bypassing the arduous, century-long journey of modernization that China has embarked on. The reification of tradition characteristic of the cultural nationalism that I have critiqued in this essay is not new in modern Chinese history. It is but another expression of the frustration and anxiety that accompanies China's modernization, which is still perceived as incomplete.[46]

---

[44] This point is raised by Zhao Yiheng (Henry Yiheng Zhao) in "Post-Isms and Chinese New Conservatism" (Houxue yu Zhongguo xin baoshou zhuyi), *Twenty-First Century* 27 (February 1995): 4–15; and by Xu Ben in "The State of 'Third World Criticism' in China Today" ("Disan shijie piping" zai dangjin Zhongguo de chujing), *Twenty-First Century* 27 (February 1995): 16–27. For an analysis of the controversy surrounding these essays, see Yeh, "International Theory and the Transnational Critic."

[45] Zhang Yiwu, "Duanlie zhong de shengzhang: 'Zhonghua xing' de xunqiu" (Growth in the midst of rupture: The search for "Chineseness"), *Shi tansuo* 13 (January 1994): 40–44; Zhang Yiwu, "Yuyan/zhuangtai: hou xinshiqi shige de xuanze" (Allegory/state of being: Poetry's choice in the post–New Era), *Shige bao* 184 (November 1994): 43–45; quotation at 43.

[46] Yeh, "International Theory and the Transnational Critic."

Finally, postmodernism is inseparable from globalization, which has been going on throughout the modern age but has accelerated dramatically in our own time. From a post-colonial/postmodern perspective, the cases of Zheng and others suggest that the quest of cultural identity is the flip side of an equally strong desire for international recognition and participation. Nationalism reinforces internationalism so long as the nation-state is still the common denominator of international transactions. To be part of the "global village" brings a sense of pride as well as anxiety. If being "international" is accorded a higher prestige and authority than ever before, the "admission ticket"—to recall Zheng's metaphor—is national culture. Hence, the paradox of the simultaneous ascendency of internationalism and nationalism around the world and, in particular, in Chinese literary and cultural studies. Zheng's appropriation of contemporary theory is itself an example of self-validation in terms of what is "new" and "international."[47]

Yet another example of the internationalism/nationalism symbiosis is the intense attention that Chinese intellectuals and writers have focused on the Nobel Prize in Literature in recent years. Not only do newspapers and magazines in Taiwan devote much space to the prize every early October when it is announced, but books have been published and conferences hosted in China on the topic. Chinese intellectuals regularly complain that the most populous nation and one with one of the longest literary traditions in the world has yet to be honored by the Swedish Royal Academy, especially in view of the fact that authors from two of its Asian neighbors, Japan and India, have been awarded the prize.[48] The anxiety seems to have escalated since Göran Malmqvist, a renowned sinologist, was appointed to the academy in 1985. In the multicultural climate of the late 1990s, it is a common phenomenon that the more China wishes to be seen as international, the more nationalist it becomes.

Taken together, the above-mentioned aspects of postmodernism cast most talk about Chinese alternatives to postmodernism, whether in or outside China, in a suspicious light. The prefix "post" has become a mantra for some critics, as if it automatically resolves the contradictions and tensions in the cross-cultural rela-

---

[47] Ibid.

[48] Dong Dingshan, "Nuobeier wenxue jiang beihou" (Behind the Nobel Prize in Literature), *Dushu* 202 (January 1996): 93–97.

tionships between China and "the West." Given the transnational cultural politics of contemporary China, any facile appropriation of postmodernism only camouflages such theoretical issues as cultural identity and modernity rather than confronting them head-on.

Glossary

Changshiji 嘗試集
Chen Duxiu 陳獨秀
Chen Pingyuan 陳平原
Dai Wangshu 戴望舒
Fei Ming 廢名
hou baihua 後白話
hou xinshiqi 後新時期
hou yuyan 後寓言
Hu Shi 胡適
Huang Zunxian 黃遵憲
Jiumeng 舊夢
Jiuyepai 九葉派
jueju 絕句
Li Jinfa 李金髮
Liang Shiqiu 梁實秋
lianhualao 蓮花落
Liu Daibai 劉大白
Mei Guangdi 梅光迪
Mu Dan 穆旦
piaoqie 剽竊
Ren Shuyong 任叔永
"Shijimo de huigu: Hanyu yuyan biange yu Zhongguo xinshi chuangzuo" 世紀末的回顧: 漢語語變革與中國新詩
shijie geming 詩界革命
Tan Sitong 譚嗣同
Wen Yiduo 聞一多
Wenxue pinglun 文學評論
"Wenxuegailiang chuyi" 文學改良芻議
"Wenxue geming lun" 文學革命論
Wang Hui 汪暉
"Wushi nian lai Zhongguo zhi wenxue" 五十年來中國之文學
Xia Zengyou 夏曾佑
Xu Ming 許明
Xu Zhimo 徐志摩
Xueheng School 學衡派
yangguizi 洋鬼子
yanshipilichun 煙士披里純
Ye Gongchao 葉公超
Yu Pingbo 俞平伯
Zhang Yiwu 張頤武
Zheng Min 鄭敏
Zhonghuaxing 中華性
Zhou Zuoren 周作人
Zong Baihua 宗白華

SIX

Postmodernism in China: A Sketch and Some Queries

HAUN SAUSSY

The various "posts" that have attracted so much attention in China lately—principally postmodernism (*houxiandai zhuyi*) and postcolonialism (*houzhimin zhuyi*), and in an idiomatic sense poststructuralism (*houjiegou zhuyi*), or as the Chinese authors conveniently call them for short, postlearning (*houxue*)—look like translations into modern Chinese idiom of terms and ideas pioneered elsewhere. But I mean by that no more than "look like." The key to making sense of them, I think, is to discard the hope that understanding them, and above all judging them, can be accomplished by reference to a more familiar "original" postmodernism. What more uncomfortable paradox can be imagined than attempting to argue that one's own postmodernism is the real, the authentic, the historically originary, the ancestrally legitimate brand? Rather than fall into the trap of saying that the Chinese post-ists have got it wrong, and trying to put them right by a more heavily supported reading of Derrida or Foucault or Lyotard, let us ask what the appropriate frame of reference for understanding Chinese post-ism is.

Because contemporary Chinese literature is not my main interest, I have relied on friends and colleagues for guidance through the dense bibliography on these questions. My biggest debts are to Zhang Kuan (who knew that I would disagree with him but generously supplied information nonetheless), Wang Youqin, and Guan Qi. I also thank Wen-hsin Yeh for inviting me to look into these issues. Errors of fact and judgment can be lodged securely with me. For two stimulating surveys of the questions discussed here, see Sheldon Hsiao-peng Lu, "Art, Culture, and Cultural Criticism in Post-New China," *New Literary History* 28 (1997): 111–33; Zhang Xudong, *Chinese Modernism in the Era of Reforms* (Durham, N.C.: Duke University Press, 1997), especially "On Some Motifs in the Cultural Discussion," 71–99.

Not that we—or our Chinese contemporaries—are quite ready to answer that question. Certainly part of the frame of reference we will require is the academic context of present-day Europe and America, in which the post-ideologies were first elaborated, distributed, and made part of the intellectual lives of scholars and readers (Chinese-speaking or not). And the availability, the relative transparence and familiarity of the words and gestures, tempts us into thinking that post-ism amounts to an application to Chinese realities of something Jameson or Rorty has already said. But that would set us on precisely the path that a cursory reading of Chinese post-ist publications causes me to fear—namely, that of taking for granted the correspondence of discursive universes to the nondiscursive, possibly unutterable, situations in which they are pronounced. Euro-American precedents are only part of the frame of reference, and far from the most interesting part.

A first gesture toward derailing the Euro-American reader's confidence—the confidence that says, If that's postmodernism, then I already know all about that (including whether I like it or not)—would be to adopt the attitude of some scholars of traditional Chinese philosophy who like to say that Chinese thought was always postmodern because it never bothered to become modern.[1] I think this is a fallacy in its original setting, but it can be helpful here for its air of paradox. The original fallacy is that of supposing that two things are alike because they are different from a third thing. That fallacy may, nonetheless, guard us from a second fallacy, that of assuming that there is only one right way to get to postmodernism, by taking the path that leads (etymologically enough) through and past modernism. Both accidental similarity and historical inevitability furnish disreputable grounds for argument. By mixing together a bit of each we may discredit both.

One might say that philosophical modernism is an attempt to regulate the relationship of fact and value and that postmodernism is the abandonment of such attempts—resulting in claims that knowledge can never be grounded, or that values are entirely arbitrary, or that trying to work out principles for either is just a thinly disguised policing of discourse. Then in traditional China one would not have the relevant illusions to discard, since generally speaking the project of Chinese thought has not been to

[1] A. C. Graham, discussing Derrida in his historical work *Disputers of the Tao* (La Salle, Ill.: Open Court, 1989), opened up this now quasi-obligatory topic.

propose transcendental guarantees for reliable knowledge or exception-free prescriptions for conduct.[2] Postmodernism then looks like an absurd detour in the Chinese context—the taking of medicine to cure ills one never suffered from. Is this the secret of the discursive vigor that has been shown in these late debates—the fact that nothing very real is at stake? What kind of critique is it in which no one's ox is relevantly gored?

But here it would be good to recall that no twentieth-century Chinese person, of whatever degree of literacy, has been able to live a purely traditional Chinese life, and therefore the imported oddities are live targets for critique. Indeed, how far back in history would we have to go to discover the inhabitants of so blissfully isolated a Peach Blossom Spring? The very ideals and models many people would distinguish from the enterprise of canonical Chinese thought have been active in the Chinese world for at least the past 150 years, furnishing one regime after another with challenges, forms of legitimacy, or aims of struggle. Their attraction survives much clumsiness in translation. The idea that one could know the world as it is, and that by knowing it one could transform it into the world as it should be, has quite a pull, and one doesn't have to be a professional philosopher to feel it.

The postmodernist gesture that I see most insistently brought forth in my readings is the rejection of modernist, cosmopolitan legitimation-devices. Are we called to submit our judgments to the court of science? To the norms of democratic constitutionalism? To the aesthetic canons of Sophocles and Phidias? If it's a norm, it's out of bounds. The fact that for most of this century the ruling standards, not to mention ideological currents and political influence, have been derived from international culture, commerce, and technology means that for mainland Chinese thinkers

---

[2] See, as an early report on this contrast, I. A. Richards's observations. Richards speaks of

> the very absence in Mencius of anything which we can recognize as a theory of knowledge.... [H]is reflections are nearly all about action, its sources and control.... [H]is arguments are less demonstrations than instructions." *Mencius on the Mind* (London: Kegan Paul, 1932), 61. More generally, "Pragmatism, as a doctrine that ideas are tools to be judged by the work they do... is a fairly modern doctrine [in the West], a result of reflection and a result still treated in most European schools of philosophy as a heresy to be refuted. In Chinese philosophy, in its main streams at least, there seems to have been no Problem of Truth as such. Reflection has not exercised itself on the question 'What do we mean when we say that a statement is true?' The place of this problem has been taken by an assumption, so initial as to be unformulated, that what is true is what had better be accepted.

Basic in Teaching: East and West (London: Kegan Paul, Trench and Trubner, 1935), 24–25.

the rejection of existing modes of legitimation is doubled with the identification of these modes as specifically Western. (I normally refuse to bow to the idol referred to by this term, but in some contexts "Western" is the only right one, however many distinctions are sacrificed by pronouncing it.) Within living memory, indigenous Chinese standards have not had the backing needed to command belief and practice, saving a few exceptionally constituted domains such as family life, specific areas of scholarship, religion (where and when tolerated), and some forms of art. The ghostly local standards can therefore furnish a comfortably vague countermodel to the models derided as hegemonic yet obsolete. I see in several authors a mood that might be paraphrased as follows: "The European Enlightenment went bankrupt—we have only to follow the postmodernist argument to see it collapse. No matter for us! We still have something to fall back on—cultural goods that escaped the crash because nobody thought to bid them unrealistically high."

As received in China, the devices and authorities of postmodernism have produced not a uniform set of doctrines but a set of opportunities variously taken. It would be folly to try to summarize them all under one ideological or sociological heading. Nor do I have the space or the learning to describe the whole intellectual ecology of 1990s China. But by exploring some of the niches in which argument grows, I may be able to describe the conditions under which these opportunities arise and guess about their likely consequences.

While I was writing this essay I made my first trip to Beijing in more than ten years and was predictably startled by all that was new and much that wasn't. Just as on an earlier trip, someone thought to take me to see the stone set up over the ashes of Edgar Snow, next to the lake on the campus of Peking University. "Edgar Snow—An American Friend of the Chinese People" reads the inscription. Snow, of course, is the American journalist who "discovered" and loyally championed Mao Zedong and his Yan'an rebels, returning several times in the 1960s and 1970s to interview Mao and tell the world that collectivization, the Great Leap Forward, and the Cultural Revolution were splendid and beneficial transformations. Taking American visitors to see Snow's tomb is a gesture of solicitude, and it would have been poor manners to say what I thought of the definition of friendship the stone implied. "The American friend of *some* Chinese people,"

I said instead, and this was all right, because it led the conversation toward Mao's personal foibles, which is a permitted, indeed encouraged, subject.

Many of the "postmodern" essays suppose that communication between China and foreigners interested in it should be held up to the ideal represented by Snow's truckling to Mao. It is no longer the charismatic leader, but rather Chineseness, to which the acceptable foreigner must pay respect. I'm less concerned about the implicit xenophobia than about what cultural nationalism does to its domestic public. Whose interests are advanced by the circuits of identification that cause people to make much of "China's ability to say No" while many individual Chinese are unable to say no to each other?[3] Is not the cause of national unity supremely useful, in peacetime, for foreclosing both majority rule and minority protections? Is "cultural democracy" a barricade worth mounting while Chinese political economy, based on a mode of production that is both low wage and increasingly high tech, works its way toward constitutional guarantees of worker docility and efficiency? The "friend of *some* Chinese people" that I am worries about these things, because I worry about them at home too.

Xu Jilin describes the conditions making for an eager reception of the anti-Enlightenment streak in postmodern thinking as in part intellectual, in part sociological:

> To consider the factors internal to epistemology, [the "anti-Western" theorists of the 1990s] all had begun by accepting the mainstream discourse of the Western intellectual genealogy. They believed that Western modernist thought should and could contribute to China's modernization adequate intellectual resources and patterns for action. As a consequence, the deeper their previous commitment, the more they were able to discover that the supposed universals of modernist theory were really nothing more than particular products of Western history or culture and were separated by a great gulf from the discourse of Chinese contemporary culture and historical tradition. This gap between Western theory and Chinese discourse made it impossible for them not to

[3] An allusion to the title of the best-seller by Song Jiang, *Zhongguo keyi shuo "bu"* (Beijing: Zhonghua gongshang lianhe chubanshe, 1996). For a brief but thoughtful discussion of such nay-saying, see Rey Chow, "Can One Say No to China?" *New Literary History* 28 (1997): 147–51. I am glad to see misgivings similar to mine expressed by Xu Ben, "Zai tan Zhongguo 'houxue' de zhengzhixing he lishi yishi" (Again on Chinese postmodernism's political character and historical consciousness), *Ershiyi shiji* 39 (February 1997): 135.

> shift their gaze from Western mainstream discourse and toward marginal discourses such as postcolonial cultural theory, analytical Marxism, and so on. They hoped to find there inspiration for a pattern of modernization that would fit Chinese conditions. ...Unlike previous cultural conservatives, these scholars' plan was not to "confront Western learning with native learning," but rather to "use the aliens to control the aliens," to use Western marginal discourses to resist Western mainstream discourse....
>
> From the external, sociological perspective, the anti-Western trend is closely connected to a series of changes in the environment at home and abroad. Following the sudden take-off of the Chinese economy, the national strength of China grew enormously; and the first reaction of a disfavored people that is emerging from its disfavored status is always to say "No" to those privileged peoples it has long been attempting to overtake. In the 1980s, China's contacts with the West were limited, conflicts of interest were rare, and intellectuals had a flattering image of the West, so that Westernization had a suitable psychological support. But from the beginning of the 1990s China began to enter the international political-economic system, and conflicts between China and the West became more and more direct: the opposition of the Western countries, and particularly the United States, to China's joining the WTO [World Trade Organization] and hosting the Olympic Games, trade frictions, the *Yinhe* incident,[4] and a series of other events caused Chinese intellectuals to lose a great part of their faith in the West. Behind their beautiful Western discourse they discovered ugly relationships of power and an unequal power relationship that the Western countries were determined to force onto China....Thus the nationalistic feeling of Chinese intellectuals was greatly awakened, so that anti-Westernism had a deep psychological foundation.[5]

One thing is missing from the chronology. If Xu's account accurately represents the thinking of Chinese intellectuals, then someone has perfected the art of spin control. Although the trade frictions and boycotts Xu lists surely harmonized with the self-

[4] The ship *Yinhe* was pursued and boarded on the open seas by an American vessel, under the suspicion (unfounded) that it was carrying arms to Iraq.

[5] Xu Jilin, "Wenhua rentong de kunjing: 90 niandai Zhongguo zhishijie de fanxihua sichao" (The difficulties of cultural identity: The anti-Western trend in Chinese intellectual life of the 1990s), *Zhanlue yu guanli* 18 (1996): 100–1. In another essay, Xu acknowledges that "the Tiananmen incident of 1989 not only brought an abrupt halt to the 'culture fever' [of the 1980s], it also caused mainland intellectuals to lose some of their passion for politics." "Bi pipan geng zhongyao de shi lijie" (Understanding is more important than critique), *Ershiyi shiji* 30 (August 1995): 131.

interest of many of China's trade partners (though not all, and certainly not for long), the proclaimed reason for denying China such badges of international recognition as WTO membership and the hosting of the Olympic Games was to punish the government for its violent repression of the popular movements of 1989. To have done otherwise would have been to display friendship for the wrong people. As "unequal power relationships" go, some are uglier than others. Better that some contracts be cancelled and some international meetings be spoiled by an unwelcome speech or two than that the memory of the dead be too quickly swept under the rug. That June 1989 marked a turning point in recent Chinese intellectual life I am sure is a fact; but it would startle me to think that the main pivot of the turn was the discovery by Westernizing scholars that foreign countries have economies of their own, advantages to protect, and a weakness for self-serving policies, especially in election years. Does no one remember the principled boycotts of Japanese goods during the Pacific War? Or was the short-lived, American-led cooling of trade relations with China such a propaganda failure that none of the people who, in China, had the best chance to learn of it could ever figure out what it was about? In any case, Xu's analysis of anti-Westernism assumes that the educated classes of China recognize the power aims of their present government as identical to their own aims, or those of the Chinese people generally—which I should think needs to be shown, even without the killings of unarmed students to inspire reflection.[6] (If Chinese intellectuals are disappointed with Enlightenment ideals, does it follow that they are delighted with obscurantism?) The critique of universalism seems to have skipped over some important steps. Or then, it may be that Xu is using an advanced Aesopian technique, and counting on us to note the omission and therefore read the whole essay ironically.

It takes a *xenos* like me to imagine that a Chinese intellectual movement is all about xenophilia or xenophobia. One ought to try to keep things in proportion, just as one ought not to assume that *houxiandai zhuyi* attempts to reproduce French or American

[6] Rey Chow, in her previously mentioned essay, names "the scarcely touched issues of *China's relation to those whom it deems politically and culturally subordinate.* I am referring, specifically, to Tibet, Taiwan and Hong Kong" (151, italics Chow's). Scarcely touched, indeed, because to discuss them would be to infringe the Four Great Principles that currently mark the boundaries of permitted debate within China.

discourses about "postmodernism." Where a Chinese writer seems to "get it wrong," to conjoin incompatible streams of thought, we need to ask if the story being told is different from the one we already know. The poet-professor Zheng Min's essay "Shijimo de huigu: Hanyu yuyan biange yu Zhongguo xinshi chuangzuo" (Retrospect at century's end: The transformation of the Chinese language and modern Chinese poetic creation)[7] is confusing—and therefore, I will argue, inspiring—on precisely these grounds. By attempting to correct its author's historical perspective or theoretical information, its readers overlook its most provocative aspect, its revision of the collective story about Chinese modernity (poetic and political).

Zheng's opening question seems calculated to address the national-interest theme: "Why is it that literature in Chinese, with thousands of years of poetic history behind it, has been unable to produce internationally recognized great works or great authors?"[8] Zheng proposes to reexamine the history of the Chinese language and literature over the last hundred years as a way of tracing the insufficiencies of modern poetry to their social and linguistic sources. The May Fourth modernizers—leaders of the vernacular literature movement and the New Literature movement—erred by

> cutting themselves off from classical literature.... They forced literary creators to turn their backs on and abandon classical poetry, and they rejected the ideas of those scholars (Zhu Jingnong, Ren Hongjun, Qian Xuantong, and others) who advocated integrating classical poetry with the new literature. Moreover it was announced by Chen Duxiu [one of the leaders of the May Fourth movement and cofounder, in 1921, of the Chinese Communist Party] that [on the adoption of vernacular language] "we must not allow our opponents any room for discussion." (Zheng, "Shijimo," 5)

Zheng sees as the cause of this dogmatism an oversimple understanding of language and meaning. Hu Shi (1891–1962) and Chen Duxiu (1880–1942) saw in language nothing more than a tool for exchanging information and therefore demanded a literal, immediately understandable, contemporary idiom (19). But for Zheng,

[7] *Wenxue pinglun* 3 (1993): 5–20.

[8] Zheng, "Shijimo," 5. Michelle Yeh surmises that the low estimate of modern Chinese poetry cited by Zheng mainly refers to Stephen Owen's review of Bei Dao, "The Anxiety of Global Influence: What Is World Poetry?" *New Republic*, November 19, 1990, 28–32.

following Saussure, "language is principally an *arbitrary, inherited* system of signs that *admits of no choice,* and its reform must be on the basis of inheritance" (emphasis Zheng's); moreover the reformers "were not aware of the gap between the signifier and the signified, a fissure that, according to the theory of J. Lacan, is never completely bridged, causing a part of every language to remain hidden from view" (10). By calling for writing to base itself on speech, rather than on previous examples of writing, Hu Shi and Chen Duxiu attempted to erase the "archi-writing" of cultural codes, of memorized literature, of the whole Chinese past. If by "language" we mean what Saussure, Heidegger, Lacan, or Derrida mean by language, then the May Fourth generation hated language. What they wanted from language simply could not be given within language. But rather than admit that they were engaged in a futile project, the modernizers simply went on the offensive against backsliders. Zheng sees in this radicalization of the modernizing movement a pattern that remained consistent in twentieth-century Chinese literary theory—

> the logic of the binary opposition: protecting this, overthrowing that. The result is that we turned the complex relations of culture, literature, and history into pairs of mutually exclusive binary oppositions: vernacular writing / classical writing; proletarian culture / bourgeois culture; traditional literature / up-to-date literature; authentic literature / inauthentic literature; poetry for the masses / Misty Poetry; revolutionary poetry / decorative poetry about little grasses and flowers. . . . This strategic logic seems to have been our normal logic ever since the May Fourth movement, and its authority has been uncontested. (Zheng, "Shijimo," 6)

In the early years of the vernacular movement, Zheng concedes, it must have been helpful to have an ideology that cast aside complexities and qualifications, splitting the world into good and bad camps. But the consequences have been severe, amounting to a public neurosis. "From 1919 onward, every cultural movement in China has been marked by the same extraordinary tensions. The unprecedented Cultural Revolution of the 1960s went from literary skirmishes to actual battles, from the flourishing of pens to the flailing of whips, resulting in a bloody revolutionary drama."[9] Zheng's reconsideration of the May Fourth reformers, then, is

[9] Zheng, "Shijimo," 7. This picture of literary modernization closely corresponds to what Jean Paulhan called "Terror": the attempt to extirpate rhetoric and style in the name of an always elusive authenticity. *Les fleurs de Tarbes ou la Terreur dans les Lettres* (1941, rpt. Paris: Gallimard, 1990).

meant to trace the radicalizing logic to its roots and to critique it, not only in its effects but in its basic structure, which she calls "precisely a closed, metaphysical way of thinking that proceeds through symmetrical contradictions" (7).

Zheng's essay puts European literary theory to strategic use, invoking "recent linguistic science" to correct the instrumentalist views of Hu and Chen and benefiting from the general intellectual climate of the present in discrediting the logic of binary oppositions. Some of her readers have been shocked by her tradition-minded reading of theory: it is surely idiomatic to put together Derrida's reading of Freud's "scene of psychic writing" and Lacan's claim that "the unconscious is structured like a language" to reach the conclusion that the more traditional a language is, the more deeply it is connected with the unconscious, and therefore that language reform represents an attack on the unconscious by the conscious mind (18–19). Her Saussure and Derrida sit on the same bench with the Eliot of *Notes toward the Definition of Culture* and Heidegger in *völkisch* mood. These and other applications of theory are bound to surprise readers more familiar with a canonical set of poststructuralist writers and positions.

Does Zheng's essay represent a postmodern understanding, or a mishmash of postmodernistic citations in an old-fashioned argument? Is it, as Zhao Yiheng puts it, an example of "a neoconservative trend that uses postmodern theory as a base or corroboration"? "Surprised" to see that "the conservative judgment on the May Fourth movement current abroad has now found its way back to the Chinese mainland," Zhao is equally astonished to find that "although the topic is an old view on an old subject, the author uses new theories: Lacan's psychoanalysis and Derrida's deconstruction."[10] He finds the essay evidence of "the neoconservative trend with, as one of its symptoms, the return to traditional culture.... Zheng Min blames modernistic poetry for 'cutting itself off from the ancients.'"[11] In a response, Zheng characterizes Zhao's objection as revealing his

> orthodox [modern] traditional viewpoint: he seeks to defend the

[10] Zhao Yiheng, "'Houxue' yu Zhongguo xin baoshouzhuyi" ("Post-ism" and Chinese neo-conservatism), *Ershiyi shiji* 27 (February 1995): 4–15. The "conservative" source mentioned by Zhao is Lin Yü-sheng, *The Crisis of Chinese Consciousness* (Madison: University of Wisconsin Press, 1979). Lin's analysis of "totalistic anti-traditionalism" bears some resemblance to Zheng's description of May Fourth "binarism."

[11] Zhao Yiheng, "'Houxue,'" 5, 9–10.

> 'evolutionary character' of the May Fourth movement, without suspecting that my article was intended precisely to bring us out of this traditional position of reducing literature to politics.... To leave behind us this binary political theory of 'revolution' versus 'conservatism' is... the urgent task of the twenty-first century.[12]

Zhao is, for Zheng, a part of the problem she seeks to diagnose (binarism, all-or-nothing-ism, triumphal history, the political immediacy of art). For Zhao, history has a sequence: it goes from right to left, and if it harks back to themes discarded in the leftward progress, this is only to be described as "conservatism."

By calling on a label like that one, Zhao apparently wishes to regain territory that might have been lost to the minions of polysemy and ambiguity. "Conservatism" underrates the revisionary force of Zheng's arguments. I think that if some peculiar interpretations can be forgiven it, the essay performs precisely the work of classical deconstruction on the territory of modern literature as studied in China. It describes a logic of airtight oppositions—for example, the polarizing of past and present in modern literary history—and tries to discover ways of subverting the distinctions, as for example with the claim that language is always and necessarily an "inheritance" from the past. Moreover, it returns to the root of a historical paradigm, partly in the mode of classical cause-seeking, but also with the aim of showing that what one history narrates as necessity and prescience becomes, in another history's telling, repression and bad faith. Zhao's response, then, shows why Zheng's article makes a difference. The disagreement between Zheng and Zhao amounts to a choice of narratives and confirms Zheng in the tacit argument that legitimacy (both literary-historical and political) grows from the barrel of a story. Zheng's critique of twentieth-century poetic language—a critique carried out almost totally without citation of poetic texts!—may seem the least consequential, most apolitical of essays, but if you want to displace a master-narrative (*yuan xushu*), the best way to start is to propose a rival master-narrative. If the adventuresomeness and determination displayed in Zheng's essay were more common, there would be more excitement and less hackwork in Chinese literary criticism. Even in its shortcomings it shows the possibility of generating within mainland literary

[12] Zheng Min, "Wenhua, zhengzhi, yuyan sanzhe guanxi de wojian" (The relations among culture, politics, and language as I see them), *Ershiyi shiji* 29 (June 1995): 120, 124.

history positions corresponding to some of the histories proposed and debated in the less rigidly ordered circumstances of Taiwan and the overseas Chinese world. And that would break down some large, publicly held "binary oppositions" indeed.

What the casual reader of Zheng's essay notices as an asymmetry—the absence of a general account of cultural constructedness, resulting in the critique of modernist vernacular literature for its artificiality and the repeated endorsement of premodern classical literature as the "house of being" proper to Chinese writers and readers, their "cultural unconscious"—suggests that some forms of nativism pass without comment in contemporary China. Part of the appeal of postmodern theories (especially postcolonialism) lies in their seeming to make room for Chineseness. If the postmodern impulse amounts to marginalizing the center and centralizing the margins, then Chinese intellectuals have nothing to lose from identifying their own central themes with the once-marginal, now-prominent values and cultures in postmodern Western discourse. Zhang Kuan seeks to take Edward Said's *Orientalism* one step further, arguing that

> Said has only critiqued a hollow "Orient" molded by the West, he has not sketched out what the real Orient ought to be like. If he is unable to supply a real Orient to replace the false Orient, then his castigations of "orientalism" are without force. Moreover, Said's critiques of the West find their moral support in the very humanism championed by Westerners. He must have forgotten that the Renaissance, when the flag of humanism was brandished most boldly, was the bloodiest period of the West's colonial expansion and that the understanding of "man" in Renaissance humanism as well as its concept of universal human nature were the moral anchors of colonialism.[13]

For Zhang, it's a package deal: if you want Montaigne, you have

[13] Zhang Kuan, "Zai tan Sayide" (On Said again), *Dushu*, October 1994, 9. In a characteristically condensed argument, Zhang states that "the cruelty of the German Fascists toward the Jewish people was the necessary consequence of the logic of Enlightenment discourse" and blames the May Fourth intellectuals for drinking at the same sources. "Wenhua xinzhimin de keneng" (The possibility of cultural neocolonialism), *Tianya*, February 1996, as cited in Lei Yi, "Shenme shi baoshou? Shei fandui minzhu?" (What is conservatism? Who opposes democracy?), *Ershiyi shiji* 40 (April 1997): 123. A more detailed discussion of the historical problems surrounding colonialism and its relation to modernization is Li Tuo, "Rang zhenglun fuchu haimian" (Let the debates rise to the surface), *Dushu*, December 1997, 52–59.

to take Cortez and the Inquisition; if you admire Matteo Ricci, you'll have to extend your appreciation to the Opium War. Zhang is able to wrap up cultures so comprehensively because his view of the Chinese past is equally without differentiation. He does not apologize for the Boxers and the Qing court, the better to praise the reformist statesmen of 1898. History for him no longer sorts out into thematic streams of "progressives" and "reactionaries" (or what-have-you) establishing their principles through internal and external struggle; rather it is primarily a field of ethnic or culturewide agency.[14] This fits with his view of the relevance of postcolonial theory to the present moment in world politics:

> The international situation since the end of the Cold War shows an ever more obvious tendency toward reorganization on the basis of ethnic characteristics and cultural identity. Ideology correspondingly pales. While the West continues to present itself as powerful, postcolonial criticism brings a bit of deconstruction to all the myths of the grandiose Western discourse—and for us this is surely a good thing. No doubt about it, Said and anticolonialism are not reasons for stopping China's processes of reform and openness in favor of closing the door and protectionism, but for the sake of strengthening the cultural self-image and ethnic solidarity of Chinese people as we go forth to face the stirrings of a "clash of cultures," these are questions that no responsible Chinese intellectual can fail to take seriously.[15]

As with Zheng, the combination and linking of sources in Zhang's writings is surprising. For the American left-liberal reader, there is no great chasm separating Said from Chomsky, and Chomsky's denunciation of the United States as "the leading violator of the three principles America claims to campaign for"[16] is often echoed by citizens critical of our country's foreign policy. Where Zhang leaves the beaten track is his disavowal of humanistic principles as such. If Chomsky were simply interested in maximizing the power of the United States, he would doubtless still be critical of his country's foreign policy, but in different ways and with different standards. To go from Chomsky's rights-based

---

[14] For examples of this narrative economy, see Zhang Kuan, "Oumeiren yanzhong de 'fei wo zulei'" (The "ethnic other" in the eyes of Europeans and Americans), *Dushu*, September 1993, 3–9.

[15] Zhang, "Zai tan Sayide," 14.

[16] Cited ibid., 12. I have been unable to locate the exact passage to which Zhang refers. A detailed presentation of the ideas involved occurs in chapter 5, "Democracy and Markets in the New World Order," in Chomsky's *Powers and Prospects: Reflections on Human Nature and the Social Order* (Boston: South End Press, 1996).

criticism to Samuel Huntington's theory of a coming "clash of cultures" based on ethnic and cultural power blocs is to travel quite a distance in terms of assumptions held and company kept.[17] (In the eyes of American liberals, Huntington's main accomplishment has been to discover a new excuse for maintaining our military budget at Cold War levels.) Zhang is able to make this transition because the language of rights appears to him only as a dialect of the "language of the powerful" used by Western countries in coercing China. Talk of human rights has no substance; the only real story is ethnic. "Reform and openness" likewise are good policies only insofar as they add to the national wealth and power.

Postmodern appropriations like Zhang's show how unpredictable the circulation of theories can be. Foucault, Chomsky, and Said gain our attention by denouncing not just abuses, but hypocrisy—the practice of claiming to be generous or objective when one is actually rather more small-minded. Their critique asks us to be as good as our word. So in the most revisionary theories there may be a core of idealism. In Zhang's picture of history there is no room for hypocrisy or its critique. Is this a consequence of Foucault's having passed through an American filter of presentation and translation (emphasizing the criticism of liberal institutions) on his way to China? In his Chinese version, Foucault is the person who described democratic society as a prison, the demolisher of Enlightenment folklore about the free individual conscience—certainly not the activist who sought "the point of linkage between ethical preoccupation and the political struggle for the respect of rights, the connection between critical reflection against abusive governmental techniques and the search for an ethics on which individual freedom may be based."[18]

Now, it is always a failure of critical sense to "absolve a certain political regime of its responsibilities in the name of the 'principles' that inspire it,"[19] but there is a difference between the

[17] Huntington's *The Clash of Civilizations and the Remaking of World Order* (New York: Simon & Schuster, 1996) was an instant success in China. "His view that America should look on China as its greatest future antagonist was exciting to a number of Chinese, because it restored to the long-downtrodden Chinese the proud feeling of belonging to a great imperial power. Many people are still drawing advances on this pride, though I cannot see what it contributes to China's present progress." Chen Xiaoming, "'Wenhua minzu zhuyi' de xingqi" (The rise of "cultural nationalism"), *Ershiyi shiji* 39 (February 1997): 37.

[18] Michel Foucault, "L'éthique du souci de soi comme pratique de la liberté," *Dits et écrits 1954–1988* (Paris: Gallimard, 1994), 4:727–28.

[19] Michel Foucault, "Discourse on Power" (interview with Duccio Trombadori), in Foucault, *Remarks on Marx*, trans. R. James Goldstein and James Cascaito (New

critique of Enlightenment theories or practices by people who think enlightenment is a good thing and its critique qua enlightenment by people who think other objectives are more worthy. In the United States, postmodernism has provided a big tent for both sorts of critique, and some prominent figures (Stanley Fish, for example) are hard to pin down as definitively belonging to one side or the other; but this coexistence is possible because postmodern critique has yet to affect the comforts and liberties of daily life in any tangible way. If there were something more important than professional standing to be gained or lost, presumably the temporary community of those who dissent from the Cartesian-Kantian model of the subject would begin to dissent from one another more vigorously. What is the purpose of dissolving the consensus around liberal society—to create more truly autonomous individuals, or to strengthen the collectivity? Without making the cultural argument that communitarianism is natural to China (that habit will come in for examination later), one can see why, under present conditions, the Foucault who comes across most easily in translation is a fragment.

One evening, I go out to Dachengfang Street to browse from the used-book carts. Among the software manuals and tales of derring-do I find *Gaige qianhou luewang lu—julong fusu* (A record of things overlooked in the reform process—the giant dragon revives) by the apparently pseudonymous Wei Da.[20] The next night's insomnia sees me reading its chapters on the Democracy Wall movement of 1979, especially "Shou che" (The tow trucks are coming), on its aftermath. Wei Da is surprisingly fierce in describing the sloppiness of the trial that convicted Wei Jingsheng of "selling state secrets."[21] Wei Da underlines the vagueness of the charges, the predetermined outcome, the flimsiness of the evidence. What I find most useful in Wei Da's account is that although he or she is able to cite foreign scholars and newspapers—Roderick MacFarquhar, the *Manchester Guardian, Le Monde,* the *Bangkok Post*—the case against Wei Jingsheng's accusers is not made by instancing some international standard of human rights. Rather, Chinese notions of consistency, proportion,

York: Semiotexte, 1991), 171.

[20] (Chengdu: Chengdu keji daxue chubanshe, 1993.) In my opinion the book is too intelligent to have been a CIA plant.

[21] Some of Wei Jingsheng's writings have been collected as *The Courage to Stand Alone,* trans. Kristina M. Torgeson (New York: Viking Penguin, 1998).

and due process are adequate to revealing the show trial as a scandal; and that is encouraging, though not yet a bill of rights. It is good to be reminded that this is possible; also that the protection of powerful outsiders is not always the protester's only guarantee. The notion that human rights are a gospel that the Chinese are only reluctantly coming to accept suits the needs of certain international organizations, along with the Chinese and American governments—it gives them all a space in which to exhibit "determination," "flexibility," and "understanding," score "victories" and make "concessions"—but it is probably worse than useless to citizens in a tight spot. Without universalistic or particularistic fanfare, counting on pedestrian, everyday reactions to unfairness, Wei Da shows how to make native rights talk work.

I carry these thoughts to dinner with a group of professors and administrators whose specialty is the teaching of Chinese to foreigners. In a discussion of the international reach of Chinese cultural figures, someone brings it up as an article of praise that "no matter how bitterly Hu Shi railed against his opponents in China, whenever he went abroad he had nothing but nice things to say about Chinese culture." In other words, Napoleon's rule about dirty linen—it's to be washed *en famille.* That the mere mention of Amnesty International or the concern of external organizations in relation to a case like Wei Jingsheng's is usually sufficient to cloud matters is made plain by historical excerpts like the following:

> How can it be that foreigners aim to bestow on the Chinese [concepts of] "human rights" and "democracy"? Impossible!... Before Liberation, the whips, knives, and guns of imperialism never breathed a word about "human rights" and "democracy." In certain parks there were signs reading: "No Dogs or Chinese Allowed."[22]
>
> What business does a millionaire who has stuffed his paunch with the blood and sweat of laboring people have preaching "human rights"?[23]

Conveniently, through such feints, all foreigners collapse into one; the writers of Amnesty letters are as one with the empire builders and union busters, the better to mold the home population into a matching ideal unity. The quotations immediately above date from 1979, but the technique, the use of supposed

---

22 *Beijing ribao,* April 2, 1979, cited in Wei Da, *Gaige qianhou,* 328.

23 *Zhongguo qingnian bao,* cited ibid., 328–29.

ethnic and national interests to discredit anything said by foreigners or through foreign channels, is very much in force twenty years later. Its ongoing persuasiveness may show that some of the themes of the Chinese postmodernists—their communitarianism, their refusal of universal ideals or narratives, their self-depiction as "decolonizers of the mind"—mirror a consensus, or a deadlock, of the moment.[24] Is the theory of postmodernism a fortuitous epicycle upon untheorized social grounds? To answer this question one would need to see into the future of China—farther than I can, at any rate.

The reader will have divined that I see in the postliberal, Huntingtonian theory of history a resource for governments that like to speak for the collectivity and show their "strength" by "standing up" to the meddling of other peoples in their "internal affairs." The question of which kinds of argument harmonize with the "official line" is often raised in essays on *houxue,* usually in the form of an accusation. Liu Kang finds that "authoritarian capitalist modernization, spread by the global cultural imaginary, has become the mainstream school of thought among Chinese intellectual and cultural figures, filling in the ideological gaps left by the declining hegemony of the Communist Party"; for Zhao Yiheng, the situation sketched by Liu amounts to "neoconservatism under the slogan of exceptionalism, with theoretical support from the various 'post-' discourses of the West and a background of cultural nationalism," putting into question the project of modernization. Xu Ben's analysis faults the postmodernists for staying well within the zone of "permitted discourse" and even chiming in with "the official discourse that says that 'the meaning of human rights is just the right to survival, food, and clothing.'"[25] Under contemporary Chinese conditions, postmodernity's antipathy to universals together with its inability to formulate a principled pluralism gives it the specific contours of an official-thought-in-

[24] The allusion is to Ngugi wa Thiong'o's work *Decolonizing the Mind* (London and Portsmouth, N.H.: James Currey / Heinemann, 1986).

[25] Liu Kang, "Quanqiuhua yu Zhongguo xiandaihua de butong xuanze" (Globalization and the distinctive choice of Chinese modernization), *Ershiyi shiji* 37 (October 1996): 145. The phrase "filling in the gaps" is ambiguous here—supplanting the CCP or supporting it?—and not, I think, just a matter of style. Zhao Yiheng, "Moxuyou xiansheng yu tamen de watiao" (The lords of unreality and their leapfrogging), *Ershiyi shiji* 38 (December 1996): 137. Xu Ben, "Zai tan Zhongguo 'houxue' de zhengzhixing he lishi yishi," 135.

waiting. For many post-ists, the specificity of their moment in history—the "post-new period"—is best defined through a contrast to the enthusiasm for civil society and liberal regimes that marked the 1980s. The 1980s were a period of "Western studies"; the 1990s, of "national studies" (*guoxue*).[26] "National" is taken in a special and rather defensive sense. Zhang Kuan: "Freedom, democracy, pluralism, the independence of authors—these have been discussed for years, but the key issue is that distinctions must be made under differing historical conditions, and we cannot embrace unconditionally this chain of capitalist concepts....Our thinking on these problems today cannot stop at the 1980s; we must take a step forward."[27] Zhang Yiwu: "The split between the new period and the post-new period has already become obvious. The old style of discourse used to interpret mainland Chinese culture has been rejected by the new cultural practices of the present."[28] So much for critique: by declaring a "post-new period" and consecrating the intellectual attitudes appropriate to

---

[26] In the early 1980s, according to Chen Xiaoming, a number of scholars began to "have second thoughts about Western studies and return to national studies" (*fanxing xixue, huidao guoxue*): "'Wenhua minzu zhuyi' de xingqi," 35. The term *guoxue* first appeared in the late nineteenth century as a calque on the Japanese term *kokugaku*. It bears the connotation of a celebratory account of national culture, often in the frame of a story about essential national characteristics (*guocui/kokusui*). The reported idols of "New National Studies" or "Post-National Studies" are Zhang Taiyan, Chen Yinke, Wang Guowei, Gu Jiegang, Liang Shuming, Zhang Junli, Du Yaquan (ibid., 36)—anticolonialists to a man, but hardly cultural chauvinists. For similar lists, see Xu Ben, "Zai tan Zhongguo 'houxue' de zhengzhixing he lishi yishi," 136; Zhang Yiwu, "Chanshi 'Zhongguo' de jiaolü" (Interpreting the concern about "China"), *Ershiyi shiji* 29 (June 1995): 134. On "national essence" thinking in the 1930s and 1940s, see Lydia Liu, *Translingual Practice: Literature, National Culture, and Translated Modernity: China, 1900–1937* (Stanford, Calif.: Stanford University Press, 1995), 239–56.

[27] Zhang Kuan, "Jiaqiang dui xifang zhuliu huayu de pipan" (Reinforcing the criticism of mainstream Western discourse), *Zuojia bao*, June 24, 1995, cited in Lei Yi, "Shenme shi baoshou? Shei fandui minzhu?" (What is conservatism? Who opposes democracy?), *Ershiyi shiji* 40 (April 1997): 124.

[28] Zhang Yiwu, "Chanshi 'Zhongguo' de jiaolü," 128. Elsewhere Zhang defines the "post-new period" of the 1990s "as a total surpassing of the 'modernity' sought by 'new period' culture from the late 1970s onward; it gives the general outline and description of the contemporary Chinese cultural situation in the global post–Cold War cultural context. It is a new period led by consumption, dominated by mass media, structured by pluralist cultural discourse, and strongly utilitarian." "Hou xin shiqi wenhua: tiaozhan yu jiyu" (Post–new period culture: Challenge and opportunity), *Zhanlue yu guanli* 2 (1994): 112–14.

it, one may hope to restrict radically the circulation of permitted ideas.

It is perhaps too much to expect anyone to adopt willingly the label of *guanfang* (official) thinker, although the post-ists seem unable to avoid positions that echo, resemble, or are convenient to the policies of China's rulers.[29] The citation-history of Zheng Min's essay on modernist poetics is instructive. That essay's redescription of the institutionalization of modern vernacular literature as a process, not of creation but of elimination, might be read as pointing the way to a more truly pluralistic politics—pluralistic in the sense of putting forward more than one legitimation-story for the community to consider. But the criticism of the May Fourth movement in that essay has also been used as a cat's-paw for the critique of all "Westernization" movements, including the 1980s influx of liberal-democratic ideas. Zhang Yiwu appropriates Zheng Min's second thoughts about the modernist movement to denounce the whole project of enlightenment: for him, "May Fourth" is simply "the completion of a process begun in the Opium Wars" whereby Chinese intellectuals "internalized the point of view of the Western subject." Even Chinese nationalism is stained by its relation to Western nation-state thinking. "This process of 'othering' one's own culture is the most important mark of modernity in China."[30] So the sooner an end to modernity is proclaimed, the better for all Chinese, goes the story. When Zhao Yiheng, descrying a conservative agenda in Zheng's essay, recited the more conventional foundation-story of modern Chinese literature, he was doubtless spurred to do so by this set of implications. What meaning does the term "conservative" have in this context? Appealing to a longer, more complex account of the Chinese past may suggest the legitimacy of rival versions of modern history, thereby breaking the monopoly of textbook triumphalism, but if a more searching discussion is impossible it may only bring grist to the mill of national-interest theoreticians who see in it a chance to discredit cosmopolitan ideals. The opening represented by some aspects of Zheng Min's essay closes down all too soon. Perhaps it is simply intolerable—intolerable because undecidable?

---

[29] The dilemma of giving aid to the official doctrine is discussed in Lu Jia, "'Fan xifang zhuyi' huichao" (The return of anti-Westernism), *Zhongguo shibao zhoukan* (Hong Kong), January 2, 1994, 17–18.

[30] Zhang Yiwu, "'Xiandaixing' de zhongjie—yige wufa huibi de keti" (The end of "modernity"—an unavoidable topic), *Zhanlue yu guanli* 4 (1994): 106.

The question of pluralism is, like the label "conservative," ambiguously dependent on the contexts of its use. The theory of "cultural democracy" developed as an annex to Chinese postcolonialism provides a case in point. According to Zhang Yiwu, it is "thanks to postmodernism [that] the basis of a powerful cultural practice, a pluralist culture, a new cultural democracy, and limitless options have all sprung up overnight."[31] Zhang's optimism is interestingly interwoven with the idea of "resistance."

> At the beginning of the 1990s, quite a few overseas scholars painted a dark and gloomy picture of mainland Chinese culture, but the vitality and richness of that culture has proved them wrong. The irony of history as it comes sharply into view at present is that the process of Chinese politics, culture, and economics has completely escaped the control of those discourse-centered "intellectuals"; it has also completely escaped the grasp of the ready-made discourses and interpretative models produced abroad or at home. China seems to have become an uncontrollable "Other."[32]

Like Zhang Kuan, Zhang Yiwu takes his cues from Edward Said, but he reads many of Said's gestures as in a mirror. Said argued that the West built a scholarly discourse around the East to dominate it. Zhang Yiwu's conclusion is that China must be incomprehensible if it is to shake off outside domination. Against "orientalism"—which he defines broadly enough to include any opinion about China that foreigners may express—Zhang Yiwu insists on "Chinese cultural specificities." The point is not to form a theory or description of Chineseness, but to "resist" foreign (or foreign-tainted) discourses about China in any way possible. Sneering is a favorite method:

> These two essays [Xu Ben's "Disanshijie piping zai dangjin Zhongguo de chujing" (The place of third-world criticism in contemporary China) and Zhao Yiheng's "'Houxue' yu Zhongguo xin baoshou zhuyi" ("Post-ism" and Chinese neo-conservatism)] have one extremely obvious common feature, a strong degree of what Homi K. Bhabha calls the "pedagogical" style. This "pedagogy"

---

[31] Cited in He Jiadong, "Houxiandai pai ruhe nayong xiandaixing huayu" (How the postmodernists have appropriated the discourse of modernism), *Zhanlue yu guanli* 27 (1998): 74.

[32] Zhang Yiwu, "Chanshi 'Zhongguo' de jiaolü," 128. The "overseas scholars" surely include Perry Link (*Evening Chats in Beijing* [New York: Norton, 1992]) and Merle Goldman (*Sowing the Seeds of Democracy in China* [Cambridge: Harvard University Press, 1994]).

> does not just take the form of ideas; it is also a rhetorical strategy. It shows a lofty condescension, a sympathetic, nay tragic understanding, as if the writer were a prophet holding the blueprint of history and surveying from a high tower the native critic in his troubled realm; it is the style of a writer in the "observer" position, taking note of the struggles and pursuits of the "observed."[33]

Moreover, persuaded that the observations or analyses of foreigners (or of Chinese-born people living abroad) are "regulated by Western cultural hegemony" and aimed at "making China an obedient 'Other'" to the West, he refuses to grant them the status of knowledge and marks this by surrounding the words "knowledge" and "China" with quotation marks. This passive-aggressive style—casting every dialogue or critique as an unequal contest—is in itself such a heavy verdict on Zhang Yiwu's intellectual self-respect that I marvel at his appetite for controversy.[34] But it is not simply a mannerism: it mirrors the substance of what he has to say.

Zhang's recommendations for criticism at the present time are not bold.

> This exploration tries, first, to find a new position: "the Other of the Other." While seeking to transcend the old condition of "Otherness," refusing to take either side of the oppositions of universal / particular, classic / modern, it reflects on both in the context of contemporary culture and offers new insights. Secondly, it implies participation in contemporary culture—it implies the Gramscian role of the "organic intellectual." It neither stands apart from culture, nor tries to transcend culture, but seeks theoretical advances from within the dialectical thought of transformations in society and culture. It maintains a critique of Western cultural hegemony, but this critique does not imply a decisively nativistic conservative perspective. This new perspective allows a new grasp on the "condition" of hybridity in contemporary China. This grasp was made possible by the appropriation of Western theories, but this appropriation does not imply the use of theory to advance interpretations of the Chinese context; rather it recognizes that the transcendence of theoretical hegemony is dependent on reflection about and critique of theory. This requires the use of theory to critique theory, using contemporary Chinese conditions to reflect on theory, and using theory to match

[33] Zhang Yiwu, "Chanshi 'Zhongguo' de jiaolü," 129.

[34] For another example, this time referring to an essay by Zhang Longxi, see Zhang Yiwu, "Zai shuo 'Chanshi Zhongguo de jiaolü'" (Once again on the "anxiety of interpreting China"), *Ershiyi shiji* 34 (April 1996): 121–26.

> contemporary Chinese conditions, to produce a two-sided hermeneutic and gain a new cultural imagination and creativity.[35]

I see a determined defensiveness in this program. It is as if Zhang has compiled a list of the current terms of abuse—"conservatism," "hegemony," "elitism," "commercialism," "radicalism," and the like—and devised postmodern-sounding formulas that steer clear of all of them. Committed to nothing, but also standing apart from nothing, it is a very safe place to be. It resembles what Roland Barthes, reporting from the bourgeois world, called "Neither-Nor criticism."[36]

A criticism without thorns or horns, seemingly—but in practice things can be quite different. After repeating some points of this program in another essay, Zhang mentions two styles of play that he finds "unhelpful": "the desire for a discourse that privileges politics" and "the desire for a discourse that privileges values." In response to a reader's objection that his resistance to human rights talk makes him sound like "the [Chinese] Foreign Ministry's official spokesman," Zhang Yiwu retorts that this amounts to "calling any 'Other' whose choices are different from one's own, whose scholarly opinions go in a different direction, a 'spokesman for the Foreign Ministry'—and the implications are so obvious that they do not need to be stated.... It all turns into a dramatic 007-style combat between the angel of freedom and the devil's advocate." Likewise, when fellow scholars argue that the attack on modernity is indiscriminate and fails to recognize the better purposes to which modernization has sometimes been put, Zhang Yiwu complains that he has been "picked out as a person with evil motives."[37] People who attack *houxue* show that they cling to "absolute values beyond experience"—and that clearly renders them unfit for the job.[38] If politics and values are both out of bounds, and the role of "theoretical reflection on theory" is to shift discussion from substantive issues to one's displeasure at being criticized—if, in short, no "privileged discourse" is permitted—then a kind of perfection of pluralism has been achieved, and the power of debate to change minds and worlds is at a standstill.

---

[35] Zhang Yiwu, "Chanshi 'Zhongguo' de jiaolü," 134–35. On "the Other of the Other," see also "'Xiandaixing' de zhongjie," 109.

[36] Roland Barthes, *Mythologies* (Paris: Editions du Seuil, 1970), 144–46.

[37] Zhang Yiwu, "Zai shuo 'Chanshi Zhongguo de jiaolü,'" 125.

[38] Zhang Yiwu, "Miandui quanqiuhua de tiaozhan" (Facing the challenge of globalization), *Ershiyi shiji* 38 (December 1996): 140.

Zhang Yiwu shares with all the "post-ists" an unfavorable verdict on the May Fourth movement with its enthusiasms for John Dewey, Bertrand Russell, and Lev Tolstoy. Like Zhang Kuan, he describes modernity as "a set of knowledge/power discourses centered on Western Enlightenment values. As far as non-Western societies and peoples are concerned, 'modernity' is a concept bound up with the colonizing process."[39] A historical coincidence perhaps? "In the Chinese context, 'modernity' meant the construction of 'enlightenment' and 'salvation' as measured by Western discourse.... 'Modernity' in China... gave rise to a body of 'knowledge' about China / the West, with the purpose of determining China's place in the world by the application of this 'knowledge.'" As we have already seen, Zhang considers the May Fourth movement to have marked the definitive self-colonization of Chinese intellectuals by their imagination of the West. "'Modernity' is a set of important 'knowledges,' the contours of which cannot be separated from the function of intellectuals. 'Modernity' and its 'knowledge' produced intellectuals who received and expressed them, and the 'intellectuals' reinforced the indubitable authority of the 'knowledge' of the discourse of 'modernity.'" The new-style intellectual was "named and scripted by Western discourse.... This 'othering' was involved in the whole process of producing 'modernity' and 'knowledge.' The classical form of this production was the making, through Chinese-Western comparisons, of a discourse of 'otherness' concerning the specificities of Chinese culture and a way of knowing in reference to China." But the promulgation of ethnic stereotypes, however unflattering, could not have undermined ethnic consciousness to the degree desired by the modernizers. That job fell to the concept of the "human," the universal Enlightenment subject: "from Lu Xun's call for 'real people' [*zhende ren*] to the 1980s theoretical thinking about 'the objectification of the intrinsic powers of the person' and 'subject-formation,' an unconditional identification with the values of universal human nature prevailed." Now, says Zhang, that is all over. "Modernity" has been shown to be an effect of "othering," all its goals are discredited as side effects of colonial false consciousness, and as a result "reflection on and critique of 'modernity' is the basic task of contemporary culture."[40]

[39] Zhang Yiwu, "'Xiandaixing' de zhongjie," 104. A critical discussion of Zhang's essay occurs in Lei Yi, "Shenme shi baoshou? Shei fandui minzhu?"

[40] Zhang Yiwu, "'Xiandaixing' de zhongjie," 105, 106, 107, 108.

"The old-time 'pathfinders,' the traditional Enlightenment intellectuals" find themselves on the wrong side of an "Althusserian epistemological break," and a new species, the "post-intellectual," has already come forth to replace them. "Thanks to pluralist culture and its multiple strategies of progress, the phase [of modernity] is on its way out."[41]

"Pluralism" and "hybridity" are occasional synonyms for the "cultural democracy" Zhang Yiwu advocates. But when actual hybrid cultures—like May Fourth modernity—come into view, he faults them for their "surrender" to foreign notions. In a proper "cultural democracy," no one would presumably compare Chinese values to Western Enlightenment values—at least, never unfavorably—and there would be no forcing of universals of any kind down the throats of autonomous people. Zhang does not give a substantive account of "Chinese culture" or tell us what is precious about it. He defends it on principle. One need only know that in the twentieth century it has been the subject of a "subaltern discourse" and the whipping boy of indigenous reforming intellectuals. If Lu Xun and Chen Duxiu were degraded, foreign-devil-worshiping Chinamen, then how pure indeed must the true, non-Othered China be! In the present, Zhang finds much to correct in

> the "knowledge" about "China" created by global cultural interests. Major cultural products about the special political circumstances of China have already become an indispensable resource for international investment. From the discourse of "human rights" advanced by Western governments to the striking use of Chinese politics in the films of Zhang Yimou and Chen Kaige, Chinese politics has become a precious cultural bit of recycled goods. "Human rights" has long been a bargaining chip in the effort to take control of Chinese markets and mastermind commerce; it is the last shadow determining the Otherness of "China." As Rey Chow has shown, the democracy represented by the [statue of] the Goddess of Democracy [in Tiananmen Square, May 1989] was "a naïve, idealistic clamor for democracy 'American style,'...converg[ing] on the symbolism of the white-woman-as-liberty."[42] And the major symbolic products about the oppres-

[41] Zhang Yiwu, "Hou xin shiqi wenhua: tiaozhan yu jiyu," 112; idem, "'Xiandaixing' de zhongjie," 109.

[42] As a matter of fact, the "Goddess" did not have the features of a white woman. See *Tiananmen yijiubajiu* (Taipei: Lianjing chubanshe, 1989), 155–56, for photos. The statue made, of course, a direct reference to an American national symbol, but ethnicity and political regimes are not identical.

> siveness of the Chinese government, just now wildly popular, ...turn this "clamor" into marketable commodities...that display the "Otherness" of China.[43]

If foreigners who address problems in China can be shown (or suspected) to have selfish motives—including the pleasurable frisson of horror at the "oppressiveness of the Chinese government"—then the problems, magically, no longer exist. Chinese objectors may, surely, be characterized as having "othered" themselves, with or without the rewards of participation in the discourse of authority. Knowledge (well-founded or not) about China becomes "knowledge" about "China," projections of a false consciousness. In his triumph, Zhang has confused autonomy with autism.

Just for the record, the fact that rascals and thieves glorify something does not make it bad. Nor does the fact that something is odious make its opposite (or supposed opposite) automatically good. One must make appropriate distinctions; otherwise it would be enough to look no farther than slogans. Postmodernism, it is good to remember, began as literary criticism and all along has excelled in showing strange relations of mutual influence between the content of cultural products and their ways of being in the world. But when the story disappears and cultural critique exclusively addresses the story about the story, or the story about the story about the story, perhaps another type of questioning better deserves the name of critique.

---

[43] Zhang Yiwu, "Chanshi 'Zhongguo' de jiaolü," 131. Zhang cites Rey Chow, "Violence in the Other Country: Preliminary Remarks on the 'China Crisis,' June 1989," *Radical America* 22 (July–August 1988 [*sic*]): 24–33; the quoted passage appears on page 27. An expanded version of Chow's article appears in Chandra Talpade Mohanty, Ann Russo, and Lourdes Torres, eds., *Third World Women and the Politics of Feminism* (Bloomington: Indiana University Press, 1991), 81–100. Chow's article shares with Zhang Yiwu the resentment against the "intrusion" of foreign news media in the Chinese physical and political scene, comparing it to the colonial-period privilege of "extraterritoriality" granted to foreign residents in China; like Zhang, too, Chow sees "democracy" as a stalking-horse for Western hegemony. "Don't they [the Chinese students of 1989] know what atrocities have been committed in the name of liberty and democracy?" she asks, citing as example "the way Margaret Thatcher's British government is treating the citizens of Hong Kong," namely, denying them any form of United Kingdom citizenship. Surely no definition of "democracy" is broad enough to contain the British government's behavior toward Hong Kong. I am unable to see in what way Chow's warnings address the problems of political and mediatic representation that concern most Chinese advocates of democratization.

The strategic role of the term "culture" varies—consider only the British study of "working-class culture" in the second-tier universities of the 1950s and 1960s, where establishing that the working class had a culture was the main task, as contrasted with the easy accreditation of "cultures" in the American system of competing interest groups. In China, "culture" (*wenhua*, with or without its newly acquired opprobrious epithet, "elitist": *jingying wenhua*) is the category through which the intellectual vanguard (carefully distanced from direct political power since 1949, but still the primary audience for state speech) can think of itself as "China." Zhang Yiwu does have some things right. He sees, for example, that modernization conferred on the educated few the right to speak for the masses, to speak as China. And Zhang, like other post-ists, sees the reorientation of Chinese society toward consumption and production for the outside market as the twilight of the intellectuals.[44] "Cultural democracy" speaks for the destitution of intellectuals' authority: it will be a pluralism, thus an absence of guiding role, carried to the one province where the educated classes might still claim leadership. The one-party consumer state no longer needs them, except as specialists in technology, management, entertainment, and advertising. The new "organic intellectuals" will be employees. Disruptions like those of 1919 and 1989 will no longer be their affair.

A certain "Chinese postmodernism" occurs outside China too. It is reliably produced under some of the same conditions that I have shown influencing contemporary Chinese critical theory. It certainly deserves the attention of all who reflect on economic and political globalization, although the currently available ways of posing the problem are doomed, as I will argue in a moment, to present it in misleadingly clear-cut fashion.

Is there any truth to the consensus of journalists and diplomats that the economic liberalization of China prepares the way for a stronger conception of personal rights?[45] Or is that theory a

[44] Zhang Yiwu, "'Xiandaixing' de zhongjie," 108.

[45] The phrase "civil rights" might be less confusing than "human rights," resting as it does on a more modest philosophical basis. The crucial distinction of vocabulary is that human rights tend to be ascribed to individuals qua humans, and civic rights to individuals qua citizens. Universalism doesn't go away—the exemplary civil-rights question is, Why should there be distinctions of privilege among citizens?—but the historical specificity of particular constitutions is preserved well into the normative part of the discussion. "Civil rights" should not be confused with Jürgen Habermas's account of the emergence of modernity from an auton-

product of inappropriate universal humanism? Postmodern thinkers, with their diagnoses of the dissolution of the freely choosing, autonomous self, should provide valuable guidance on this point. Comparative philosophy, too, deals with conceptual differences, and with its frequent admission that "rights as defined in the classical Western tradition entail assumptions that are in many ways incompatible with Chinese social considerations" it should be able to start the discussion from a more or less neutral ground.[46] In fact nothing is less certain. The comparative philosophers, when they have an actual text to analyze, are almost always found working with the language of Confucius (551–479 B.C.) or Mencius (4th c. B.C.). Or when they look to modern China, what they see is timeless and unspecific. Hall and Ames, for example, contrasting the Chinese idea of "ritual" (*li*) to the modern European notion of "rights," find that

> *li* is not passive deference to external patterns or norms: it is a "making" of society that requires the investment of oneself, one's judgment, and one's own sense of cultural importances.... Beyond any formal social patterning is an open texture of ritual that is personalized and reformulated to accommodate the uniqueness and the quality of each participant.... There are variable degrees of personalization in ritual practices, and as a consequence, the roles they establish are hierarchical. These roles form a kind of social syntax that generates meaning through coordinating patterns of deference.... It follows, then, that individuality in the liberal democratic sense of autonomy and independence is anathema to ritually constituted society, suggesting even idiocy and immorality.[47]
>
> Ritual-based order seeks to guarantee tolerance, for it is the basic nature of harmony, the aspiration of ritual practice, that it is enhanced by a coordinated diversity among its elements.[48]

The optimism of this account is obvious; the problem, however, is to figure out whether the "ritually constituted society" Hall and Ames speak of existed in the fifth century B.C., the twelfth century

omous "public sphere" or "civil society," a theory much discussed in China in the 1980s but vitiated by its use to stand for another thing China "lacked."

[46] Donald Hall and Roger Ames, *Thinking from the Han* (Albany: State University of New York Press, 1998), 276.

[47] Ibid., 271. It would be an exaggeration to say that a ritually constituted life appears to a liberal society's ideology as "idiotic" and "immoral" (maybe just premoral), but consider the connotations of the English word "ritualistic" as explored in Hall and Ames, 271.

[48] Ibid., 281.

A.D., the eighteenth century, or the present, or in all and none of these as an "ideal type." The China that is currently (as some would put it) withstanding an assault of rights language from outside is, in any case, a late-twentieth-century collection of more or less interdependent areas of Chinese language and culture, and it would be useful to know whether any of these is a working "ritually constituted society," and if so, whether the rites do produce order for all and protection for those in need of it. Hall and Ames sketch a present-tense realm of communitarian ritual creativity in which one might detect a version of the modern People's Republic:

> In China, political directives appear to take the form of broad and abstract slogans promulgated in the public institutions and the press. What is not apparent is the degree to which such directives require interpretation and application as they ramify back down through society. Communication and consensus is, in fact, arrived at by a much less abstract mechanism than would be characteristic of a society constituted of strictly autonomous individuals. This is true in a large measure because the Chinese conception of humanness does not presuppose any notion of a moral order transcending the consensual order that could justify either demagogic appeals or appeals to individual conscience, and that might disrupt the consensus.[49]

On a good day, this might be a very fine system indeed, allowing me as much room for choice and creativity as does ballot-box democracy (if not more); but constitutional safeguards are designed for the bad days, and it would be unconvincing to describe twentieth-century Chinese history as a "consensual order" immune to both "demagogic appeals" and "appeals to individual conscience." It has not all been self-regulating harmony, nor have all the destructive influences come from outside.

Leaving comparative philosophy aside, another reason for confusion in the discussion of democratic culture and its spread is that there is at present no way to know whether people want more democracy than they have. The spokesmen, self-appointed or not, are always unreliable (though the "they don't have it and they don't want it" argument is, I think, particularly suspect). Satellite television, often described as the inevitable herald of democracy, teaches more about consumption and celebrities than about autonomy. It is after all imaginable that the majority of

[49] Ibid., 279.

Chinese people (or for that matter, American people) are persuaded that economic growth, international prestige, social order, and a thriving culture are best achieved without the distractions of democracy and rights talk; and in that case, it will be futile to tell them otherwise—though no one has asked them yet in any way that counts. The very thought of asking them would be a tremendous departure from the history of Chinese modernization, not to mention postmodernization.

The question about democracy comes down, finally, not to a matter of concepts or culture but to a matter of speech in the most pragmatic sense. Who has the floor? Can the floor be shared? Can it be yielded? The greatest cause of distortion in the *houxue* democratization debate is that the conversation takes the form of intellectuals asking each other what they think about concepts and principles. It is not as a concept that democracy is valuable, but as a practice. In 1989 students, teachers, office personnel, factory workers, small merchants, casual laborers, and others took to the streets to ask for a broadening of reform. These innovations in social action have not been repeated since, however often issues of "elitism," "vulgar culture," "market values," and intellectuals' "participation in contemporary culture" have been invoked in the 1990s debate. The term "culture" has expanded so relentlessly in its passage from Euro-American literary theory to Chinese "post-" studies because it allows the issues to be handled as matters of verbal discrimination, not of things done in shops, buses, prisons, and streets; and intellectuals are at home with verbal discriminations, while new forms of relation underpinned by economics, for example, escape their guidance.

What people need, if modernity—and postmodernity, for that matter—is to make good on its promises, is more narratives, more debate about what goes on and why; which is to say that unlicensed citizens need to speak and be heard. Of course, debate is a form of practical action, and it emerges on the basis of other practices. The most oppressive thing about Zhang Yiwu's "cultural democracy" is that it is conducted in a sort of last-round international chess tournament space, where his tales of postcolonial resistance are all alone with the Fukuyama-CNN-IMF modernization narrative. Where are the veterans of China's regional conflicts? the soldiers of June 1989? the people who produce export goods of higher and lower added value? No one but fellow intellectuals who share a great deal of background with the contenders has even a supporting role. That is more discouraging practically than theoretically. The historiography of the Taiwan liberation movement, for example, is deeply flawed—irresponsible and transparently self-serving on many counts—but in the event of reunification the independence movement's narratives are not going to be debated, merely suppressed (along with their authors, no doubt) as contrary to public order. Authentic pluralism would protect from punishment the fashioners of these and many more sorts of narrative. But this is not what the emitters or the receivers of human rights and democracy talk are bargaining about, as the transcript of President Clinton's speeches in China shows.[50]

Reform under tightly controlled conditions—that could summarize not only the last twenty years of Chinese internal politics, but the ambitions for the future expressed by Chinese "post-" studies. The capitalization of "Chinese political cruelty" denounced by Zhang Yiwu is a predictable consequence of Chinese governmental decisions, at the beginning of the economic reform process, to open up some areas of history for reconsideration (the Hundred Flowers, the Cultural Revolution, the cult of Mao Zedong) while keeping the rest under lock and key. It was a strategic move—redirecting criticism toward safe targets. Postmodernism with its particular pluralisms offers a similarly limited critique. But pluralism with a checklist is plural only in the barest numerical sense. It is still answerable to the grantors. Although its metaphysical background is dodgy, the concept of universal, natural, or inborn rights has the practical advantage of favoring the subject claiming a right at the moment of justification. Would you rather have your liberties as an assumption, the limitation of which needs special argument, or as a privilege to be sought on every occasion of their use? If the people of China were sure of their ability to form peaceful assemblies, petition for redress, and coordinate labor actions, the result would be a pluralism worth listening to—and ample compensation, if it came to that, for the

[50] The parallel press conference conducted by the two leaders often took the following form: Clinton would urge the adoption of a right or principle; Jiang replied that the right in question already existed in China but followed this reassurance with a reminder that the inappropriate exercise of any right would be punished by the law. The talk of rights began to seem more and more a hollow exercise without the fashioning of means of recourse—these being beyond the concerns of the diplomatic script. At the writing of this essay (August 1998), transcripts were available at <http://www.whitehouse.gov/WH/New/China/speeches.html>.

fading-away of the leadership of the educated class. The opposition, beloved of comparatist scholars in a hurry, between Western individualism and Chinese communitarianism reposes on silences of long standing. In principle, every community with a grievance is capable of producing its "organic intellectuals." And every community has a grievance—that is what spawns narratives and maintains communities. At present, however, China, like its postmodernists, recognizes only one community. So what we should be talking about, if the consensus of modernity really is at an end in China, is forming the preconditions for the practices the Western countries, with their curious theologies and ethical assumptions, describe as the exercise of individual rights. But none of this will come to pass so long as Chinese nationhood has the monopoly on requests for representation and "cultural identity" in the global information order.

Contributors

Stanley Abe is Assistant Professor of Art History, Duke University.

Patricia Berger is Assistant Professor of Art History, University of California, Berkeley.

Rey Chow is Andrew W. Mellon Professor of the Humanities at Brown University; she teaches in the Department of Comparative Literature and the Department of Modern Culture and Media.

Wendy Larson is Professor of East Asian Languages and Literatures, University of Oregon, Eugene.

Haun Saussy is Associate Professor of Asian Languages and Comparative Literature at Stanford University, where he chairs the Department of Asian Languages.

Michelle Yeh is Professor of East Asian Languages and Cultures, University of California, Davis.

Wen-hsin Yeh is Professor of History, University of California, Berkeley.

INSTITUTE OF EAST ASIAN STUDIES PUBLICATIONS SERIES

CHINA RESEARCH MONOGRAPHS (CRM)

36. Suzanne Pepper. *China's Education Reform in the 1980s: Policies, Issues, and Historical Perspectives,* 1990
sp. Phyllis Wang and Donald A. Gibbs, eds. *Readers' Guide to China's Literary Gazette, 1949–1979,* 1990
38. James C. Shih. *Chinese Rural Society in Transition: A Case Study of the Lake Tai Area, 1368–1800,* 1992
39. Anne Gilks. *The Breakdown of the Sino-Vietnamese Alliance, 1970–1979,* 1992
sp. Theodore Han and John Li. *Tiananmen Square Spring 1989: A Chronology of the Chinese Democracy Movement,* 1992
40. Frederic Wakeman, Jr., and Wen-hsin Yeh, eds. *Shanghai Sojourners,* 1992
41. Michael Schoenhals. *Doing Things with Words in Chinese Politics: Five Studies,* 1992
sp. Kaidi Zhan. *The Strategies of Politeness in the Chinese Language,* 1992
42. Barry C. Keenan. *Imperial China's Last Classical Academies: Social Change in the Lower Yangzi, 1864–1911,* 1994
43. Ole Bruun. *Business and Bureaucracy in a Chinese City: An Ethnography of Private Business Households in Contemporary China,* 1993
44. Wei Li. *The Chinese Staff System: A Mechanism for Bureaucratic Control and Integration,* 1994
45. Ye Wa and Joseph W. Esherick. *Chinese Archives: An Introductory Guide,* 1996
46. Melissa Brown, ed. *Negotiating Ethnicities in China and Taiwan,* 1996
47. David Zweig and Chen Changgui. *China's Brain Drain to the United States: Views of Overseas Chinese Students and Scholars in the 1990s,* 1995
48. Elizabeth J. Perry, ed. *Putting Class in Its Place: Worker Identities in East Asia,* 1996
sp. Phyllis L. Thompson, ed. *Dear Alice: Letters Home from American Teachers Learning to Live in China,* 1998
49. Wen-hsin Yeh, ed. *Landscape, Culture, and Power in Chinese Society,* 1998
50. Gail Hershatter, Emily Honig, Susan Mann, and Lisa Rofel, comps. and eds. *Guide to Women's Studies in China,* 1999
51. Wen-hsin Yeh, ed. *Cross-Cultural Readings of Chineseness: Narratives, Images, and Interpretations of the 1990s,* 2000
52. Marilyn A. Levine and Chen San-ching. *The Guomindang in Europe: A Sourcebook of Documents,* 2000
53. David N. Keightley. *The Ancestral Landscape: Time, Space, and Community in Late Shang China,* 2000

KOREA RESEARCH MONOGRAPHS (KRM)

13. Vipan Chandra. *Imperialism, Resistance, and Reform in Late Nineteenth-Century Korea: Enlightenment and the Independence Club,* 1988
14. Seok Choong Song. *Explorations in Korean Syntax and Semantics,* 1988
15. Robert A. Scalapino and Dalchoong Kim, eds. *Asian Communism: Continuity and Transition,* 1988
16. Chong-Sik Lee and Se-Hee Yoo, eds. *North Korea in Transition,* 1991
17. Nicholas Eberstadt and Judith Banister. *The Population of North Korea,* 1992
18. Hong Yung Lee and Chung Chongwook, eds. *Korean Options in a Changing International Order,* 1993
19. Tae Hwan Ok and Hong Yung Lee, eds. *Prospects for Change in North Korea,* 1994
20. Chai-sik Chung. *A Korean Confucian Encounter with the Modern World: Yi Hang-no and the West,* 1995
21. Myung Hun Kang. *The Korean Business Conglomerate: Chaebol Then and Now,* 1996

24. Lewis R. Lancaster and Richard K. Payne, eds. *Religion and Society in Contemporary Korea*, 1998
25. Jeong-Hyun Shin. *The Trap of History: Understanding Korean Short Stories*, 1998
26. Hyung Il Pai and Timothy R. Tangherlini, eds. *Nationalism and the Construction of Korean Identity*, 1999

JAPAN RESEARCH MONOGRAPHS (JRM)

8. Yung H. Park. *Bureaucrats and Ministers in Contemporary Japanese Government*, 1986
9. Victoria V. Vernon. *Daughters of the Moon: Wish, Will, and Social Constraint in Fiction by Modern Japanese Women*, 1988
10. Steve Rabson, trans. *Okinawa: Two Postwar Novellas* by Ōshiro Tatsuhiro and Higashi Mineo. Introduction and afterword by Steve Rabson. 1996 (2d printing, corrected and updated [1989])
12. James W. White. *The Demography of Sociopolitical Conflict in Japan, 1721–1846*, 1992
13. Winston Davis. *The Moral and Political Naturalism of Baron Katō Hiroyuki*, 1996
14. Michael H. Gibbs. *Struggle and Purpose in Postwar Japanese Unionism*, 2000

RESEARCH PAPERS AND POLICY STUDIES (RPPS)

24. Joyce K. Kallgren, Noordin Sopiee, and Soedjati Djiwandono, eds. *ASEAN and China: An Evolving Relationship*, 1988
29. Richard Holton and Wang Xi, eds. *U.S.-China Economic Relations: Present and Future*, 1989
30. Sadako Ogata. *Normalization with China: A Comparative Study of U.S. and Japanese Processes*, 1989
32. Leo E. Rose and Kamal Matinuddin, eds. *Beyond Afghanistan: The Emerging U.S.-Pakistan Relations*, 1990
33. Clark Neher and Wiwat Mungkandi, eds. *U.S.-Thailand Relations in a New International Era*, 1990
34. Robert Sutter and Han Sungjoo, eds. *Korea-U.S. Relations in a Changing World*, 1990
35. Harry H. Kendall and Clara Joewono, eds. *Japan, ASEAN, and the United States*, 1990
36. Robert A. Scalapino and Gennady I. Chufrin, eds. *Asia in the 1990s: American and Soviet Perspectives*, 1990
37. Chong-Sik Lee, ed. *In Search of a New Order in East Asia*, 1991
38. Leo E. Rose and Eric Gonsalves, eds. *Toward a New World Order: Adjusting U.S.-India Relations*, 1992
39. Harumi Befu, ed. *Cultural Nationalism in East Asia: Representation and Identity*, 1993
40. Yufan Hao. *Dilemma and Decision: An Organizational Perspective on American China Policy Making*, 1997
41. Frederic Wakeman Jr. and Wang Xi, eds. *China's Quest for Modernization: A Historical Perspective*, 1997
42. Loraine A. West and Yaohui Zhao, eds. *Rural Labor Flows in China*, 2000
43. Shalendra D. Sharma, ed. *The Asia-Pacific in the New Millennium: Geopolitics, Security, and Foreign Policy*, 2000

INDOCHINA RESEARCH MONOGRAPHS (IRM)

1. William J. Duiker. *China and Vietnam: The Roots of Conflict*, 1986
2. Allan E. Goodman. *The Search for a Negotiated Settlement of the Vietnam War*, 1986
3. Tran Tri Vu. *Lost Years: My 1,632 Days in Vietnamese Reeducation Camps*, 1989
4. Ta Van Tai. *The Vietnamese Tradition of Human Rights*, 1989
5. Douglas Pike, ed. *The Bunker Papers: Reports to the President from Vietnam, 1967–1973*, 3 vols., 1990
6. Judith Banister. *Vietnam Population Dynamics and Prospects*, 1993

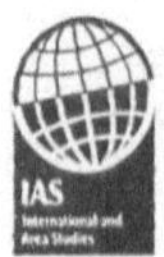

INTERNATIONAL AND AREA STUDIES

David K. Leonard, Dean

International and Area Studies at the University of California, Berkeley, comprises four groups: international and comparative studies, area studies, teaching programs, and services to international programs.

INSTITUTE OF EAST ASIAN STUDIES
UNIVERSITY OF CALIFORNIA, BERKELEY

The Institute of East Asian Studies, now a part of Berkeley International and Area Studies, was established at the University of California at Berkeley in the fall of 1978 to promote research and teaching on the cultures and societies of China, Japan, and Korea. It amalgamates the following research and instructional centers and programs: the Center for Chinese Studies, the Center for Japanese Studies, the Center for Korean Studies, the Group in Asian Studies, and the East Asia National Resource Center.

Cover: Luochuang (*ca.* 13th century), "Hanshan Reading a Scroll," Yuan dynasty, hanging scroll, ink on paper. University of California, Berkeley Art Museum. Calligraphy from title page of Xu Bing's *A Book from the Sky*.